ANGE[illegible]

Fifteen Le[illegible]

A. P. ROSSITER

Angel with Horns

FIFTEEN LECTURES ON SHAKESPEARE

Edited by

GRAHAM STOREY

and with an Introduction by

PETER HOLLAND

Longman

London and New York

Longman Group UK Limited,
Longman House, Burnt Mill, Harlow,
Essex CM20 2JE, England
and Associated Companies throughout the world

Published in the United States of America
by Longman Inc., New York

First published 1961
Re-issued, with an Introduction, 1989

British Library Cataloguing in Publication Data
A CIP Catalogue record for this book is available from the British Library

ISBN 0-582-01499-9

Library of Congress Cataloguing in Publication Data
Rossiter, A. P. (Arthur Percival), d. 1957.
Angel with horns.

Includes index.
1. Shakespeare, William, 1564–1616—Criticism and interpretation. I. Storey, Graham, 1920–
II. Title.
PR2976.R66 1989 822.3′3 88–32608
ISBN 0-582-01499-9

Produced by Longman Group (FE) Ltd
Printed in Hong Kong

CONTENTS

ACKNOWLEDGMENTS

We are grateful to Hodder & Stoughton Ltd for permission to reproduce the chapter ‘Ambivalence: The Dialectic of the Histories’ by A. P. Rossiter from *Talking Shakespeare* by Dr. John Garrett.

Preface

A. P. ROSSITER's lectures on Shakespeare were an experience that few of his audience—whether in the Cambridge English Faculty or the Shakespeare Summer School at Stratford—are likely to forget. They undoubtedly owed much of their effect to their delivery: Rossiter was a born lecturer, with a manner entirely his own, and (as those who heard his broadcast talks, 'Our Living Language', will remember) a passionate belief in the effectiveness of the spoken word. But their more enduring appeal came from another source—from a mixture of allusiveness and closeness to contemporary life that was always exciting and often—as it was meant to be—disturbing. Through Shakespeare he invariably forced his listeners to reconsider their own attitudes to living.

Two of Rossiter's books bear intimately on Shakespearian studies: his edition of the anonymous *Woodstock* (1946), in which he examined the Morality tradition underlying the Histories; and *English Drama from Early Times to the Elizabethans* (1950), which shows convincingly Shakespeare's indebtedness to his Gothic predecessors. But, though Shakespeare himself remained his central interest, he published relatively little directly on him. After a series of excellent articles in the *Durham University Journal*, almost all his work on Shakespeare—and certainly the work he regarded as his most important—went into his lectures, which he constantly rewrote. Only one of them, 'Ambivalence and the Dialectic of the Histories' (Rossiter apologized later for its somewhat alarming title), has been published before.[1] It is reprinted here, and gives the fullest account of terms he uses in many of the others.

[1] In *Talking of Shakespeare*, ed. John Garrett, 1954.

Rossiter died in January 1957, after a motor accident; and as his literary executor, and one of his original Cambridge audience, I felt convinced that these lectures should be published. They are drawn from his more recent ones and from those which existed in something approaching printable form. They do not cover the whole Shakespearian canon: their range was in any case limited by the special requirements of his two audiences. But the plays in which he was most interested—the Histories, Problem Plays and Tragedies—are nearly all here;[1] and in them he was able to explore deeply what was, to him, Shakespeare's unique preoccupation: an inquisition, operating through an increasingly critical use of the comic and the tragi-comic, into the equivocal nature of the State, of Man, and finally of Nature itself. To that extent, they have a theme, although a complex one: the title-lecture points to it, and the three more general lectures—'Ambivalence', 'Shakespearian Tragedy' and 'Comic Relief'—examine it from different angles. But this is emphatically not a study of 'Shakespearian themes'. Rossiter continually challenges schematic 'solutions'—the 'Tudor-moral version of the Histories', for example, or the allegorical interpretation of the Problem Plays; and insists throughout on Shakespeare's complexity and the loss that results from trying to over-simplify him.

Substantially these lectures are, I hope, much as they were given. But I am only too aware that in print they have lost something of their personal quality. Rossiter prepared them expressly for delivery: he used his own devices for emphasis, and he made great play with parentheses and asides—turns of phrase that needed the speaking voice. Only he could have produced a really faithful transcript of the lectures just as he gave them (as he did with that on 'Ambivalence': see his note at p.64); and I did not feel able to attempt this myself.

As each lecture was written to stand on its own, there were

[1] *King Lear* is an apparent exception, but is discussed fully in 'Shakespearian Tragedy' and 'Comic Relief'.

inevitably some repetitions, both of ideas and illustrations. Some I have removed, but the removal of others would have upset the argument. Again, these were in a sense 'occasional' lectures: and some of the occasions—a particular Stratford performance or a new edition of the play concerned—provoked at the time what might seem a disproportionate amount of comment now. I have taken out what appeared mainly topical. On the other hand, there has been space to include passages Rossiter had to omit through lack of time. The few notes that I have added are in square brackets to distinguish them from Rossiter's own. All references to Shakespeare are to the text of *The Complete Works,* edited by Peter Alexander (Collins, 1951).

The following lectures were given to the Shakespeare Summer School at Stratford: 'Shakespeare and Wordsworth' (1950: to mark the centenary of Wordsworth's death); 'Ambivalence and the Dialectic of the Histories' (1951); 'Coriolanus' (1952); 'Angel with Horns: The Unity of Richard III' (1953); 'Troilus and Cressida' (1954); 'All's Well That Ends Well' (1955); and 'Othello' (1956). The remainder were given during approximately the same period to the English Faculty at Cambridge.

I am very grateful to Mrs. Barbara Rossiter, who has given me advice on many points in addition to checking the proofs; and to Mrs. John Talbot, who typed the lectures from a difficult MS. Thanks are also due to Messrs. Hodder & Stoughton for permission to reprint 'Ambivalence and the Dialectic of the Histories'.

GRAHAM STOREY

Cambridge,
August 1960.

Introduction

Jeremy. Sir, I have the seeds of Rhetorick and Oratory in my Head – I have been at *Cambridge.*

Tattle. Ay; 'tis well enough for a servant to be bred at an University: But the Education is a little too pedantick for a Gentleman.

A. P. Rossiter set this snatch of dialogue from Congreve's *Love for Love* as the epigraph to his only novel, *Poor Scholars,* published in 1932. Set in Cambridge in 1926, this novel of university life follows the careers, academic and amorous, of twins Philip and May Chesterfield, including the bizarre irruption of the General Strike into the university's limited and measured world. Rossiter pursues as a central theme of the novel the difficulty for Philip of evaluating the worth of scholarship and of maintaining his own commitment to it. When, at the end of the novel, Philip receives a telegram with the news that he has gained a first with distinction in his final examinations, he rushes off to tell his sister only to find her embracing her fiancé on the beach. For Philip academic work seems suddenly unimportant:

> Sitting on a sunbaked rock and staring into the sand, Philip knew that his solution was a failure: that the abstract and bookish life was only a device of his cowardice in its desperate search for safety... Scholars were like termites, patiently eating each other's leavings till the final product was so digested and devitalized that, decay being impossible, the ponderous ant-hill of erudition could be built out of it, standing high and grey above a levelled world. (pp. 351, 353)

Philip poses his dilemma as a conflict: 'Could he, then, bring life to his scholarship, or carry back his scholarship to life?' (p. 353). It does not take long before Philip can reaffirm his belief in scholarship, triumphantly though with a full awareness of the limitations of that triumph:

> It was not futile, though it was little enough to put before his lust of living: the maintenance of a tradition, the renunciation he had once seen in a classical building of noble proportions, the quiet disdain for all transient catchpurse success, shaping truth slowing from all man's stored-up wisdom. In a sense he was confirmed in the faith in which he had vaguely set out. Cambridge was for learning, for scholarship; not to be made paying or practical; not to cater for the career, but to shape full men, heedless of money and business as in the middle ages. Yet never reactionary from a timid fear of development: a home of the spirit of man seeking truth where alone it can be found: in the study of the widest body of human knowledge without consideration of creed or place or time. (p.354)

Philip's academic credo is also Rossiter's. The gap between literary scholars and the poets they write about is one Rossiter found in Yeats's poems, particularly 'The Choice' and 'The Scholars', a poem from which he was fond of quoting:

> Bald heads, forgetful of their sins,
> Old, learned, respectable bald heads
> Edit and annotate the lines
> That young men, tossing on their beds,
> Rhymed out in love's despair
> To flatter beauty's ignorant ear.

The humanist belief in the essential value of scholarship as the place for the shaping of 'full men' validates the connection between scholarship and 'life'. It is a liberal and now unfashionable justification but one that underlies all Rossiter's work. In his writing it creates a vitality and energy that contrasts sharply with the dry authority of most of our academic criticism.

Angel with Horns is a posthumous collection of Rossiter's Shakespeare lectures. First published in 1961 it quickly established itself as a crucial and powerful work of Shakespearean criticism. If its significance rests finally on what it argues about the nature of Shakespearean drama it seems to me necessary to begin a reassessment of it by recognising its origins as lectures. For lectures were for Rossiter the centre of his educative method. His undeviating commitment to clarity of argument led him to an equally strong commitment to the persuasive power of lectures, immensely stylish arguments that depended on the honest trickery of the spoken word.

In *Our Living Language* (1946), a collection of broadcast talks, he wryly quotes from Dr Johnson: 'People have now-a-days...got a strange opinion that everything should be taught by lectures. Now, I cannot see that lectures can do so much good as reading the books from which the lectures are taken' (p. 132). But, realising that 'few readers can say with Swift, "When I am reading a book, whether wise or silly, it seems to me to be alive and talking to me" ' (p. 133), he set out to prove the efficacy of the lecture, using all his rhetorical skills to create a style that rejected jargon and obscurity.

Rossiter aimed at a simplicity and lucidity that was the product of complex thought, working his ideas through until they could be fully expressed in apparently straightforward statements. As a style it is of a piece with his years of work on the project for Basic English, for the belief that complex expression in English was practicable with a remarkably small vocabulary. While his brilliant study of *English Drama from Early Times to the Elizabethans* (1950) included quotations from French, German and Latin with translations at the back 'for those who cannot read other tongues' (p. 164), the lectures which make up *Angel with Horns* avoid any hint of patronising the listeners with a rash of references to the whole range of European literature. Shakespeare, as Rossiter constructs him, is clear and sufficient to Rossiter and he makes his conception of him clear to his audience. Since, apart from 'Ambivalence: the Dialectic of the Histories', the lectures were never intended for publication, they manage, as a result, to retain those qualities and advantages of the spoken word which he used with such incisive brilliance. The result is that the style in itself connects *Angel with Horns* with those lectures that have become some of the major and determining works in the whole history of Shakespearean criticism, the writings of Coleridge and A. C. Bradley.

While Coleridge's Shakespeare criticism is a resource of at times unyielding complexity and Bradley's book on *Shakespearean Tragedy* is now, unjustifiably, more mocked than read, the view of Shakespeare Rossiter develops in *Angel with Horns* prefigures much of the best Shakespearean criticism published since. It epitomises many of the major concerns manifest in most recent Shakespeare study: the revaluation of neglected plays in the corpus of Shakespeare's work, the problem of history and the anxiety of uncertainty.

Angel with Horns by no means covers the whole of Shakespeare's work. Rossiter has little to say about the comedies (apart from the outstanding study of *Much Ado About Nothing*), the Roman plays apart from *Coriolanus* or the late plays. Even the chapters on the Tragedies, fine and invigorating though they are, do not show him at his most brilliant and radical. Instead the core of the book is the study of the English Histories (chapters 1 to 3) and of the 'problem plays' (chapters 5 to 8).

It is perhaps in his response to the latter that Rossiter's important attempt to redefine significance is at its most revolutionary. If for us the group of three plays, *All's Well That Ends Well, Measure for Measure* and *Troilus and Cressida*, have come to occupy a position of near-centrality in the recognition of Shakespeare's achievement, our recognition of these plays' curiously emphatic modernity is founded largely on Rossiter's reassessment. Though there had been worthwhile earlier studies, to which Rossiter pays careful and generous attention, his work succeeds for the first time in taking the plays on their own terms and finding in them strange and unnerving qualities.

It is not enough for him to identify a cynical or satiric doubt in the plays about conventionally accepted views. While he is concerned to determine accurately and extensively the radical ideologies embodied in these works Rossiter comes again and again to a position in which satire or cynicism is inadequate for a description of the plays' overall paradoxes. Alongside the violent subversions of establishment orthodoxies, the plays contain qualities of the traditional ideals which cannot be seen as being simply overturned, subverted or rejected. Conventional nobility is frequently presented in a way or a context that it would be awkward to read ironically.

The analysis of the multiplicity inherent in Shakespeare's presentation of conflicting perspectives cannot for Rossiter remain a purely cerebral activity. As for Philip Chesterfield, the recognition of the nature of the work that scholarship reveals is both vital and taxing. The emotional impact of Shakespearean drama seems at present to be a topic of marginal significance but Rossiter belongs with Dr Johnson and Coleridge in his preparedness to admit to the emotional consequences of reading or watching the plays. It is vital to his understanding of the problem plays that he admit to his discovery of the plays' revelations of 'a bad reality beneath fair appearances of things' as 'painful in the extreme – and we are *made to feel the pain'* (p. 126 – his italics). It is part of his scrupulous care in the attempt to define the seemingly indefinable that Rossiter should want to admit that the plays '*do* bother us' (p. 127) but the anxiety is also the logical outcome of his concentration. Much of the plays' strategy of disruptive subversion is revealed by Rossiter's analysis but that does not allow him to tidy the plays into place. They simply refuse to be neatened off, trapped by analytical expertise into singleness: they 'throw opposed or contrary views into the mind: only to leave the resulting equations without any settled or soothing solutions' (p. 128).

Rossiter does not seem to be a Shakespeare critic much influenced by the theatre. He rarely makes a point based on a stage-centred perception of the plays and he does not refer to contemporary production as a significant resource for the interpretation of the plays. Yet his revaluation of these plays is exactly contemporary with their rediscovery by Peter Hall and John Barton with the Royal Shakespeare Company. *Troilus and Cressida*, a play virtually without a stage-history until the 1950s, is now one of the most frequently performed. If Rossiter slightly overemphasises the possibility of the play's having been written for an Inns of Court audience, his recognition of the play's strange demands on the audience to follow its complex legalistic debates enables him also to appreciate the brutal twists and turns achieved by the play's narrative and its unexpected juxtapositions. But it is also both characteristic of Rossiter's aims and important to his larger argument in the lectures that the play should not appear to be an oddity. The play is seen as having common concerns with the *Henry IV* plays and *Othello* just as much as with the other problem plays.

The teasing-out of puzzles of superficially logical argument are one aspect of Rossiter's interest in the language of the play but he is also intrigued by two further aspects of the language of these plays: the frequent disjunction between language and speaker and the problematic nature of the plays' verbal ambiguity. Ulysses's speech on degree marks the first problem acutely: the gap between the received wisdom of the speech and the action Ulysses undertakes in the rest of the play. At times Rossiter seems to want to find Shakespearean characterisation less problematic. Helena in *All's Well* is, as he well outlines, a mass of contradictions but if the analysis 'only results in confusion' (p. 106) it is not therefore enough to suggest that the analysis should not take place and that Helena is to be taken 'for granted'. The play's obsessive fascination with the gap between its romance plot and the incompatible and awkward reality of the principal characters leads Rossiter to brilliant perceptions of Parolles but he backs away from a comparable analysis of Helena. Perhaps the only major concern of recent criticism that Rossiter does *not* anticipate is feminist analysis of Shakespeare.

In his exploration of Shakespeare's verbal ambiguity Rossiter is the inheritor and equal of William Empson whose *Seven Types of Ambiguity* (1930) lies behind *Angel with Horns*. For Rossiter local verbal complexity interconnects with broader questions of the plays' polysemous and multivalent techniques. Hence his identification of Shakespeare's frequent use of the rhetorical form *hendiadys* in the problem plays (p. 163) is part of his analysis of the plays' 'doubleness'. Particular examples of ambiguity are therefore seen as part of the plays' web of clashing ideologies, clashes not susceptible to resolution. As such the problem is of a piece with his analysis of his term 'ambivalence', a concept broader than Empsonian ambiguity and one which he develops most fully in examining the English histories.

Rossiter's repeated concern in the problem plays with questions of 'nobility' and 'virtue' return in his extraordinary study of *Coriolanus,* another neglected play which he does much to set at the centre of Shakespeare studies. For Rossiter is prepared to accept the play as political, as Shakespeare's most political or most evidently political play. While the studies of the problem plays only gesture elliptically in passing to the need to provide a Jacobean cultural and political context for the problem plays (as in the tantalising comment on *All's Well* that 'reference to the Jacobean social context only makes [Helena] more difficult' (p. 107)), Rossiter's analysis of *Coriolanus* is firmly located in the need to see the play in terms of the socio-political context of 1607, the year of the play's writing.

But in analysing the play as a work about politics, he also connects it with emotional affect; the play is not narrowly about political conflict but conflict in terms of 'political feeling' (p. 239), the excitement of concern, by the audience as well as the characters, with 'what happens to the Roman State' (p. 240). Rossiter's discussion of a posited authorial position in the play aligns Shakespeare's view of the plebeians closer to Coriolanus's than I would accept the play as necessarily demanding. The long tradition of anxiety about the mob is substantially rethought in the play: *Coriolanus* is not *Julius Caesar*. But his refusal to approach the play primarily as tragedy, defined by his recognition of the disappointment the play provokes when viewed as individualist tragedy, enables him to see the play's different strengths and to judge it '*one of* Shakespeare's most assured artistic successes' (p. 252).

Since Rossiter undervalues *Coriolanus's* willingness to understand the position of the plebeians he inevitably blurs something of the play's dialectic. But it is with the concept of a dialectic of ideologies, coupled with the concept of 'ambivalence', that *Angel with Horns* sets out Rossiter's analysis of the English Histories. Rossiter, rejecting as ever any attempts to straitjacket the plays, refuses to subscribe to the providentialist reading of the plays, a reading which still surfaces in a variety of guises. Rossiter does not find the opposition to the supposed Tudor orthodoxies in anything as simple as the outlining of an alternative Elizabethan theory of history. Instead he finds the providentialist interpretation of the processes of history opposed by a generic contrast. It is found, for instance, in the conflicting views of Richard III himself: as the Elizabethan tradition of Richard as 'Devil-King...a ready-made Senecan tyrant' (p. 21) and as Shakespeare's redefinition of him as 'a ruthless, demonic comedian with a most un-Senecan sense of humour' (p. 21). What prevents *Richard III* being the exposition of 'moral history' is, for Rossiter, Shakespeare's invention or espousal of 'comic history' (p. 22). The paradoxes contained in the comic view of history lead him to link Richard with Iago, Macbeth and Coriolanus and the last link means that 'you are past the great tragic phase and back in history again' (p. 22). The tensions inherent in comic history reappear throughout *Angel with Horns*, in the chapters on the problem plays and in the attempt to describe Shakespearean tragedy in terms of the alternative view offered by comedy and embraced within the tragedies themselves (chapters 13 and 14).

It is salutary at a time when much Shakespeare study seems content to bind Shakespeare into an inescapable net of Renaissance orthodoxies to see Rossiter finding him playing in consciously theatrical ways on those orthodoxies for distinctly subversive ends. Rossiter argues, for instance, that the emphatic verbal patterning of the language of *Richard III* is available to Shakespeare as a source of irony as well as orthodox assertion. Comic history infects language even in emphatically non-comic scenes, such as the scene of the women's lamentations (IV.iv).

Rossiter subsumes 'dramatic irony', the critic's conventional stand-by term, into 'ambivalence'. Instead of "one-eyed' simplifications', Rossiter finds in the Histories 'two opposed value-judgements' so that the 'whole is only fully experienced when both opposites are held and included in a "two-eyed" view' (p. 51), though in his account the reader seems to need many more 'eyes' to encompass the complexity of these plays. Taking his cue from what is for him a pregnant passage in Wordsworth's *The Borderers,* 'Suffering is permanent, obscure and dark' (quoted on p. 43), Rossiter develops his sense of the plays as revealing a 'chill and deeply saddening' mystery beneath the surface. Comic history, the possibility explored in *Richard III* and *1* and *2 Henry IV,* is not in itself sufficient: 'what isn't Comic History in the Histories is what I can only call 'Obscure Tragedy'' (p. 63). At moments like this, the climax of 'Ambivalence: the Dialectic of the Histories', perhaps Rossiter's finest achievement, the subtlety of Rossiter's thinking, trying to match himself to the subtleties of the plays, makes magnificently compatible the complexity of his ideas and the clarity of his expression.

Ambivalence is not, for Rossiter, a tidy concept. The recognition of the way that the English Histories work for him is profoundly disturbing. It is something he also found in a play he considered seminal in the development of

Shakespearean history, the anonymous and unpublished Elizabethan history play known as *Woodstock* which he edited as *Woodstock: A Moral History* (1946). If the introduction to the edition anticipates many of the themes that found their most crystalline expression in *Angel with Horns,* the view of 'moral history' he develops in the lectures might have led him to discard the phrase from the title of his edition. 'Moral history' is reassuringly conventional in precisely the way that neither *Woodstock* nor Shakespeare's Histories are. Instead the confrontation with the plays shows that the connection of life and scholarship over which Rossiter's Philip Chesterfield agonised is awesome and anxiety-ridden.

Reading *Angel with Horns* now is to see Rossiter's work in its own dialectic of history. If there are, as I have been suggesting, so many features of the book that are as powerful and necessary for our consideration of Shakespeare as they were when the book first appeared in 1961, there are, of course, others that belong to a past era of Shakespeare study. Inevitably for a man so aware of the tradition of academic Shakespeare scholarship, Rossiter often feels obliged to engage in argument with critics now forgotten. He is, too, unable to avoid a certain biographism, to read the plays in terms of a single generating consciousness, as the product of an author rather than as a body of texts. But, faced with so much that is as provocatively fresh as when it was first spoken in Cambridge lecture-rooms, the reader cannot treat the book as a historical curiosity. The issues in Shakespeare that matter to Rossiter are no less important now. *Angel with Horns* is as helpful as ever in the liberal studies to which Rossiter was committed, 'the study of the widest body of human knowledge without consideration of creed or place or time' *(Poor Scholars,* p. 354).

The publication of *Angel with Horns* was never Rossiter's intention. The book was edited from the lectures, after his death, by his colleague Graham Storey. As Graham Storey's student and colleague, I am glad to have the opportunity, writing this Introduction in the month of his retirement, to pay brief tribute to his editing. The care with which he undertook the presentation of Rossiter's work is no less than Rossiter's care in presenting Shakespeare's – I can find no higher terms of praise.

Cambridge,
September 1988.

PETER HOLLAND

I

Angel with Horns: The Unity of Richard III

'Let's write "good angel" on the devil's horn'—*Measure for Measure, II.* iv. 16

IN THE Second Part of *Henry IV* (III. i.) the King and Warwick are talking away the midnight, or the King's insomnia; and the King remembers how Richard spoke like a prophet of the future treachery of the Percies. Warwick replies that those who look for rotations in history can indeed appear to be prophets:

> There is a history in all men's lives,
> Figuring the nature of the times deceas'd;
> The which observ'd, a man may prophesy,
> With a near aim, of the main chance of things
> As yet not come to life, who in their seeds
> And weak beginnings lie intreasured.
> Such things become the hatch and brood of time.

Richard, he explains, had observed 'the necessary form' of the events he had seen happen; and from that he could 'create a perfect guess' of some that were to ensue as 'the hatch and brood of time'.

Men have always looked for such a predictability in history: it gives the illusion of a comfortably ordered world. They have also often read—and written—historical records to show that the course of events has been guided by a simple process of divine justice, dispensing rewards and punishments here on earth and seeing to it that the wicked do *not* thrive like the green bay-tree (as the Psalmist thought), and that virtue is not 'triumphant only in theatrical performances' (as the humane Mikado put it: being a Gilbertian Japanese, not an Elizabethan Christian). The story-matter of the Henry VI plays and of *Richard III* accepted both of these comforting and comfortable principles.

When I say 'story-matter' I mean what the Chronicles gave the author (or authors) of these four plays, and I wish to remain uncommitted as to whether their *plots* (and especially that of *Richard III*) work entirely within those reassuring limitations.

I am averse to source-study, as material for lectures. Yet sad experience of human nature (and perhaps of historians) leads me to remind you how the Richard III myth ('*story*') came to reach Shakespeare. In the play, you remember, the Bishop of Ely, Morton, plots with Buckingham and runs away to join Richmond (Henry Tudor). He duly became one of Henry's ministers; and Thomas More grew up in his household—and later wrote the life of Richard III. It would only be human if Morton recounted all the worst that was ever said of the master he had betrayed: it is not surprising that Edward Halle should accept More's account, in writing his vast book on the 'noble and illustre families of Lancastre and York'; and still more human that Raphael Holinshed (whom no one could call a historian) should copy extensively from Halle—and so leave room for all those since Horace Walpole who have had doubts about the historical character of this terrible monarch and the events of his times.

To think that we are seeing anything like sober history in this play is derisible naïvety. What we are offered is a formally patterned sequence presenting two things: on the one hand, a rigid Tudor *schema* of retributive justice (a sort of analogy to Newton's Third Law in the field of moral dynamics: 'Action and reaction are equal and *apposite*'); and, on the other, a huge triumphant stage-personality, an early old masterpiece of the art of rhetorical stage-writing, a monstrous being incredible in any sober, historical scheme of things—Richard himself.

I will talk about the first, first. The basic pattern of retributive justice (or God's vengeance) is well enough illustrated in Holinshed, in the passage telling how Prince Edward (Henry VI's son and Margaret's) was murdered at the Battle of Tewkesbury. The Prince was handed over to Edward IV on the proclamation of a promise that he would not be harmed; he was brought before the King, asked why he 'durst so presumptuously enter into his realm' and replied courageously 'To recover my father's kingdom and heritage' (and more to that purpose)—but let Holinshed say the rest:

> At which words king Edward said nothing, but with his hand thrust him from him, or (as some saie) stroke him with his gantlet; whom incontinentlie, George duke of Clarence, Richard duke of Glocester, Thomas Greie marquesse Dorcet, and William lord Hastings, that stood by, suddenlie murthered; for the which cruell act, the more part of the dooers in their latter daies dranke of the like cup, by the righteous iustice and due punishment of God.

There you have the notional pattern, in little, of the whole framework of *Richard III*: Clarence—'false, fleeting, perjur'd Clarence' (who took the sacrament to remain true to Henry VI of Lancaster and deserted him); Gray—one of the group of Queen Elizabeth Woodeville's relations, who fall to Richard and Buckingham next after Clarence; Hastings, who says he will see 'this crown of mine hewn from its shoulders/Before I see the crown so foul misplaced' (on Richard's head)—and *does* (if a man can be said to see his own decapitation). Holinshed really understates the matter in writing 'the more part of the dooers . . . dranke of the like cup'; for of those he names, everyone did. On the one hand, that is what *Richard III* is about: what it is composed of. A heavy-handed justice commends the ingredients of a poisoned [cup].

This notional pattern of historic events rigidly determined by a mechanical necessity is partly paralleled by, partly modified by, the formal patterns of the episodes (or scenes) and the language. By 'formal patterns' I mean the unmistakably iterated goings-on in scenes so exactly parallel that if the first *is* passable on a modern stage as quasi-realistic costume-play stuff, the second (repeating it always *more* unrealistically) cannot be. The two wooing-scenes (Richard with Anne and Elizabeth) are the simplest case; but in the lamentation-scenes—where a collection of bereft females comes together and goes through a dismal catalogue of *Who was Who* and *Who has lost Whom* (like a gathering of historical Mrs. Gummidges, each 'thinking of the old 'un' with shattering simultaneity)—there, even editors have found the proceedings absurd; and readers difficult. When Queen Margaret, for example, says:

I had an Edward, till a Richard kill'd him;
I had a husband, till a Richard kill'd him:
Thou hadst an Edward, till a Richard kill'd him;
Thou hadst a Richard, till a Richard kill'd him. (IV. iv. 40–43),

a reader may *just* keep up (and realize that the last two are the Princes in the Tower, so that Queen Elizabeth is being addressed); but when the Duchess of York takes up with

I had a Richard too, and thou didst kill him;
I had a Rutland too, thou holp'st to kill him,

it is likely that you are lost, unless your recollection of *3 Henry VI* and the ends of Richard, Duke of York and his young son (Edmund) is unusually clear.

It is not only the iteration of scene that is stylized: the stiffly formal manipulation of echoing phrase and sequence of words within the scenes is even more unrealistic. A closely related parallelism exists in the repeated occurrence of a sort of 'single line traffic' in sentences: the classicist's *stichomythia*. One speaker takes from the other exactly the same ration of syllables, and rejoins as if under contract to repeat the form of the given sentence as exactly as possible, using the maximum number of the same words or their logical opposites, or (failing that) words closely associated with them. I describe the game pedantically, because it *is* an exact and scientific game with language, and one of the graces and beauties of the play Shakespeare wrote. If we cannot accept the 'patterned speech' of *Richard III*, its quality must remain unknown to us. 'Early work' is an evasive, criticism-dodging term. Early it may be; but the play is a triumphant contrivance in a manner which cannot properly be compared with that of any other tragedy—nor of any history, except *3 Henry VI* (where the manner takes shape, and particularly in III. ii.) and *King John* (which is not half so well built or integrated as this).

I have emphasized the stylization of verbal patterning (with its neatly over-exact adjustments of stroke to stroke, as in royal tennis), because the sequence of most of the important events offers very much the same pattern. I might remark, in passing, that these verbal devices were offering to the Elizabethans an accomplished English equivalent to the neat dexterities they admired in Seneca (a point made by T. S. Eliot years ago; though he did not examine how the dramatic ironies of the action run in parallel with these counter-stroke reversals of verbal meaning, and form a kind of harmony). But we miss something more than Shakespeare's rhetorical game of tennis if merely irritated by, e.g.:

Anne: I would I knew thy heart.
Richard: 'Tis figured in my tongue.
Anne: I fear me, both are false.
Richard: Then never man was true.

Those reversals of intention (*heart-tongue*; *false-true*) are on precisely the pattern of the repeated reversals of human expectation, the reversals of events, the anticipated reversals (foreseen only by the audience), which make 'dramatic irony'. The patterned speech of the dialogue—the wit that demonstrates that a sentence is but a cheveril glove, quickly turned the other way—is fundamentally one with the ironic patterns of the plot. 'Dramatic irony' here is verbal *peripeteia.*

You will see that simply exemplified if you read Buckingham's speech at the beginning of Act II, where he calls a curse on himself if ever he goes back on his reconciliation with the Queen (and is quite specific about it); then turn straight to his last lines in V. i., when he is on the way to execution: 'That high All-seer, which I dallied with.' He has got exactly what he asked for. He did not mean the words he used, but they have been reversed into actuality, in exactly the same way as verbal terms are reversed in the tennis-court game of rhetoric.

The same irony plays all over *Richard III*. It lurks like a shadow behind the naïvely self-confident Hastings; it hovers a moment over Buckingham when Margaret warns him against 'yonder dog' (Richard), and, on Richard's asking what she said, he replies, 'Nothing that I respect, my gracious lord' (I. iii. 296) —and this at a time when Buckingham is under no threat whatsoever.

Its cumulative effect is to present the personages as existing in a state of total and terrible uncertainty. This is enhanced if we know the details of what comes into the play from *3 Henry VI*, but is there even if we know only a few bare essentials of what has gone before. We need to know who Margaret is; how Lancaster has been utterly defeated, and King Henry and his son murdered; how Clarence betrayed his King and returned to the Yorkists; and how Richard, his younger brother, has already marked him as his immediate obstruction on his intended way to the crown. We need to know too that the Duchess of York is mother to that unrewarding trio, Edward IV, Clarence, Gloucester; that Edward IV has married an aspiring commoner, Elizabeth Grey (*née* Woodeville); and that she has jacked up her relations into nobility. Beyond those half-dozen facts we do not need back-reference to *3 Henry VI* for any but the finer points—so far as the essential ironies of the plot go.

Far more important than these details is the simple overriding principle derived from the Tudor historians: that England rests under a chronic curse—the curse of faction, civil dissension and fundamental anarchy, resulting from the deposition and murder of the Lord's Anointed (Richard II) and the usurpation of the House of Lancaster. The savageries of the Wars of the Roses follow logically (almost theologically) from that; and Elizabeth's 'All-seeing heaven, what a world is this!' says but half. It is a world of absolute and hereditary moral ill, in which *everyone* (till the appearance of Richmond-Tudor in Act V) is tainted with the treacheries, the blood and the barbarities of civil strife, and internally blasted with the curse of a moral anarchy which leaves but three human *genera*: the strong in evil, the feebly wicked and the helplessly guilt-tainted (such as the Princes, Anne—all those despairing, lamenting women, whose choric wailings are a penitentional psalm of guilt and sorrow: England's guilt, the individual's sorrow). The 'poor painted Queen's' 'What a world' needs supplementing with the words of the pessimistically clear-sighted Third Citizen:

> All may be well; but, if God sort it so,
> 'Tis more than we deserve or I expect. (II. iii. 36)

I have in effect described the meaning of the framework of the play: presented it as 'moral history', to be interpreted in abstract terms. But the play itself is also a symphonic structure which I can only describe in terms of music: a rhetorical symphony of five movements, with first and second subjects and some Wagnerian *Leitmotifs*. The play-making framework is Senecan revenge, the characterization largely Marlovian; but the orchestration is not only original, but unique. It can be sketched like this.

The first movement employs five 'subjects': Richard himself, his own overture; the wooing-theme (to be repeated in the fourth movement); Richard among his enemies (repeating the duplicity with which he has fooled Clarence); Margaret's curse; and the long dying fall of Clarence. It occupies the whole of Act I.

The second movement includes Act II. and scenes i.-iv. of Act III. It begins with the King's feeble peace-making—in which Buckingham invites his curse—and its other subjects are: a lamentation after the King's death (repeated in the fourth movement); the fall of the curse on Rivers, Grey and Vaughan (when the curse is remembered), and on Hastings (the curse briefly recalled again). The future subject of Richard's moves against the Princes is introduced between-whiles.

The third movement cuts across the Act-divisions and runs from III. v. to IV. iii. Its main subject is the Gloucester-Buckingham plot for the crown, with the magnificently sardonic fooling of the London *bourgeoisie* with a crisis-scare, a brace of bishops, and the headline-story that here is a highly respectable unlibidinous monarch for decent England. On its success, Anne is called to be Queen, and thus to meet the curse she herself called on Richard's wife before he wooed her in that humour and won her (the first movement is here caught up). Buckingham now makes himself one of Richard's future victims by showing reluctance for the plot against the Princes, and Richard throws him off with a snub. The Princes are dealt with (the account of Forrest and Deighton echoing that of the murderers of Clarence, one of whom had a temporary conscience); and Richard concludes with a brisk summary and prospectus:

> The sons of Edward sleep in Abraham's bosom,
> And Anne my wife hath bid this world good night;

and so, since Richmond plans to marry 'young Elizabeth, my brother's daughter,' 'To her go I, a jolly thriving wooer'. (Richard's last jocularity). The movement ends with the first murmurs of Richmond. Previously there has been slipped in the trivial-sounding prophecy about 'Rugemount', besides Henry VI's prophecy (IV. ii. 99 f.). The flight of the Bishop of Ely (Morton) really troubles Richard.

The fourth movement brings down the curse on Buckingham (V. i. is obviously misplaced, so the movement runs from IV. iv. to V. i. inclusive). Mainly it repeats themes heard before: with a long lamentation-scene (the Blake-like weeping Queens); a repetition of Margaret's curse with the curse of Richard's mother added; the second wooing-scene; the subject of Nemesis repeated by Buckingham. In it the sound of Richmond's advance has become clearer; and Richard's self-command and certainty begin to waver.

The fifth movement is all at Bosworth: the fall of the curse on Richard himself. There is the dream-prologue of the procession of contrapuntal Ghosts (including all those so qualified from the four previous movements) and, like all ghosts, they are reminiscent and repetitive. The play ends with the epilogue to the Wars of the Roses—spoken by Queen Elizabeth's grandfather—calling a blessing on the English future, and inverting the opening lines of Richard's prologue:

> Now is the winter of our discontent
> Made glorious summer . . .

The deliberateness of this highly controlled workmanship needs but little comment. I shall take up a single musical phrase: one that intertwines its plangent undertones throughout the whole symphony, a true *Leitmotif*.

At first sight, Clarence's dream (I. iv. 9 f.) appears to contribute little to the play, nothing to the plot; and it may seem a rhetorical indulgence, even if we accept Mr. Eliot's judgement that it shows 'a real approximation in English to the magnificence of Senecan Latin at its best. . . . The best of Seneca has here been absorbed into English.'[1] But first recollect the setting. Clarence has been sent to the Tower, by the machinations of the Queen's party (so he thinks), and he is confident that his brother Richard will stand good friend to him. He believes Richard's worried 'We are not safe, Clarence; we are not safe'; cannot possibly see the ironical joke Richard is cracking with himself; has no idea that he has been first on Richard's list since that moment in *3 Henry VI* (v. vi. 84) when his brother muttered, 'Clarence, beware; thou keep'st me from the light'.[2] (A line that follows a passage predetermining the gulling of both Clarence and Anne to follow:

> I have no brother, I am like no brother;
> And this word 'love', which greybeards call divine,
> Be resident in men like one another,
> And not in me! I am myself alone).

Clarence had not been there to hear that: knows nothing of the

[1] *Selected Essays*, 1932, p. 90; reprinted from Introduction to *Seneca His Tenne Tragedies*, 1927.

[2] This contradicts R. G. Moulton, *Shakespeare as a Dramatic Artist*, 1885 (p. 92), who says Richard is *not* 'ambitious' (as Macbeth is): 'never found dwelling upon the prize in view.' This presumes a complete disconnection between *3 Henry VI* and *Richard III*. No such assumption is acceptable nowadays—nor was it sensible even then.

typically sharp reversal of Richard's solemnly hypocritical fooling now with:

> Go tread the path that thou shalt ne'er return.
> Simple, plain Clarence, I do love thee so
> That I will shortly send thy soul to heaven,
> If heaven will take the present at our hands. (I. i. 117–20)

Clarence has his nightmare in the Tower: a vision prophetic of doom, and thick with curdled guilt. He dreams that Richard blunderingly knocks him overboard from a vessel; he drowns; goes to hell; and his guilt-sick mind spews up its own evil:

> *Keeper:* Awak'd you not in this sore agony?
> *Clarence:* No, no, my dream was lengthen'd after life.
> O, then began the tempest to my soul!
> I pass'd, methought, the melancholy flood
> With that sour ferryman which poets write of,
> Unto the kingdom of perpetual night.
> The first that there did greet my stranger soul
> Was my great father-in-law, renowned Warwick,
> Who spake aloud 'What scourge for perjury
> Can this dark monarchy afford false Clarence?'
> And so he vanish'd. Then came wand'ring by
> A shadow like an angel, with bright hair
> Dabbled in blood, and he shriek'd out aloud
> 'Clarence is come—false, fleeting, perjur'd Clarence,
> That stabb'd me in the field by Tewkesbury.
> Seize on him, Furies, take him unto torment!'
> (I. iv. 42–57)

It is as fine a passage in that style as English can offer: calculated to leave its solemn music in even half-attentive ears. In the second movement of the play (II. ii. 43 f.), Queen Elizabeth announces the King's death:

> If you will live, lament; if die, be brief,
> That our swift-winged souls may catch the King's,
> Or like obedient subjects follow him
> To his new kingdom of ne'er-changing night.

It is scarcely a proper-wifely expectation of the fate of her husband's spirit: but the echo of 'Unto the kingdom of perpetual night' is the effect intended, not Elizabeth's notions. The actors who put together the Q. text of 1597 showed that they appreciated, if clumsily, the author's intention. They made it 'To his new kingdom of perpetuall rest': catching the echo rightly, while missing the point.

The same 'dark monarchy' awaits all these people: they are the living damned. That is the translation of this echo-technique of *Leitmotifs*; and why I call the play's anatomy 'musical'. Nor is that all: the phrase returns again. But before I come to that, remark how Hastings philosophizes on his fall at the end of the second movement:

> O momentary grace of mortal men,
> Which we more hunt for than the grace of God!
> Who builds his hope in air of your good[1] looks
> Lives like a drunken sailor on a mast,
> Ready with every nod to tumble down
> Into the fatal bowels of the deep. (III. iv. 98–103)

We have heard that surging rhythm before. And with it the feeling of being aloft, in air, unbalanced: the rhythm of Clarence dreaming:

> As we pac'd along
> Upon the giddy footing of the hatches,
> Methought that Gloucester stumbled, and in falling
> Struck me, that thought to stay him, overboard
> Into the tumbling billows of the main. (I. iv. 16–20)

Pattern repeats pattern with remarkable exactitude. 'Into the fatal bowels of the deep' is where the giddy Hastings also goes. 'O Lord, methought what pain it was to drown' might be extended to all these desperate swimmers in the tide of pomp and history. The elaboration of the dream is no mere exercise in fine phrase on Latin models: it offers a symbol of choking suspense above black depths (the ocean, and perpetual night) which

[1] Qq. faire.

epitomizes the 'momentary grace' of all these 'mortal men' and women. And the sea as figure of 'the destructive element' appears again in Elizabeth's lines in the second wooing-scene:

> But that still use of grief makes wild grief tame,
> My tongue should to thy ears not name my boys
> Till that my nails were anchor'd in thine eyes;
> And I, in such a desp'rate bay of death,
> Like a poor bark, of sails and tackling reft,
> Rush all to pieces on thy rocky bosom. (IV. iv. 229–34)

'Bay' of death suggests also an animal at bay; just plausibly relevant, since Richard (the boar) would be at bay when she *could* scratch his eyes out. But the repetition of the rather too emphatic anchors and the eyes from Clarence's dream is much more striking.

You will find a further echo of the 'night-motif' in the last movement. Richard suspects Stanley (confusingly also called Derby), and reasonably so: for he was husband to the Countess of Richmond, Henry Tudor's mother, the famous Lady Margaret Beaufort; and therefore keeps his son, George Stanley, as hostage. Before Bosworth, he sends a brisk message to warn the father of the black depths beneath the son; and again Shakespeare sounds his doom-music from the Clarence sequence:

> bid him bring his power
> Before sunrising, lest his son George fall
> Into the blind cave of eternal night. (V. iii. 60–2)

Need I remark that Clarence was 'George' too, and lightly called that by Richard when he was afraid that King Edward might die before he signed his brother's death-warrant?

> He cannot live, I hope, and must not die
> Till George be packed with post-horse up to heaven.
> (I. ii. 145)

I could further exemplify the play's tight-woven artistry by taking up that very remarkable prose-speech on 'conscience' by Clarence's Second Murderer (I. iv. 133 f.), and following the word into Richard's troubled mind in Act v. before Margaret's curse attains its last fulfilment. But to reduce attention to Richard himself in his own play, beyond what I am already committed to by my insistence on taking the play as a *whole* (as a dramatic pattern, not an exposition of 'character'), would be to do it—and Shakespeare—an injustice.

Richard Plantagenet is alone with Macbeth as the Shakespearian version of the thoroughly bad man in the role of monarch and hero; he is unique in combining with that role that of the diabolic humorist. It is this quality which makes it an inadequate account to say that the play is 'moral history', or that the protagonists are the personality of Richard and the curse of Margaret (or what it stood for in orthodox Tudor thinking about retributive justice in history)—for all that these opposed 'forces' *are* central throughout. The first movement establishes both, and emphatically. First, Richard, stumping down the stage on his unequal legs, forcing his hitched-up left shoulder and his withered arm on us, till we realize that *this* is what the 'winter of our discontent' in *3 Henry VI* has produced, *this* the proper 'hatch and brood of time'; and then, Richard established, his cruel and sardonic effectiveness demonstrated on Clarence and Anne, there arises against his brazen Carl Orff-like music the one voice he quails before (if but slightly): the sub-dominant notes of Margaret and her prophecy of doom, to which the ghosts will walk in the visionary night before Bosworth. It is a conflict between a spirit and a ghost: between Richard, the spirit of ruthless will, of daemonic pride, energy and self-sufficiency, of devilish gusto and *Schadenfreude* (he *enjoys* wickedness even when it is of no practical advantage to his ambitions or to securing himself by murder: it may be only wickedness in *words*, but the spirit revealed is no less evilly exultant for that); and the ghost, as I call her—for what else is Margaret, Reignier's daughter picked up on a battlefield by Suffolk and married to that most etiolated of Shakespeare's husbands, Henry VI, but the living ghost of Lancaster, the walking dead, memorializing the long, cruel, treacherous, bloody conflict of the years of civil strife and pitiless butchery?

You can, of course, see more there if you will. Make her the last stage or age of woman-in-politics: she who has been beautiful, fiercely passionate, queenly, dominating, master of armies, *generalissima*; now old, defeated, empty of everything but fierce bitterness, the illimitable bitterness and rancour of political zeal. What did Yeats write of *his* equivalent symbol? It is in *A Prayer for my Daughter.* For her he prays:

> An intellectual hatred is the worst,
> So let her think opinions are accursed.
> Have I not seen the loveliest woman born
> Out of the mouth of Plenty's horn,
> Because of her opinionated mind
> Barter that horn and every good
> By quiet natures understood
> For an old bellows full of angry wind?

Margaret is that, if you like; but, not to go beyond Shakespeare, I cannot but think that when the old Duchess of York sits down upon the ground for the second lamentation-scene (to tell 'sad stories of the death of kings'), the *author's* mind ran more upon Margaret as he wrote:

> Dead life, blind sight, poor mortal living ghost, . . .
> Brief abstract and record of tedious days,
> Rest thy unrest on England's lawful earth,
> Unlawfully made drunk with innocent blood. (IV. iv. 26, 28–30)

Here Shakespeare devises a new variation on the Senecan visitant from another world howling for revenge, by making the spectre nominal flesh and blood; the tune of the Dance of Death to which all dance to damnation is played by Margaret; and one aspect of the play is our watching the rats go into the Weser, compelled by that fatal tune.

But Richard himself is not simply the last and most important (and worst) of the victims—if those justly destroyed can be called 'victims'. That is just where the label 'moral history' is inadequate. For Richard has grown a new dimension since his abrupt and remarkable development in *3 Henry VI*: he has become a wit, a mocking comedian, a 'vice of kings'—but with a clear inheritance from the old Vice of the Moralities: part symbol of evil, part comic devil, and chiefly, on the stage, the generator of roars of laughter at wickednesses (whether of deed or word) which the audience would immediately condemn in real life. On the one hand, his literary relations with the Senecan 'Tyrant' (author of 'In regna mea Mors impetratur', etc.) are clear enough; as they are with the Elizabethan myth of 'the murderous Machiavel' ('feared am I more than loved/ Let me be feared,' etc.): enough has been written on them. But only the medieval heritage—from the comic devils with their *Schadenfreude*, and the Vice as comic inverter of order and decency—can fully explain the new Richard of this apparent sequel to the *Henry VI* series.

I have said that the Christian pattern imposed on history gives the simple plot of a cast accursed, where all are evil beings, all deserve punishment. Look, then, with a believing Tudor eye, and ought you not to *approve* Richard's doings? *Per se*, they are the judgment of God on the wicked; and he

> *Ein Teil von jener Kraft*
> *Die stets das Böse will, und stets das Gute schafft.*[1]

But that is not all. Richard's sense of humour, his function as clown, his comic irreverences and sarcastic or sardonic appropriations of things to (at any rate) *his* occasions: all those act as underminers of our assumed naïve and proper Tudor principles; and we are on his side much rather because he makes us (as the Second Murderer put it) 'take the devil in [our] mind', than for any 'historical-philosophical-Christian-retributional' sort of motive. In this respect a good third of the play is a kind of grisly *comedy*; in which we meet the fools to be taken in on Richard's terms, see them with his mind, and rejoice with him

[1] 'A part of that Power which always wills evil and yet always brings about good.' (Goethe's *Faust*)

in their stultification (in which execution is the ultimate and unanswerable practical joke, the absolutely final laugh this side of the Day of Judgment). Here, Richard is a middle-term between Barabas, the Jew of Malta (*c.* 1590) and Volpone (1606). He inhabits a world where everyone deserves everything he can do to them; and in his murderous practical joking he is *inclusively* the comic exposer of the mental shortcomings (the intellectual and moral deformities) of this world of beings depraved and besotted. If we forget to pity them awhile (and he does his best to help us), then his impish spirit urges us towards a positive reversal of 'Christian charity' until the play's fourth movement (which is when the Elizabethan spectator began to back out, I take it)—or even beyond that point.

An aspect of Richard's appeal, which has, I fancy, passed relatively unexamined,[1] is one that we can be confident that William Shakespeare felt and reflected on. I mean the appeal of the actor: the talented being who can assume every mood and passion at will, at all events to the extent of making others believe in it. Beyond question, all our great actors have regarded the part as a fine opportunity. The extent to which the histrionic art (as Shakespeare thought and felt about it) contributed to the making of this great stage-figure is to me more interesting.

The specific interest here is the *power* that would be in the hands of an actor consummate enough to make (quite literally) 'all the world a stage' and to work on humanity by the perfect simulation of every feeling: the appropriate delivery of every word and phrase that will serve his immediate purpose; together with the complete dissimulation of everything that might betray him (whether it be his intentions, or such obstructive feelings as compunction, pity or uncertainty of mind). This appears at once when Gloucester first takes shape as the man self-made to be King, in the long soliloquy in *3 Henry VI* (III. ii. 124 f.). The closing lines are specifically on histrionic genius:

[1] [J. Middleton Murry, *Shakespeare*, 1936, pp. 125–6, quotes the theatrical metaphors and remarks briefly on the conception of Richard as an actor.]

Why, I can smile, and murder whiles I smile,
And cry 'Content!' to that which grieves my heart,
And wet my cheeks with artificial tears,
And frame my face to all occasions. (ibid. 182–5)

And then, after a little bragging prospectus on his intended deadliness, he ends:

I can add colours to the chameleon,
Change shapes with Protheus for advantages,
And set the murderous Machiavel to school.
Can I do this, and cannot get a crown?
Tut, were it farther off, I'll pluck it down. (ibid. 191–5)

M. R. Ridley notes here that 'Machiavelli . . . seems to have been to the Elizabethans a type of one who advocated murder as a method of cold-blooded policy.'[1] It is true that that marks off one point of difference between the 'Senecan' tyrant-villainy (which is primarily for revenge) and the 'Machiavellian' (which is for power, or self-aggrandizement: 'We that are great, our own self-good still moves us'): though I do not think that the distinction can be maintained, if you read Seneca. But surely Ridley's note misses the point, in its context? What the 'Machiavel' allusion represents is, I believe, Shakespeare's recognition that the programme set before the Prince in *Il Principe* is one that demands exactly those histrionic qualities I have just described: a lifelong, unremitting vigilance in relentless simulation and impenetrable deception. There, precisely, lies the super-humanity of the Superman. The will-to-power is shorn of its effective power without it. He is an *artist* in evil.

Now Richard in his own play shows this power—these powers—to perfection. Except to the audience, he is invisible; but the audience he keeps reminded not only of his real intentions, but equally of his actor's artistries. The bluff plain Englishman, shocked at ambitious go-getters and grievingly misunderstood, is perfectly 'done' before the Queen's relations:

[1] *New Temple* edn., p. 140.

Because I cannot flatter and look fair,
Smile in men's faces, smooth, deceive, and cog,
Duck with French nods and apish courtesy,
I must be held a rancorous enemy.
Cannot a plain man live and think no harm
But thus his simple truth must be abus'd
With silken, sly, insinuating Jacks? (I. iii. 47–53)

A little later, it is: 'I am too childish-foolish for this world,' (ibid., 142); and even: 'I thank my God for my humility'. (II. i. 72).

Then, left to himself and the audience, after egging on all their quarrels:

But then I sigh and, with a piece of Scripture,
Tell them that God bids us do good for evil.
And thus I clothe my naked villainy
With odd old ends stol'n forth of holy writ,
And seem a saint when most I play the devil. (I. iii. 334–8)

The stage-direction, '*Enter two Murderers*', caps this nicely. It is not simply that Richard is a hypocrite and (like other stage-villains) tells us so. The actor's technique of 'asides' is the essence of his chuckling private jokes—made to 'myself alone'. (You might say that Shakespeare is giving not merely 'the acting of drama', but also 'the drama of consummate *acting*').

The same reminders, nudging the audience's attention, appear in his swift-switched actual asides: e.g., his thoroughly unholy reception of his mother's blessing, spoken as he gets up off his dutiful knees:

Amen! And make me die a good old man!
That is the butt end of a mother's blessing;
I marvel that her Grace did leave it out. (II. ii. 109–11)

Or, again, we have Richard's insinuating equivocations in talking to the prattling little Princes; in one of which he acknowledges his theatrical-historical legacy from the Moralities: 'Thus, like the formal vice, Iniquity,/I moralize two meanings in one word.' (III. i. 82–3). Over and above this there is that striking passage (III. v. 1–11) where he and Buckingham are working up a crisis (appearing ill-dressed in old rusty armour, as if they had armed in desperate haste), when Richard specifically inquires whether Buckingham can 'do the stage-tragedian':

Richard: Come, cousin, canst thou quake and change thy colour,
Murder thy breath in middle of a word,
And then again begin, and stop again,
As if thou wert distraught and mad with terror?
Buckingham: Tut, I can counterfeit the deep tragedian;
Speak and look back, and pry on every side,
Tremble and start at wagging of a straw,
Intending deep suspicion. Ghastly looks
Are at my service, like enforced smiles;
And both are ready in their offices
At any time to grace my stratagems.

It is all sardonically jocular; but nothing shows more clearly the artist's delight in his craft: call it illusion or deception, it makes no odds. It is this dexterity that his other rapid reversals of tone keep us aware of; whether he is half-amazedly rejoicing in his conquest of Anne, or poking unfilial fun at his mother (a performance more shocking to Elizabethans than to our more child-foolish days).

Yet again, there is that admirable moment when the Londoners are being fooled into believing that he must be persuaded to be king; when Buckingham pretends to lose patience, with 'Zounds, I'll entreat no more.' And Richard, bracketed aloft with two Bishops, is distressed: 'O, do not swear, my lord of Buckingham.' (III. vii. 220). (It is like the moment in *Eric or Little by Little* (ch. 8) when Eric refers to the usher as a 'surly devil'; and the virtuous Russell exclaims: 'O Eric, that is the first time that I have heard you swear.') It is this unholy jocularity, the readiness of sarcastic, sardonic, profane and sometimes blasphemous wit, the demonic gusto of it all, which not only wins the audience over to accepting the Devil as hero, but also points us towards the central paradox of the play. And, through that, to a full critical awareness of its unity: with a few remarks on which I shall conclude.

To begin with Richard. On the face of it, he is the demon-Prince, the cacodemon born of hell, the misshapen toad, etc. (all things ugly and ill). But through his prowess as actor and his embodiment of the comic Vice and impish-to-fiendish humour, he offers the false as more attractive than the true (the actor's function), and the ugly and evil as admirable and amusing (the clown's game of value-reversals). You can say, 'We don't take him seriously.' I reply, 'That is exactly what gets most of his acquaintances into Hell: just what the devil-clown relies on.' But he is not only this demon incarnate, he is in effect God's agent in a predetermined plan of divine retribution: the 'scourge of God'. Now by Tudor-Christian historical principles, this plan is *right*. Thus, in a real sense, Richard is a King who 'can do no wrong'; for in the pattern of the justice of divine retribution on the wicked, he functions as an avenging angel. Hence my paradoxical title, 'Angel with Horns.'

The paradox is sharpened by what I have mainly passed by: the repulsiveness, humanely speaking, of the 'justice'. God's will it may be, but it sickens us: it is as pitiless as the Devil's (who is called in to execute it). The contrast with Marlowe's painless, dehumanized slaughterings in *Tamburlaine* is patent.

This overall system of *paradox* is the play's unity. It is revealed as a constant displaying of inversions, or reversals of meaning: whether we consider the verbal patterns (the *peripeteias* or reversals of act and intention or expectation); the antithesis of false and true in the histrionic character; or the constant inversions of irony. Those verbal capsizings I began by talking about, with their deliberate reversals to the opposite meaning in equivocal terms, are the exact correlatives of both the nature of man (or man in power: Richard) and of the nature of events (history); and of language too, in which all is conveyed.

But, start where you will, you come back to history; or to the pattern made out of the conflict of two 'historical myths'. The orthodox Tudor myth made history God-controlled, divinely prescribed and dispensed, to move things towards a God-ordained perfection: Tudor England. Such was the *frame* that Shakespeare took. But the total effect of Shakespeare's 'plot' has quite a different effect from Halle: a very different meaning. Dr. Duthie may write, 'But there is no doubt that Shakespeare saw history in the same light as Halle saw it.'[1] I say there *is* doubt. Dover Wilson has nothing to offer but what he summarizes from Moulton, but his last sentence points my doubting way: 'it appears, to me at least, unlikely that Shakespeare's "main end" in *Richard III* was "to show the working out of God's will in English history".'[2] (The quotation he is discussing is from Tillyard's *Shakespeare's History Plays* (1944), p. 208.) He can go no further because his own limitations on *Henry IV* inhibit his ever observing that the comic Richard has no more place in Halle's scheme than Falstaff has.

The other myth is that of Richard the Devil-King: the Crookback *monstrum informe, ingens* whom Shakespeare *found* as a ready-made Senecan tyrant and converted into a quite different inverter of moral order: a ruthless, demonic comedian with a most un-Senecan sense of humour and the seductive appeal of an irresistible gusto, besides his volcanic Renaissance energies. They are themselves demoralizing: *Tapfer sein ist gut*[3] is the antithesis of a Christian sentiment.

The outcome of this conflict of myths was Shakespeare's display of constant inversions of meaning; in all of which, two systems of meaning impinge and go over to their opposites, like the two 'ways' of the cheveril glove. This applies equally to words and word-patterns; to the actor-nature; to dramatic ironies; and to events, as the hatch and brood of time, contrasted with opposite expectations.

As a result of the paradoxical ironic structure built from these inversions of meaning—built above all by Richard's demonic appeal—the naïve, optimistic, 'Christian' principle of history,

[1] G. I. Duthie, *Shakespeare*, 1951, p. 118.
[2] *Richard III* (*New Cambridge* edn., 1954), p. xlv.
[3] 'To be bold is good.'

consoling and comfortable, modulates into its opposite. The 'Christian' system of retribution is undermined, counterbalanced, by historic irony. (Do I need to insist that the coupling of 'Christian' and 'retribution' itself is a paradox? That the God of vengeance is *not* a Christian God; that his opposite is a God of mercy who has no representation in this play. If I do, I had better add that the so-called 'Christian' frame is indistinguishable from a pagan one of Nemesis in which the 'High all-seer' is a Fate with a cruel sense of humour.)

But do not suppose I am saying that the play is a 'debunking of Tudor myth', or that Shakespeare is disproving it. He is not 'proving' anything: not even that 'Blind belief is sure to err/ And scan his works in vain' (though I think that is *shown*, nevertheless). Contemporary 'order'-thought spoke as if naïve faith saw true: God was above God's Englishmen and ruled with justice—which meant summary vengeance. This historic myth offered absolutes, certainties. Shakespeare in the Histories always leaves us with relatives, ambiguities, irony, a process thoroughly dialectical. Had he entirely accepted the Tudor myth, the frame and pattern of order, his way would have led, I suppose, towards writing *moral history* (which is what Dr. Tillyard and Dr. Dover Wilson and Professor Duthie have made *out* of him). Instead, his way led him towards writing *comic history*. The former would never have taken him to tragedy: the latter (paradoxically) did. Look the right way through the cruel-comic side of Richard and you glimpse Iago. Look back at him through his energy presented as evil, and you see Macbeth. And if you look at the irony of men's struggles in the nets of historic circumstance, the ironies of their pride and self-assurance, you will see Coriolanus; and you are past the great tragic phase and back in history again.

2

Richard II

THE ANCIENTS had a thrifty habit of scrubbing parchments and using them again: these written-over documents are called palimpsests. It is a pity that frugal Elizabethan dramatists did not use parchments for play-books: we should not then need to rely on the hazardous ultra-violet of interpretative criticism or the infra-red of critical bibliography, to decide whether to treat a play as a palimpsest or some other kind of problem, such as lack of coherence in its author's mind, divided aims, and the like. We only want to know things like this where immediate or considered subjective reaction makes us feel some kind of discontinuity, or inconsistency, in the *stuff* (a vague term, used deliberately: ultimately, the arrangements of words and their effects).

Over *Richard II* most critics have felt this. Pater is an exception: for him it does possess 'like a musical composition . . . a certain concentration of all its parts, a simple continuity, an evenness in execution, which are rare in the great dramatist'.[1] Dover Wilson echoes this; but elsewhere excludes the Fifth Act, which he wants blamed on to one of his 'old plays': the lucubrations of that Master William Hypothesis, energetic researcher but no poet, who 'assembled' Shakespeare's plots. Other commentators are bothered by inconsistencies or discontinuities; and I share their view. Whether you approach *Richard II* from the angle of the texture of the verse, the verse-styles, character, plot or theme, you encounter what geologists call 'unconformities':

[1] *Appreciations*, p. 210.

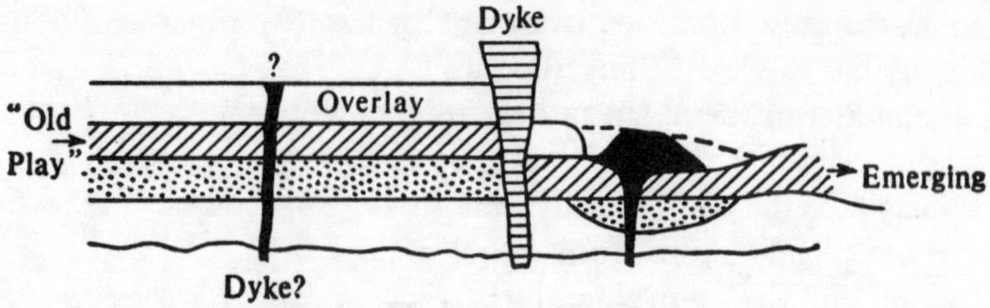

The strata right of the 'dyke' are said to be 'unconformable'; and as geology has an overriding time-scheme, the dykes and upper layers are 'later' than the rest. Applied to a play, it is only a rough analogy; although 'old play' and 'revisionist' theories will accept it as descriptively diagrammatic. I only use it to clarify the word 'unconformable': implying 'the whole *may* be consistent; but only if we have a theory of derangements or interruptions'.

If ours is the character-approach, we find a lack of continuity between the Richard of Acts I and II and the melancholy introvert re-imported from Ireland. Those who praise the play as character-piece most highly, seem to *begin* their reading with Act III; and to 'explain' the autocratic, capricious Richard of the first two acts as an imperious adolescent play-acting. This does not cover up the *lack of inside* in the early Richard; and when Coleridge remarks on 'a constant flow of emotions from a total incapability of controlling them . . . a waste of that energy which should have been reserved for action', he as clearly labels the *second* Richard as he misses the *first*, who shows uncontrolled *action* and a lack of *feeling*. He makes him a Hamlet of the sentiments: i.e. what Coleridge thought 'thought' was to Hamlet, he made emotion to Richard.

Dowden, in a study mainly very sound in what it points to, leaves him as sentimentalist, dreamer and dilettante; with a wistful charm, but condemned morally for want of what Newman called 'seriousness of the intellect: the adult mind'. That at any rate gives a firm line. There is something in Richard which calls out the latent homosexuality of critics; and I am gratified to find Dowden resisting it. Pater[1] is all the other way: Richard

[1] *Appreciations: Shakespeare's English Kings.*

is 'an exquisite poet . . . from first to last, in light and gloom alike, able to see all things poetically, to give a poetic turn to his conduct of them' (and so on, to be softly echoed in a dozen school editions). 'What a garden of words!' as Pater says. Others take the diametrically opposite view of exactly the same matter: plainly more from moral than dramatic reasons. And for all but the stern moralists, Richard's physical beauty is almost a main characteristic. You can dodge all contradictions by taking Aristotle's *ὁμαλῶς ἀνώμαλον*[1]; but, despite Aristotle, I think that such a character cannot be tragic: it surely lacks the perspicuity which makes logic of the tragic action.

About the other characters the critics are fairly agreed. Bolingbroke is an outline—a strong one; Gaunt is made rather too much of, considering he is gone by Act III; the Favourites are zeros; York 'an incomparable, an incredible, an unintelligible and a monstrous nullity' (Swinburne) or (G. M. Young) 'the first civil servant in our literature'.[2] (I do not offer these as synonyms.) In short, they are mainly orchestra: Gaunt, the wood-wind Queen, Messengers, marches and noises-off.

If we consider the play's themes, we find that although political approaches—making the play historical-epical-moral—do something to smooth-in the Duchess of Gloucester (I, ii.), the omens, the Gardener and the substance of Gaunt, they cannot make the beginning unragged, nor the rumpus in Westminster Hall (the second Quarrel-scene) clearly relevant; nor do anything to put the York-Aumerle scenes into any sort of order or 'degree'. To generalize, most commentators direct attention to parts of the play which they *can* manage, and tacitly divert it from 'misfits' they cannot; and in this there is no great critical difference between 'character' and 'thematic' approaches. Both do vaguely agree in taking measures to smooth over a kind of 'fold' between Acts II and III; and both, in different ways, have difficulties over Shakespeare's not very pellucid method of

[1] 'consistently inconsistent'.

[2] In a private letter to Dover Wilson quoted in the *New Cambridge* edn. of *Richard II*, p. iv.

presenting some of the essentials of the story, over the awkward way in which he leaves us to guess here and there, mainly in, or as a result of, Acts I and II. This also applies to his artistic intentions. The view of the play as 'ceremonial'; Dover Wilson's contention that 'it ought to be played throughout as ritual . . . it stands far closer to the Catholic service of the Mass than to Ibsen's *Brand* or . . . *St. Joan*'; the lyrical-tragedy view;[1] the poet-king view: all show a similar smoothing-over of unconformities, once taken back to the text.

If we look at the verse, it is a crude discrimination to say there are three styles: rhyme (mainly couplets) and two sorts of blank verse—that of the Deposition, say, and an 'earlier' kind. The 'early' type in fact ranges from a flattish competence (Act I, or Bolingbroke at V. iii. 1–12, 'Can no man tell me of my unthrifty son? . . .') to a jumbled incompetence, aptly described by York's comment on the state of England at II. ii. 121–2:

> All is uneven,
> And everything is left at six and seven.

The couplets vary as much, although this is less striking, as Shakespeare wrote within a convention that did not *hear* bad couplets as we hear them; and in Acts I and II especially they pop in and out most disconcertingly. The worst in both kinds, rhyme and blank verse, is distressingly or comically bad. As a *formal* type of play in what Dover Wilson[2] calls 'deliberately patterned speech', it contrasts strikingly with the operatic consistency of *Richard III*.

Examine the texture of the verse, and Eliot's 'patterned speech' *is* there; mainly in the 'early' type of verse, but also in some of the other. It is easiest seen where not very good: where it represents the heavily over-written Elizabethan High-Renaissance manner, over-ingenious with a mainly *verbal* wit, and obtrusive. It is obtrusive, I mean, in Keats's sense: 'Poetry should be great and *unobtrusive*, a thing which enters into one's

[1] If this is what Dover Wilson's relation of it to *Love's Labour's Lost* means (op. cit., p. xi).
[2] ibid., p. xii.

soul and does not startle or amaze it with itself, but with its subject.'

e.g. The setting sun, and music at the close,
As the last taste of sweets, is sweetest last,
Writ in remembrance more than things long past.
(II. i. 12–14)

There is a marked degree of what Keats would call 'obtrusiveness' in such writing. Frigid ingenuities accompany it, such as this from Northumberland:

And hope to joy, is little less in joy
Than hope enjoy'd. (II. iii. 15)

or the Queen's tortuous lines where she has conceived a grief, and wrenches her imagination to find out what has caused it:

Bushy: 'Tis nothing but conceit, my gracious lady.
Queen: 'Tis nothing less: conceit is still deriv'd
From some forefather grief; mine is not so,
For nothing hath begot my something grief,
Or something hath the nothing that I grieve;
'Tis in reversion that I do possess—
But what it is that is not yet known what,
I cannot name; 'tis nameless woe, I wot. (II. ii. 33–40)

That is really far worse than York's simple Kyd-pattern:

Grace me no grace, nor uncle me no uncle.
I am no traitor's uncle; and that word 'grace'
In an ungracious mouth is but profane.
(II. iii. 87–9)

lines all right as patterned, although what follows—'Why have those banish'd and forbidden legs . . .'—is not easily taken seriously.[1]

It is not only that there is more wit in the word-connections

[1] York's lines embarrass most Yorks; and so much of him is a fussy, incompetent old gentleman, that I wonder whether he always *was* a bit of a joke: a mild one, and perhaps poorly and misguidedly imitated from the comical side of Woodstock.

than in the thought (and the 'wit', even when called 'metaphysical', is always rather shallow); it is that these 'formal' tricks, like the eruptions of couplets, upset and confuse the *tone* both for reader and actor. Take, for instance, Bolingbroke's lines in III. i., 'Bring forth these men . . .': blank verse in neither the 'early' nor the 'more mature' style, but extremely fluent, very competent, totally without flourish. He has a statement of a heart-felt grievance to make, and he makes it: with force, clarity and cool dignity. Look back at Bolingbroke's lines in Act I, and you see at once how difficult two such disparate manners are for the best of actors.

The result tends to be recitation in a pageant, where dress and décor are everything (bar, of course, Richard). Once again, there is a kind of fold (or 'fault') in the play: Acts I and II are on one side of it, III and IV on the other; and in Act V something comes up to the surface which one is very strongly tempted to call 'half-revised Old Play'. I cannot pretend that the division in verse-texture is as sharp as all that; but the view of the play as 'ceremonial' rests heavily on the Quarrel, the Lists and the 'patriotic' oration of Gaunt; and in Act III there does come a marked change. Richard's

> Well you deserve. They well deserve to have
> That know the strong'st and surest way to get (III. iii. 200–1)

has, for example, in context, a sinewy force, an essential *unobtrusive* poetry, which is totally absent in Acts I and II (say what you will of Gaunt's melodious lamentation on England gone to the dogs).

It is on the assumption of that unconformity of Acts I and II that I shall rest my further examination of the play: accepting, that is, a discontinuity in character; some marked incoherences and dubieties in the story; a related uncertainty in the theme (tragic or political); and more than one kind of inconsistency in the texture of the verse. In so doing, I shall seem to be quarrelling with the 'political' view of the play: that here we have the fall of a rightful king, brought about by wilful rebellion, the lifting of 'an angry arm against God's minister', his Deputy; and that the curse that this brings on Lancaster and England is the uniting theme of an English dramatic-epic, in Shakespeare's peculiar double tetralogy. I am not really refuting the political pattern, although it has been given too much emphasis, and also, I think, made too *simple*. What I really question is the *unity*, the integral quality of the sequence.

Richard II, as the first play, seems to me to have no real beginning; a coherent middle; and a ragged, muddled end, only some of which can be explained as a Shakeapearian parallel to the famous 'end-links' of Chaucer. Taken by itself, if we stand back far enough, it does look like the Aristotelean 'simple' tragedy: the sort he thought inferior, having neither *peripeteia* nor any real *anagnorisis*. Richard seems to slip steadily into calamity, mainly through 'force of circumstances'; and his *hamartia* (unless we accept all the Bradleyan critics tell us) is a fatal step, a *blunder*, the mishandling of a quarrel between two violent noblemen. But go near enough to grasp the *action*, sticking tight to the text, and you will find that this alleged first term in a coherently planned series is thoroughly uncertain about its own start, and uncertain at the simplest level of the story, as well as on the major matter of essential (or political) rights and wrongs.

From now on, I shall dogmatize: state my case, and leave it to your verdicts.

Richard II's value as first term in an epic-historical series is seriously flawed by its peculiar dependence on *Woodstock*:[1] peculiar since Shakespeare not only took items from it, but also *left behind* in it explanations badly needed in his play, items taken for granted, or as read, which produce puzzles that cannot be cleared up without reference to the earlier play. To some extent, then, *Richard II* as a play does not contain within itself the reason why it is thus and not otherwise. If so, the alleged epic scheme is faulty, since the 'beginning' is not a beginning.

[1] Egerton MS. 1944, ed. Frijlinck, M.S.R., 1929; A. P. Rossiter, *Woodstock: A Moral History*, Chatto & Windus, 1946.

Richard II is about the fall and deposition of a King. The fall results from two events: (*a*) the quarrel of Bolingbroke and Mowbray, which Shakespeare invites us to focus down to the pin-point *hamartia* of throwing down the warder in the lists (see Mowbray's son in *2 Henry IV*, IV. i. 125–9); and (*b*) the falling-away of York, and all England, on Bolingbroke's landing. This second event has to do with Richard's failings as monarch: with 'the state of England', which some critics make a main theme, although (Gaunt's reproaches apart) there is very little about it in the text. Ross (at II. i. 246) says, 'The commons hath he pill'd with grievous taxes'; but that, as it happens, is a direct echo from *Woodstock* (I. iii. 112),[1] where 'Plain Thomas', being mocked about his homespun frieze, says: 'did some here wear that fashion,/They would not tax and pill the commons so.' In short, the connection between favourites and extravagance, extravagance and exaction, exactions and Richard's loss of power, is crystal-clear in *Woodstock* and nowhere else. In *Richard II* Willoughby takes up Ross with a mention of 'daily new exactions', 'As blanks, benevolences, and I wot not what'; and we wot not what neither. *Editors* tell us; but the fact is, there is precious little in Holinshed about 'blanks'; nothing about 'benevolences' (devised by Edward IV!); and one sentence about a *rumour* 'that the King had set to farme the realme of England unto sir Wm. Scroope earle of Wiltshire . . . to Sir Jno. Bushie, sir Jno. Bagot, and sir Hy. Greene knights' (iii. 496, col. i. *ad fin.*). If we look at *Richard II*, taking it as it comes (as an audience *must*), we find: (1) *Before* Gaunt's accusations, only one inexplicit line by Richard, 'We are enforc'd to farm our royal realm' (I. iv. 45); a bit more on blank charters following it, but no connecting of either with the evil influence of favourites. (2) It is only 190 lines *after* Gaunt's 'Bound in with . . . inky blots and rotten parchment bonds', that Ross growls, 'The Earl of Wiltshire hath the realm in farm' (II. i. 256). (3) *Between* these references lie Gaunt's two nearly-unintelligible charges: 'rotten parchment bonds' and 'Thy state of law is bond-

[1] Refs. are to Rossiter's edn.

slave to the law' (II. i. 64 and 114). The Arden edition notes show these *are* obscurities: both notes are nonsense.

Now these things are perfectly clear and straightforward to anyone who reads *Woodstock*, Acts II, III and IV of which are concerned with the rise to power of the favourites, headed by the villainous Lord Chief Justice Tresilian; their financial iniquities when *in* power (III and IV); and what 'blanks' meant to the Commons (IV. iii.). I can make but one point: the author of *Woodstock* scrambles and hashes history to make Richard's extortions a matter of *legal* iniquity: slavery to bonds, regal servitude to the law of contract.[1] And he therefore *stages* Richard presented with a legal instrument (a bond or lease), giving the favourites full command of the Exchequer and all the royal estates etc. in exchange for a monthly stipend of £7,000. That is what Gaunt is alluding to; and the whole difficulty of the financial wickedness of both Richard and the favourites in *Richard II* is simply that Shakespeare *alludes* and never explains. Nor is that all. Gaunt's accusations are not only explained by *Woodstock*: his terms of reproach derive from that text. England is

> now leas'd out . . .
> Like to a tenement or pelting farm;

and later:

> Landlord of England art thou now, not King.
> Thy state of law is bondslave to the law. . . .
> (II. i. 59–60; 113–14)

In *Woodstock*, IV. i., where Richard is presented with the bond, later read by Tresilian in full, and before the flattering Greene twists him round to it, Richard has a (cancelled) speech of apprehension or self-reproach: 'We shall be censured strangely . . .' (when people think of the Black Prince)

[1] He shifts back the fiscal tyranny from 1498 to a mythical date before 1488 (when Tresilian was hanged). Why does he do this? Because he was a Common-Law man, writing a moral history against the King's-Law men (i.e. Bacon as *versus* Coke). Hence the contradiction between his play and Shakespeare's on kingly right, as stated by Gaunt in *Richard II*, I, ii.

> . . . And we his son, to ease our wanton youth
> Become a landlord to this warlike realm,
> Rent out our kingdom like a pelting farm,
> That erst was held, as fair as Babylon,
> The maiden conqueress to all the world (IV. i. 146)

The term 'landlord' is applied to Richard four times in this play: *inter alia* by the Ghost of Edward III:

> Richard of Bordeaux, my accursed grandchild . . .
> Becomes a landlord to my kingly titles,
> Rents out my crown's revenues . . . (V. i. 86 f.);

and by Gaunt himself:

> England now laments . . .
> Her royalties are lost: her state made base;
> And thou no king, but landlord now become
> To this great state that terrored christendom (V. iii. 104 f.)

The emphasis of iteration and the word 'lease' (not in Holinshed) show how Shakespeare's Gaunt has, so to speak, his past political experience in mind—in a play much rather than a Chronicle. This is not simply a source-hunter's game: it affects the whole moral complexion of Richard in Acts I and II, and alters both the colour of the theme and Shakespeare's reading of history.

It also bears on what we make of the *personæ*, as 'characters' or as 'symbols': especially the favourites, but, by repercussion, Gaunt too. In *Richard II* the blank-charter iniquity is less skimped; but only in *Woodstock* does the wickedness of income-tax returns signed 'blank' (leaving the collector to invent the income) receive the emphasis we can call 'normal'. Nor, in Richard, is the dressy extravagance of favourites and Court made a clear cause. Shakespeare's Bushy, Greene and Bagot are nearly 'blank-charters' themselves: once again because they are taken as *seen* (in their bad habits as they lived—on the stage); and 'recognised' as shadows of vanity, flattery and contempt of good counsel, opposed symbolically and morally to what Gaunt stands for (which is identical with what he and York and

Thomas of Woodstock stood for in *Woodstock*: in flat defiance of Chronicle and truth). Shakespeare's play leaves us wondering what vices they had; for apart from Bolingbroke's accusations of homosexuality (refuted by the Queen's behaviour throughout), they do not get beyond being a *1066 and All That* 'bad thing'.

Their real evil, which Shakespeare presents only by allusion, is that they *were* the political and moral opposites to Richard's 'good old uncles', all of whom, in both plays, are economy, retrenchment, conservatism, public service and plain-Englishry. A phrase here points incontrovertibly to *Woodstock*. Gaunt's 'My brother Gloucester, plain well-meaning soul' (II. i. 128), refers solely to the other play. 'Plain homespun Thomas', who wears frieze at Court and is comically mistaken for a groom by an overdressed popinjay (III. ii.), is, historically, a male Mrs. Harris. In Chronicle there is no such person: he is purely a *dramatis persona*, partly modelled on the good Duke Humphrey of *2 Henry VI* and with comparable moral functions. Against Dover Wilson's attempt to extract a 'good' Gaunt from Froissart, I find that Shakespeare's Gaunt is the same 'form' (or 'shadow' in an allegory of State) as Thomas. By this I do not mean that either lacks 'character': only that moral function, not history, determines their forms.

The most unquestionably historical thing that Woodstock does is to get murdered; and here the events of *Woodstock*, assumed to be known, have their most important bearing on the moral structure of Shakespeare's play: on the character of Richard, the mechanism of his fall, and the essential rights and wrongs behind the quarrel. No one can read *Richard II* and not encounter the problem, 'Who killed Woodstock?' Bolingbroke accuses Mowbray of it; Gaunt tells the Duchess of Gloucester that Richard was responsible; Bagot and Fitzwater say it was Aumerle: they imply, moreover, that the murder took place *after* Bolingbroke was banished, and add that Mowbray said so (IV. i. 80). To say they are all liars is no more than they all say to one another. The whole thing makes sense, and makes the plot of Acts I and II far more coherent, as soon as we know that Woodstock was (1) kidnapped in a masque, with Richard and his favourites present; (2) conveyed to Calais, the Governor of which is called Lapoole in the play, but *was* Thomas Mowbray; and (3) there put to death (in a stirring scene) not by the Governor, but rather against his will, and by two experts in tidy murder sent from England.

Thus in the quarrel, Mowbray knows that Richard knows the truth, and that Bolingbroke knows most of it. Hence Richard's desire to quiet the pair, and his saying *he* will calm Norfolk, while Gaunt calms Bolingbroke. Hence his 'How high a pitch his resolution soars!' (I. i. 109), when Bolingbroke has said that Gloucester's blood cries 'to me for justice and rough chastisement'. Hence, too, the riddling lines where Mowbray says:

> . . . For Gloucester's death—
> I slew him not, but to my own disgrace
> Neglected my sworn duty in that case. (I. i. 132–4)

Reference to *Woodstock* suggests at once that the allusion is to Act V. i. where Woodstock appeals to Lapoole 'by virtue of nobility' and 'on that allegiance/Thou ow'st the offspring of King Edward's house' (V. i. 145 f.), when he fears murder. The lines in Shakespeare mean, then, that Mowbray admits he was Governor (which is known to everyone), and that he failed in his sworn duty to protect the blood royal (which again is obvious). But simultaneously he reminds Richard of *why* he failed (Richard threatened his life if Woodstock was not killed), while giving nothing away. For 'I slew him not' is perfectly true of Lapoole himself: Woodstock was killed by agents, and all Lapoole-Mowbray did was not to prevent them.[1]

[1] Before dismissing *Woodstock*, let me remark that several of Dover Wilson's notes on *Richard II* (*New Cambridge* edn.) are unreliable, mainly because of his predisposition to lay a non-Shakespearian 'old play' behind Shakespeare's, written by a wide-reading historian who potted many recondite chronicles. But the puzzle he makes of Bagot (who loses his head *en route* for Ireland and then apparently comes back to life again) vanishes if *Woodstock* is consulted; York's reference to 'nor my own disgrace' (II. i. 168) is not a loose end, but alludes to the same

This criminal collusion with Mowbray *could* supply the motive for the stopping of the single-combat at Coventry. The principle of trial-by-arms is that it gives 'the judgement of God'; and we may plausibly make the induction that Richard is afraid that God will give the right verdict. But it is only a reasonable *induction*, for Shakespeare gives no hint of Richard's motives. Character-critics are content to see here only an exhibition of Richard's exhibitionism: his self-regarding theatricality in the kingly role—even, perhaps, the actor-manager's vanity, in dramatically focusing all eyes on himself and dragging them away from the combatants (like a film-star at a prize-fight). That is there, no doubt: the Deposition-scene supports it, with Richard in a complex pageant of vanity, as the Middle Ages regarded it: stripping himself of kingly vanities, the pomps and glories of temporal rule; gazing in the glass of vanity; and yet, vanity of vanities, still making himself the focus of a dramatic contemplation of the essential human vanity, persistent though the robe is stripped, the mirror shivered.

But this act of throwing down the warder is of fatal consequence: fatal and fateful. From that one act a strict logic of events throws down Plantagenet and, inside ninety years, throws up Tudor. The logic of the eight-play series *and* the exact apprehension of the 'tragedy' demand that we should know if it was *guilt* (and guilt of royal blood) which started this momentous sequence. If not, where is the beginning of the epic-drama? Further back. Then it has no unity. And in this case we cannot delve into *Woodstock* for the answer and come out certain.

We must be satisfied with a fair degree of probability and the absence of final certainty. The explanation of the King's desertion by England is writ large in *Woodstock*: favourites, vanities, extravagances, taxation, extortion, antipathy to sound counsel: all these are kingly vices. The explanation of the quarrel is

Duke's 'Disgraced our names and thrust us from his court' (*Woodstock*, III. ii. 4); and his attempt to make the phrase 'upon pain of life' (I. iii. 140 and 153) a link with Froissart ('I have not found the phrase in any of the sources except Froissart . . .') fails completely, as it is used in *Woodstock*, IV. iii. 171.

there too: briefly, 'Woodstock's blood', the wanton murder of a royal prince, epitome of the right-mindedness and political and social responsibility which are expressed in Gaunt. Integrate the causes of Richard's fall, and his confused actions throughout Acts I and II derive from a guilt, or guilts, out of which there is no clear path. Shakespeare knows this—indeed too well: he slips into the lecturer's commonest fault, of assuming that everybody must know what, as it happens, many do *not*. But this applies mainly to the first two acts alone. It explains Richard as he there appears, and explains too why a different Richard arrives from Ireland in Act III. It also suggests why Bolingbroke's intentions about the crown are left rather obscure. I believe that the *historic* fact is that there was a well-contrived conspiracy, leading to a well-timed landing. But Shakespeare took Halle's hint that Bolingbroke had no glimmer of what fate had in store for him: that chance would have him King (as we should say), and so chance crowned him. It is, after all, what he tells Warwick before his death:

> . . . God knows, I had no such intent,
> But that necessity so bow'd the state
> That I and greatness were compell'd to kiss.
> (*2 Henry IV*, III. i. 72–4)

If, though, we accept the many hints in *Richard II* that Richard was a guilty *King*—and it is the guilt of the King, much rather than the innate wickedness of the man, that *Woodstock* emphasizes—then Bolingbroke's walk-in to kingship is itself one more instance of that process of retributive reaction which is the really *tragic* element in the History plays (the judgement of God in the process of history, as I suppose Professor Butterfield would call it). This retributive reaction, as a divinity that shapes the ends of England, is a principle which makes sense and logic of Bolingbroke's incredibly easy usurpation. Richard is *wrong*, but Bolingbroke's coronation is *not right*; and Richard's murder converts it to the blackest wrong. This greatly reduces the possibility of regarding Richard as a 'royal martyr' or 'sacrificial-king'. It should also prevent our making Shakespeare a kind of sentimental conservative, looking nostalgically back, like Walter Scott, to the 'great age' of Chivalry and showing us 'the waning of the Middle Ages'.

It implies a conception, or apprehension, of *history*. If the ills of England do not begin with Richard's deposition, then there is a dreary endlessness in this long sample of human affairs, sometimes cyclical, but always a conspectus of half-blinded actions and unpremeditated reactions, apparently with neither end nor beginning. Thus Shakespeare '*ends*' with the triumph of Henry V, pointing straight to Henry VI and all *that*: 'Another Troy will rise and rot, another lineage feed the crow.' The effect is to present the 'historical process' as *obscure tragedy*, in which men are compelled, constrained, baffled and bent by circumstances in which their actions do *not* express their characters. Even in *Richard II* there are many light touches of irony, mainly the irony of frustration: for what makes such tragedy 'obscure' is a kind of *stupidity* in events (in men and things), something far more confused and uncertain than Fate or Destiny. Hence the weariness of both Richard ('Learn, good soul,/ To think our former state a happy dream': v. i. 17 f.) and King Henry (his invocation of sleep: *2 Henry IV*, III. i.). The times are always out of joint: and the weak men, strong men, good men and bad men who try to re-articulate them, are *all* fumblers, or so compromised that their very skill is vain. As Pater said, 'No! Shakespeare's kings are not, nor are meant to be, great men.'

But if we turn to *Hamlet*, is not that, too, in a different sense, an 'obscure tragedy'? Obscure, in the sense that *Othello* is not, nor *Coriolanus*, nor *Antony and Cleopatra*. And though 'the mystery of things' is heavy enough within *Macbeth* and *Lear*, they bear the mind beyond that iron curtain which shuts about the 'History' world. *Hamlet* stands between: and its two worlds of action and sensibility have their somewhat shadowy counterparts in *Richard II*. It is not a dream of 'sensibility' in any way like Hamlet's: rather, of sentiments, of the sentimentalist, as defined in Meredith's aphorism, quoted by Stephen Dedalus to Malachi Mulligan: 'The sentimentalist is he who would enjoy without incurring the immense debtorship for a thing done.'

The central experience in *Richard II* is its *middle*, the substance of Acts III and IV. The ceremonial or ritual scenes and styles do matter: although only six scenes out of nineteen can be called 'ritualistic' or formalized. They matter because of what they *contrast* with; for in that contrast there is a tonal and visual rendering of the contrast of Richard and his group and Bolingbroke and his, but more as *Weltanschauungen* or aspects of human experience than as just 'characters'.

However and whenever *Richard II* is played, the pageant-element is important (as much for 1955 as for 1595). But this element is double, not single. After the lists, etc., a new tone begins to emerge at the end of II. i, in the huddle of sullen earls plotting together after the fops have gone. Northumberland emerges there; and a grim meaning is given him at once in:

> Not so; even through the hollow eyes of death
> I spy life peering . . . (II. i. 270)

That is more than 'character'. When Bolingbroke lands, Northumberland is there beside him; and in III. i. and III. iii. I am sure that the *visual* contrast between these armed campaigners and the toy warfare of the lists, the brilliant and vapid refinement of the Court, are part of the play as images. Elizabethan eyes saw iron as we see khaki battle-dress and camouflage. And, significantly, Richard's words in banishing Bolingbroke foreshadow this very change: he would *avoid* the

> . . . harsh-resounding trumpets' dreadful bray,
> And grating shock of wrathful iron arms. . . . (I. iii. 135–6)

But the iron comes; and with it a touch of iron in the verse: as witness Bolingbroke's opening lines in the scenes before and after Richard's speech on landing in Wales, 'Dear earth, I do salute thee with my hand. . . .' The answer to that is the efficient staff-officer's: 'So that by this intelligence we learn/The Welshmen are dispers'd.' (III. iii. 1). It is more than character-contrast: the verse, backed by the hardening of the human exteriors, the steel-framed faces, jars two worlds together. The same jar is in the Deposition-scene. It gives the play its meaning and experience, as a kind of tragic drama: the obscure tragedy, unclear, interesting, rather disheartening, of 'Shakespearian history'.

The nature of the jar—the nature of those two worlds—makes Richard less than the fully tragic hero. One is the half-fantasy world of the Court, where Richard's half-dream kingship reigns, with angels at his beck and serpents for his foes; the other is that other dream, of action, will and curt-worded decision, in which he is nothing, or a passive sufferer, a king of woes (or merely a king of words). In the mirror-episode the two dreams doubly confront each other. This it is that makes the Arden editor, following Pater, tell us Richard's nature is 'that of the poet who has unfortunately had kingship thrust upon him'. One need not reply, 'If so, surely a very *bad* poet'; for the answer is in Dowden, or in what Dowden quotes from Kreyssig: '. . . he affords us the shocking spectacle of an absolute bankruptcy, mental and spiritual no less than in the world of outward affairs, caused by one condition only: that nature has given him the character of a Dilettante, and called him to a position which, more than any other, demands the Artist.'[1]

[1] Kreyssig, *Vorlesungen über Shakespeare* (ed. 1874), i, p. 189, quoted (in original) by Dowden, *Shakespere: His Mind and Art* (ed. 1892), p. 195.

3

Ambivalence: The Dialectic of the Histories

First, my Feare: then, my Curtsie: last, my Speech. My Feare, is your Displeasure: My Curtsie, my Dutie: And my Speech, to Begge your Pardons.

If you looke for a good speech now, you vndoe me: For what I have to say, is of mine owne making: and what (indeed) I do say, will (I doubt) prooue mine owne marring.

But to the Purpose, and so to the Venture.

STRATFORD 1951, a Shakespeare Memorial Theatre playing a sequence of History-plays in a fixed unchanging Elizabethan-house-front stage-set. Stratford 1612, a man writing his last History: *Henry VIII*, first performed 29 June 1613, when in a sense it 'brought the house down', for The Globe was set on fire. . . . And as far as I know, no Shakespeare History-play was staged with Elizabethan décor—or non-décor, if that suits you better—till this year, 1951. We should hope to find *some* curtains taken away (from the mind, I mean), *some* unanticipated continuities revealed, *some* unexpected groupings, interconnections, echoes. . . .

The Man was 48; had begun writing Histories some twenty years back, perhaps as early as 1586, when he left home and twins, and was perhaps 'a Schoolmaster in the Country' (as Beeston jun. told Aubrey). How did he *end* by thinking of History? Had he any coherent 'view' of the Historic Process: from John—with a jump to Richard II (1398) and thence more or less consecutively to Bosworth and 1485, the Tudor dawn... ?

His last play—or his and Fletcher's—ends with the dazzle of the Elizabethan sunrise: with the christening of the baby Elizabeth, and Cranmer in the role of 'prophet new inspired'. Yes; but in 1612 the Queen was nine years dead; the great age was dying before her; and this Man, who had seen so deeply, so terrifyingly, into human experience could not be blind and deaf to the *ironies* of his last stage-situation. To say no more: Could he, who had staged so many 'poor painted Queens', be nescient of the irony of Anne Bullen's triumph—he knowing all that followed . . . . ? And with the noble, pathetic, fallen Katherine in the selfsame play?

Looked at *one* way, the Histories present a triumphal march of the destinies of England. But look at them another way—at the individual lives of men and women—and your conclusion will be nearer to what Yeats wrote (also *At Stratford on Avon*):

> He meditated as Solomon, not as Bentham meditated, upon blind ambitions, untoward accidents, and capricious passions; and the world was almost as empty in his eyes as it must be in the eyes of God.

I find that apposite to the Histories; for though Shakespeare gives but few generalizations applicable to 'the Historic Process' (as we grandly call it . . .) yet Yeats catches the note that rings beyond the melancholy brooding of Richard II on the fates of Kings: the note of the helpless Henry VI at Towton (Pt. 3, II. v); it is near to the feeling of Henry V's 'idol Ceremony' speech; it generalizes for Margaret of Lancaster, for Isabella of France, for Katherine of Aragon . . . (Proud Names!) . . . for all the long line of women broken in the course of great events. And it most precisely fits that generalizing moment when the weary sleepless Henry IV is turning over in his midnight mind the history of his own times:

> O God! that one might read the book of fate,
> And see the revolution of the times
> Make mountains level, and the continent,
> Weary of solid firmness, melt itself
> Into the sea . . . how chances mock,
> And changes fill the cup of alteration
> With divers liquors! O, if this were seen,
> The happiest youth, viewing his progress through,
> What perils past, what crosses to ensue,
> Would shut the book and sit him down and die.
>
> (Pt. 2. III. i. 45.)

Those melancholy tones are familiar enough: they are what makes the burdened man-beneath-the-Crown a major symbol in the Histories. The voices murmur on behind the tapestries: 'sad stories of the deaths . . .' 'all murdered . . .' 'Upon the King . . .' 'Uneasy lies the head . . .' They mind me of Chaucer's lines (on quite another theme):

> What? Is this al the Ioye and al the feste?
> . . . Is al this peynted proces seyd, alas,
> Right for this fyn?
> (*Troylus and Crysede* ii. 421 f.)

But though there is a 'Doubleness' here: in the conflicting values set by the Greatness (the Triumph) of the National Destiny, and the Frustration, the inadequacy, of the Individual (the frail Man within the robe)—there is nothing complex in that 'Doubleness'. It falls just short of the tragic; where Man's greatness is asserted in his destruction. That falling-short is characteristic of the Histories.

These kings and great persons are all sub-tragic. They lack a degree (or some degrees) of freedom; are caught in nets of events by which they are frustrate and less than their potential selves. In Rilke's phrase, they are *Verwirrt mit Wirklichkeit*: bondsmen to a 'reality' which is that of the world of action, therefore temporary, pragmatic, unreal. And they (to quote Yeats again):

> Constrained, arraigned, baffled, bent and unbent
> By those wire-jointed jaws and limbs of wood,
> Themselves obedient,
> Knowing not evil and good;
> Obedient to some hidden magical breath.
> (*The Double Vision of Michael Robartes*)

The mechanism to which they are subjected is that process of 'retributive reaction' which is the only *tragic* component of the Histories.

Retributive Reaction is my name for the principle of the simplest of the patterns in these plays; of which pattern we see only a short and misleading section in the Richard-to-Henry V tetralogy. *There*, the usurpation of Bolingbroke (exactly described in terms of consequences by Carlisle), with Richard's death by murder, leads on to the Unquiet Time of Henry IV—to the Percies' Rebellion, and the father's fears that Prince Hal is just another Richard; and so up to the death-scene in 'Jerusalem' and 'God knows, my son . . .' followed by the advice to 'busy giddy minds/With foreign quarrels': which is—despite all that Archbishops may say—the political reason for Henry V's French campaign. That is victorious, and the curse of usurpation seems to sleep. Yes, to *sleep*; it is not dead.

The closing chorus of Henry V refers back to the Henry VI series, the loss of France—'which oft our stage hath shown'. Thus the sequel to *Henry V*, in the complete pattern, is 'Hung be the Heavens with black' and the Roses series, where 'civil dissension' carries forward the curse of royal murder, uncertain or divided right, brother against brother, for the sixty years to Bosworth Field.

The pattern can be extended the other way, to *Henry VIII* (I mean in Wolsey as antagonist to Katherine, and what we know of Anne Bullen, the usurperess). It is one of Shakespeare's constants. But when I say 'retributive reaction' I mean just that; for whether it is 'justice' or not, God knows . . . (Professor Butterfield would have it that *he* knows too, and that it *is* all the Will of God. To me, it is obscure, ironic, *and*—as far as Shakespeare shows me the scheme of things—seemingly endless.) Taken all together, the Histories are a dark glass, where we gaze *per speculum in enigmate*. The mystery beneath the surface of the magic mirror with its shows of kings is chill and deeply saddening.

> Action is transitory; a step, a blow,
> The motion of a muscle, this way or that,
> 'Tis done, and in the after-vacancy
> We wonder at ourselves like men betrayed;
> Suffering is permanent, obscure and dark,
> And shares the nature of Infinity.
>
> (Wordsworth: *The Borderers*)

This pattern of 'obscure tragedy' runs, for me, far deeper than any feelings *I* can derive from knowing the 'philosophic' system which modern scholarship has extracted from the plays (and other Elizabethan sources *undique coemptis*). I must briefly outline it, (*a*) because it is indubitably 'there' as a pattern of thought, and (*b*) because it offers simplifications which are in danger of diminishing the true complexity of Shakespearian History—and in the best plays. Remember, then, that I am *not* arguing anything *away*: a pattern is *there*, and it is like Edward Halle's. But Halle's theory of history is naïve, and though the Elizabethan reader found it as satisfying as the Chronicles of Israel and Judah (with similar formulae on how King So-and-so did that which was evil in the sight of the Lord and followed after the ways of Jeroboam the son of Nebat who made Israel to sin), yet I cannot find it in my reading of Shakespeare to suppose that his mind was quite as naïve as all that. There is more in the dark glass than the moral history of the Lancastrian House of Jeroboam and the happy ending in the dawn of Tudarchy.

On Order, Degree, and so on, let me be brief: the essentials only need recall; let me remind you:

The State, as monarchy, is ordained by God; its structure is hierarchical, and in health all its orders or degrees are 'congreeing in a full and natural close/ Like music' (as Exeter says in *Henry V*, I. ii). To all orders as way of life there is 'fixed as an aim or butt/ Obedience'—as the Archbishop goes on to say, using bees as ideals or exempla. (The whole speech is very serious; whatever Stratford producers may choose to do with comic clergymen.) From the principle of Obedience—which really means a complete system of proper respects towards all superiors from parents upwards—it follows that the rightful King is, as it were, the organic nucleus of the cell-State; and that without due and rightful succession all Order (all its vital processes) is put in jeopardy. The only right way with a bad King is non-resistance: biding God's good time in Christian patience—as Gaunt tells the wronged Duchess of Gloucester—

for ill Kings are as much ordained by God as good ones.

The curse of usurpation is that it confuses Right, endangers all Order. That of rebellion is that it commits the Luciferian sin of pride, and destroys all Order: by the assumed 'law' that men who will revolt against the highest loyalty (to God's Deputy) cannot be bound by any other loyalty, nor decency. The rebel abrogates all respects; and since the King-enucleated State is ordained by God, by Natural Law, therefore he is a thing *unnatural*: a boil, a plague-sore, a carbuncle of corrupted blood.

This system of notions, with its hysterical terror of treason, is alien to our minds. We can see why the Tudors wanted England convinced that no worse chaos than the Roses civil war had ever come upon the English; especially in the late 1590s, when the Queen was old and had been flattered too much and too long on her immortality to be at all inclined to contemplate her own mortality and fix on her successor. We can see that Shakespeare has this nexus of thought in an astonishing intensity: especially over his horror of the mob—as a hydra-headed incarnation of disorder. I still feel the need of an approach less Tudor-moral. I find it in a MS. note of Coleridge's: 'What a world of Love and Bee-like Loyalty and Heart-adherence did the Stuarts trick and tyrannize away.'[1]

If we think of the ideal State as bound together like that, by happily unquestioning devotions, we come much nearer at the 'politics' of the Histories than by making them rigid, frigidly-patterned Moralities of State-right and State-wrong. (Like Halle, or the Homilies.)

There is real danger of that simplification; and one important ill-effect is on Falstaff. The Dover Wilson Sir John Paunch is dangerously near usurping the place of a much greater man: because any ideological view which makes *Henry IV* into a princely morality reduces Falstaff to little more than a symbol of all the fat and idle temptations which royalty rejects. There is something in John Dover Wilson which makes him a little like that *Lord* John of Lancaster—lays him open to *Sir* John's com-

[1] K. Coburn: *Inquiring Spirit*, p. 249.

ment, 'This same sober-blooded boy doth not love me, nor a man cannot make him laugh. . . .' Already semi-deflated Falstaffs are reaching the stage—Welfare-State Falstaffs, shrunk in the moral wash, or preconditioned for pricking before they have got so far afoot as Shrewsbury. That is not only sad. The effect is to neglect all the comic criticism which Falstaff himself supplies; and also all the complexities of the Henry IV plays, which often result from the use of comic parallelism of phrase or incident. That is, of parody, critically used; or of travesty-by-parallel.

Parody of this kind operates by juxtapositions of opposites; by contrasts so extreme as to seem irreconcilable. In this sense Falstaff at Shrewsbury is a 'parody' of knighthood: everything a knight in battle ought *not* to be; that is, IF men are all that theoretical codes assume. . . . It is this travesty-by-parallel which makes Sir John more than a bigger and a greater Bluntschli, in this other inquiry into *Arms and the Man*: as much greater as sherris sack is finer, nimbler, more forgetive than chocolate-creams. Parody is used again when Hotspur and Lady Percy have appeared in Act II. sc. iii., with Hotspur taking an easy leap out of Kate's bed to pluck bright Honour (in a traitorous conspiracy), and rudely ignoring her questions. He calls a servant, asks about a horse—a roan, a crop-ear was it not?—and then pretends he has forgotten all her inquiries. In the next scene, in Eastcheap, the Prince suddenly thinks of Hotspur. What follows?—An exact parallel, a travesty of the Percy *ménage*; and in dialogue, too:

> I am not yet of Percy's mind, the Hotspur of the north; he that kills me some six or seven dozen of Scots at a breakfast, washes his hands, and says to his wife, 'Fie upon this quiet life. I want work.' 'O my sweet Harry', says she, 'how many hast thou kill'd today?' 'Give my roan horse a drench', says he; and answers 'Some fourteen', an hour after, 'A trifle, a trifle.'

The parallelism is manifest. The next sentence reminds us how farcical travesty *by play-acting* is an intrinsic part of the East-cheap critique. The Prince continues thus: 'I prithee, call in Falstaff. I'll play Percy, and that damned brawn shall play Dame Mortimer his wife.'

The 'switch' that happens in this kind of parody is not unlike the technique of the modern periodical called *Lilliput*: an interesting collection of the earlier successes in it was published under the name of *Chamberlain and the Beautiful Llama* (Hulton Press, 1940). The wit of *Lilliput* is, moreover, sometimes used in this Shakespearian way—I mean, to make the conventionally-respected suddenly absurd: as Hotspur's 'Honour-and-Glory tough-with-the-women' stuff is deflated by the Prince's echo of it in a different tone or key.

It would be merely a mistake to attach this bit of parody to the 'character' of Prince Hal and only that; it is a quality of the play. As you can see from the scene at Bangor (III. i.), where it is *Hotspur* who is the plain-man parodist—of the fantastic Welsh-nationalism and supernaturalism of Glendower. Again (I cannot discuss it in detail)—there is the recurrent theme of Falstaff's bogus repentances: all in a play framed on the crude subject of a wild and prodigal Prince's unlikely reformation. The best is in the opening speeches of Act III. iii.; which follow immediately on the moving and earnest scene of the Prince's vows to repent and reform—the scene with his father. The switch to Falstaff telling Bardolph, 'I'll repent and that suddenly, while I am in some liking' (and so on) is another sign of how comic parallelism is thematic in the entire play. I shall next explain my term 'Ambivalence' in my own way, and then return to these items, to argue whether these *Lilliput*-like switches are tricks, or mere farce, or something more significant.

Ambivalence

It is hard to persuade everyone that what is laughable may also be serious; or that a man who laughs at something is 'thinking', or 'as good as thinking' (and maybe better). That is, unless it is when a satirist laughs at things we delight in or revere; then we call it 'mocking' and say he's a horrid fellow. All that being so, I will use an example into which amusement doesn't enter.

Wordsworth's *A slumber did my spirit seal* is a familiar poem. But if you think of it as 'One of the Lucy poems', I must tell you at once that those poems were never a Wordsworthian sequence. Ward's *English Poets* (1880) puts three poems together, with this one last; the *Golden Treasury* has a sequence of four; but in neither does *Strange fits of passion* appear, though why that *isn't* a 'Lucy poem' is beyond any man's discerning. Of the Ward trio, the *first* is the eighth of Wordsworth's Poems of the Affections, the *second* is the tenth among Poems of the Imagination; and '*A slumber did*' is Imagination No. 11. If we are concerned with *Wordsworth's* poems, we must disembarrass our minds of the superfluous fictions generated by editors, and take this poem as Wordsworth offered it—as a single separate lyric on a 'she' who is dead. At all events, that must be the first approach: until you know all that's in a poem, you can't tell what cross-references are relevant, nor what to be after looking for in other poems on what superficially appears to be 'the same subject'. Try, then, to listen to the poem 'unseen' as it were; I'm going to repeat it now, without 'expression' (as far as I can)—I don't want to bias a hearer either way.

> A slumber did my spirit seal;
> I had no human fears:
> She seemed a thing that could not feel
> The touch of earthly years.
>
> No motion has she now, no force;
> She neither hears nor sees;
> Rolled round in earth's diurnal course,
> With rocks, and stones, and trees.

Now that first line is ambiguous—'A slumber did my spirit seal' —and the ambiguity lies in the little word DID: a word often used for mere poetic emphasis or intensification, but also capable of referring to *time*. I'll take the first first; never mind the second.

Taking *did* as a poetic intensive, you have an emphatic perfect tense: a slumber really sealed up my spirit. As in that other poem:

> Among thy mountains did I feel
> The joy of my desire . . .

or the six-winged seraph in *Isaiah*: 'With twain he covered his face, with twain he covered his feet, and with twain he did fly.'

On this reading, which I'll call the A-version, the poem is a record of immediate experience: of a dream or visionary state, in which all his 'human fears' were gone, and his mind was filled with an overpowering sense of her immortality. No christian, but a pantheistic immortality, in which she is one with all the wide world's being, its greatness and its mystery. The tone is rapt. The closing lines have a triumphant sweep; and the energy and magnitude of suggestion of 'Rolled round in earth's diurnal course' contradicts, no, obliterates the suggestions of 'No motion . . . no force' or any deadness in 'She neither hears nor sees.' The *seems* in 'She seemed a thing . . .' is the seems of *wonder*, the visionary recalling the magic of his slumber; not the very different *seems* of recognized illusion. If I had to characterize this A-version out of Wordsworth, I would use those *Tintern Abbey* lines describing a 'serene and blessed mood' of mystical self-annihilation in which

> we are laid asleep
> In body, and become a living soul . . .

The B-version is quite other. As I said, DID can refer mainly to *time*. On this, the B-reading, *did* is an emphatic form of the imperfect tense (not the perfect); and the line means, 'I was utterly asleep': my senses *were* sealed up in a slumber (but they are not so now). At once there is a marked contrast of tone between stanza 1 and stanza 2. The first reports on what *was*—till she died; the second is the hurting record of what *is*—now she is dead. A simple paraphrase of this version would run thus: 'The eyes of my mind were shut as in deep sleep, and my sense of normal human dangers and our fears for those we love was stopped up. In that unseeing condition she seemed to be a thing which would never have any touch from the normal changes of life, would never be damaged by time. . . . But now. . . . How wrong that sleeping was. She is a dead thing, without power to move or do: deaf: blind: a bit of material substance rolled about day by day with the earth, and as dead-ly—like stone or wood.' No mysticism there, no serenity or blessedness of mood. It becomes a very painful poem, of a certain kind of self-reproach, and the pain than which Dante said there was none greater. ('Nessun maggior dolore . . .') But no less Wordsworthian—as witness those other lines:

She died, and left to me
This heath, this calm and quiet scene,
The memory of what has been
And never more will be.

Or again:

But she is in her grave, and O
The difference to me.

Now experiment shows that if a number of people are asked to paraphrase the poem, they come down about equally on either side, A or B; and it is very rare for anyone to doubt that it can be read in any other way than his. Yet closer verbal analysis would show that in both A and B readings there are words which would point to the opposite interpretation, if they could take the bit in their teeth.

I say, therefore, that the question 'Which is right, A or B?' is a no-question: the poem is *ambivalent.* It subsumes meanings which point to two opposite and irreconcilable systems of values; and the two are related only by the fact of death. If there *is* a spiritual or real Life in all things, then 'Lucy' is one with that life, and this is felt in the visionary moment. But perhaps in that only. For if there is no Pantheistic All, only a material earth of a-spiritual non-human stuff, then 'Lucy' is dead among the deadness. As there is no certainty either way, Wordsworth's poetic mind produced his ambivalent poem: a poem only fully felt when the reader has responses to both the readings I have separated. Yet each of those readings implies, ultimately, a system of thought: a philosophy: values. (And to a sincere and thinking Christian, both aspects are delusions.)

That is what I mean by 'Ambivalence': that two opposed value-judgements are subsumed, and that both are valid (i.e. for that work of art or the mind producing it). The whole is only fully experienced when both opposites are held and included in a 'two-eyed' view; and all 'one-eyed' simplifications are not only falsifications; they amount to a denial of some part of the mystery of things.

Return now to Shakespeare. I can do no more but only remark in passing how irony—including 'dramatic irony'—is a display of an essential ambivalence. Dramatic irony causes an exact juxtaposition of opposites in the mind of the audience: opposites, in that the 'true' for one hearer (the stage Persona) must exclude the 'true' for other hearers, who take the same words in a far extended sense, of which the hearing Persona is known to be unaware. ('Fail not our feast', e.g.) Yet both meanings only happen in the same mind: the audience's or reader's. The emotive effect is a terrifying belittlement of human prescience or judgement, as in tragedy, when we project the simple meaning on to the mind of a Macbeth, then contemplate it, as it were, against the ironized, unsimple meaning. Or, where sympathy lacks, the effect is some kind of detached sardonic amusement: as in some of Richard III's ironies, or, perhaps, in watching Falstaff and Co. scampering up to London for Harry's coronation, with Shallow in tow and all to the tune of: 'Let us take any man's horses. The laws of England are at my commandment. Happy are they which have been my friends; and woe unto my Lord Chief Justice.'

We have seen the Prince reconciled to the L.C.J.—we know the rest. But though this is still irony, it is now Comic Irony: in which pathos, derision, a sad wry smile and a malicious grin strive together—and all 'belong'. A modern Mirror-for-Magistrates view, to which Falstaff is only the 'Vice' to be formally discarded in a moral interlude of princely education, leaves just nothing of all that doubleness of feeling.

But Shakespearian History plays double tunes on far more than the comic aspects of the misfortunes of an old fat cynical reprobate—even when they do (as here) symbolize the absurd vanity of human wishings (which supply all beggars with dream-horses at the twinkle of a main-chance). Consider how in both parts of *Henry IV* the shady and seamy sides of glorious War are presented; and comically. In Part 1 Falstaff explains how he damnably misuses the King's press (Act IV. sc. ii.). In Part 2 a full-length exposition of the game is given (in III. ii.), with Feeble as the unwittingly ironical commentator—laughed at for a fool, yet the only man's-size voice in Gloucestershire:

> By my troth, I care not; a man can die but once; we owe God a death. I'll ne'er bear a base mind. An't be my destiny, so; an't be not, so. No man's too good to serve's Prince . . .

The Mug is the Hero, without prejudice to his mug-dom: the Fool is the only clear-seer. Ambivalence again. And all comic; though implicitly all these 'King's press' episodes are serious commentary on the wickedness and irresponsibility inseparable from WAR. Damnably wrong, clean contrary to all the war-values associated with Crécy, Agincourt or Harfleur . . . and *therefore* a critical comic commentary on a set of human facts which the 'Agincourt-values' insist on viewing (if at all) with one eye only. 'Two voices are there', as Wordsworth said in quite another connection: 'This is damnably wicked', says the one. 'It's damn' funny', says the other. Historian Shakespeare heard both.

I shall not labour to explain how the famous 'Honour' catechism comically balances the accounts of that main term in *1 Henry IV*; but I must remark on the beautifully complicated parallelisms generated when Falstaff tells the Prince how his father has sent for him, and that he had best rehearse before he goes to the palace to explain himself. It is a scene which travesty-parallels the true meeting later (in III. ii), and it is Eastcheap interlude-acting played to the height.

First, KING Falstaff rebukes his 'son' (with a parody of Puritan oratory), allowing that he *has* observed *one* virtuous man in Harry's company: 'If that man should be lewdly given, he deceiveth me; for, Harry, I see virtue in his looks.' Next, the Prince insists that they change roles, and we have the Prince (as King) pretending just what he will *have* to pretend when he *is* King: viz. that Falstaff is 'an old white-bearded Satan', a 'villainous misleader of youth'. The picture is the obverse of Falstaff's; but now Shakespeare goes one better still, and makes Falstaff as Prince offer a final turn of defence—ending with 'Banish not him thy Harry's company. . . . Banish plump Jack, and banish all the world.' To which the King-Prince replies—as the Prince-King will have to in earnest—'I do, I will'.

In that three-move epitome you have all the special technique of the *Henry IV* plays: a constant shifting of appearances, like the changing lights of an opal, so that every event, every person becomes equivocal—as Falstaff made Honour. That Gadshill robbery is not mere farce. If we 'realize' it, in an Usurper's state where Henry's right is only that of might, might only—then what are the Percies and Bolingbrokes but Gadshills, Bardolphs, Petos in Bigger Business?

> Thieves for their robbery have authority
> When judges steal themselves

so says Isabella in *Measure for Measure*. The comic robbing of the robbers is comically parallel to what the King would do with Percy's Scots prisoners; and the difficulty of establishing the Right in anything, in an England under no rightful king, is paralleled and parodied throughout in Falstaff's 'manner of wrenching the true cause the false way'—whether in the inventive proliferation of buckram men, in belying Mrs. Quickly to the Lord Chief Justice, or bamboozling her into vigorous denials of her own (perhaps not impeccable) virtue. I mean where he calls her an otter, and explains 'She's neither fish nor flesh; a man knows not where to have her.' To which the wronged woman replies in great moral indignation, 'Thou art an unjust man in saying so. Thou or any man knows where to have me, thou knave thou.'

It is in all such places—in Falstaff as the Wit: the witty equivocator who turns all to mirth, destroying ideals and seriousnesses with a turn of the word—that the Comic Histories go beyond anything that Shakespeare attempted in *Richard II*. There, too, that the narrowly Tudor-political or 'moral' approach will most oversimplify, and thin, the true Shakespearian vintage. The 'moral-historical' approach diminishes Falstaff as Wit, leaving him with little more than the rascally quick-wittedness which gets Eulenspiegels and Harlequins out of tight corners. Sir John is more. He is not only witty in himself (No, I'm not going on with Familiar Quotations)—he is Wit ipse. And wit is critically destructive—of ideal systems which assume that human nature is what it isn't. The doubleness of implicit values in those situations which are ambivalent; those which can be seen as serious *and* farcical: as pathetic *and* absurd: as abominable *and* laughable: as fine-and-admirable *and* as all-very-fine-and-large; all that centres on Falstaff. To read it as simply 'evil' (or 'the antithesis of the Princely virtues') and to make 'evil' the opposite of the Order required by the military State of a Henry V, is too naïve. And I don't mean just 'too naïve for 1951', I mean 'Too naïve for the mind of a Shakespeare, in 1599'. As Walter Raleigh wrote:

> This is indeed the everlasting difficulty of Shakespeare criticism, that the critics are so much more moral than Shakespeare himself, and so much less experienced. . . . The ready judgments which are often passed on Shakespeare's most difficult characters are like the talk of children. Childhood is amazingly moral, with a confident, dictatorial, unflinching morality. The work of experience . . . is to undermine this early pedantry . . . to teach tolerance, or at least suspense of judgment.

That's a 'period-piece', no doubt, and I wouldn't endorse its rather shapeless liberalism, which half suggests the (to me absurd) conclusion that Shakespeare is not moral at all—let alone one of the greatest of moralists. But Raleigh didn't have the word 'doctrinaire' to hand, I suppose. The warning he gives is by no means out of date, I should say.

I hope I'm not slipping towards (what he would call) the surprising moral immaturity of some of our doctrinaire contemporaries,[1] if I say that there is, in Falstaffian wit, something of the devaluating skill of The Devil. Let me hide behind Coleridge to advance my point. In table-talking on 16 February 1833, Coleridge gave a long account of a Faust play he had designed before ever he read Goethe. (I don't believe him, but that's unimportant.) He said, 'My Devil was to be, like Goethe's, the Universal Humorist, who should make all things vain and nothing worth, by a perpetual collation of the Great with the Little in the presence of the Infinite.' Now surely that is very near to what Falstaff does, when most the Clown critical. 'The perpetual collation of the Great with the Little' is no bad formula for what Shakespeare is repeatedly doing in both *Henry IV* plays.

In Part 2, however, the Universal Humorist is a far more sardonic one than before. Not only in that Old Age, in its failings, its brags, its pavidities and follies, is a major theme; nor only that Lord John of Lancaster's 'victory' is disgracefully won; there is more besides. To hint that 'more', I'll glance at the very first speech: '*Enter Rumour painted full of tongues*'.

[1] An instance I may have had in mind in 1951 will be found in Mr. D. A. Traversi's study of *1 Henry IV* in *Scrutiny* XV. I. pp. 24 f. Having fixed 'moral' prejudices from the start, Traversi damns Douglas with a supreme moral confidence, ascribing his own notions to the Prince. Thus: 'when he describes him he stresses the same lack of imagination . . . later found in the Greek heroes of *Troilus and Cressida*. Douglas is the man who 'kills me six or seven dozen of Scots at a breakfast and then complains of "this quiet life", the man who is not above filling out his prowess in battle with unimaginative boasting &c.' (p. 27). Later we find, 'Douglas is as the Prince has described him a brainless butcher . . .' (p. 31: the rest continuing the Wilson Knight formula from *Troilus and Cressida* in *The Wheel of Fire*). Traversi never sees that his quotation is about *Hotspur*, nor that Scotticide is improbable in a Douglas. School-children produce just such fantasy-figures, with similarly misapplied quotations. *Sed quis custodit* [? *scrutinat*] *ipsos Scrutineres?*

Open your ears; for which of you will stop
The vent of hearing when loud Rumour speaks?
I, from the orient to the drooping west,
Making the wind my post-horse, still unfold
The acts commenced on this ball of earth.
Upon my tongues continual slanders ride,
The which in every language I pronounce,
Stuffing the ears of men with false reports.
I speak of peace while covert enmity,
Under the smile of safety, wounds the world;
And who but Rumour, who but only I,
Make fearful musters and prepared defence,
While the big year, swoln with some other grief,
Is thought with child by the stern tyrant war,
And no such matter? Rumour is a pipe
Blown by surmises, jealousies, conjectures,
And of so easy and so plain a stop
That the blunt monster with uncounted heads,
The still-discordant wavering multitude,
Can play upon it. But what need I thus
My well-known body to anatomize
Among my household? Why is Rumour here?

That is the first part of the speech. It is followed by a list of the tales which are spreading from the Battle of Shrewsbury, and the piece concludes thus:

The posts come tiring on,
And not a man of them brings other news
Than they have learnt of me. From Rumour's tongues
They bring smooth comforts false, worse than true wrongs.

Rumour's prologue offers a theme which runs right through the whole play; a theme which invites a sardonic, detached, unsympathetic or coldly-critical attitude towards all the agents in the historic field. *False-report befools everyone.* Not only in the rumoured rebel victory at Shrewsbury; not only in the false (favourable) report of Falstaff's prowess—to which Coleville surrenders, and which even the L.C.J. makes some allowance for. Falstaff's own trust in the Prince and his star is also 'smooth comforts false': as is old Shallow's trust in Sir John and the smell of Court. So too—false—is this same Shallow's roaring-boy Past in London. And Pistol is false-alarm personified: mouthfuls of Theatre masquerading as a man—whereas he is nothing but wind. And thus the parallel to 'Sir John to all Europe': the vain delusion to which Coleville surrenders, as the northern rebels surrender to 'smooth comforts false' from Westmorland and Prince John. Finally, the King—King Hal the First—that Falstaff expected to find in London is only a delusion; and the laugh is on Falstaff—with a grating edge to the amusement. (A. C. Bradley only encountered this unhappy Mixed Feeling at the Rejection. In fact it starts much earlier in the play. Modern 'moral' critics apparently never meet it at all.)

These shifting mirage-like effects of unstable appearances relate Part 2 to the so-called 'Problem Plays' (which *I* call 'Tragi-comedies'). They develop from, e.g., the Honour theme of Part 1, but go well beyond that historical Comedy.

And if you wonder why—talking on 'The Histories'—I say so little about *Richard II* and *Henry V*, my answer is: I am diagnosing their shortcomings by focusing attention on Shakepearian History at its highest development. (I say 'History'. If you want to see this kind of thing taken on, in later work, go to the Galley-scene in *Antony and Cleopatra*: a similar comedy, sardonic comedy, of the frailty of the Great: the strange absurd chances that turn the fate of worlds.) But in *Richard II*—either Shakespeare was bent on following Marlowe and writing an unEnglish tragedy (i.e. without comic interplay: though *Woodstock* put it directly before him); or he knew instinctively that the preciosity and self-regarding sentiment of Richard *could not stand* comic criticism or even lapse of seriousness.

In *Henry V* his aim was changed. Whatever he once intended (and that last speech, by the Dancer, in *2 Henry IV*, does show the *intention* to export Falstaff to France), what he produced was a propaganda-play on National Unity: heavily orchestrated for the brass. The sounding—and very impressive—Rhetoric shows how something is being stifled. The wartime-values demand a determined 'one-eyedness'; the King fails to reach the fullest humanity because of that demand. He *has* banished Plump Jack; and 'all the World' has been banished with him. At least, the 'Allness' is gone. The play is 'fracted and corroborate'.

Without going all the way with 'Q', to say that Falstaff must go to 'Arthur's bosom' because he can kill Harry with a look, I do agree that Sir John had to be dead; for fear of the damage he must needs have done by babbling of (not 'green fields') . . . by killing the heroics with a jest. When the ranks are closed, and to question is to lack Will, to falter, then there is not so much freedom of mind as will say *outright* what every sane man knows (however brave): 'I like not such grinning Honour as Sir Walter hath. . . . Give me Life, say I.'

There are fine things in *Henry V*; but much of the comedy has lost touch with the serious matter. It's a play Shakespeare had finished with well before he finished it. His falling-back on the old *Famous Victories* for that slapdash stuff—treating the Princess of France like a Free Frenchwoman, etc.—that shows it. It surprises me that our London dramatic critics should have been surprised to find that as a climax to the 1951 Stratford historical tetralogy it does not come off. The truth is, the heart of Shakespeare's insight into English History (which means a good deal more than the History of England)—the *heart* is in the middle of the sequence: in the *Henry IV* plays, where he turned back from the sentimental seriousness of *Richard II*, back to the kind of Comic History he had made rough beginnings with in Parts 2 and 3 of *Henry VI*. (Where he had achieved something remarkable in the grotesque, Hieronymus-Bosch-like sarcastically-comic scenes of Cade's rebellion.)[1]

To see why *comic* History was his true genre, it is needless to

[1] I mean such Bosch paintings as *Ecce Homo* and the Veronica picture, where the mob is not only grotesque—absurd and half-diabolic—but also presents itself as a kind of hydra: *belua capitum multorum*; cf. Rumour's 'the blunt monster with uncounted heads', etc. The phrase was a commonplace, unoriginal even in Horace's day; but Bosch actualizes it in paint, as Shakespeare does in drama. A European tradition is shared by the Flemish painters and Shakespeare. I explored a fringe of it in an article on *Breugel's Ambivalences* in *The Cambridge Journal* for December 1948.

go back to the evolution of the Elizabethan Drama and its Miracle-play and Morality-play underlays. 'Mungrell tragy-comedy' *was* the mere-English genre, but never mind that now. Look only at *King John*—those lines by the Bastard on 'Commodity' ('Mad world, mad kings . . . etc.')—and you will see how they take the gilded lid off the lofty illusions of theoretical Tudor Politics (I mean *Stage*-politics). By-passing all the ideals of Order, Degree, Non-resistance, Right-divine and God's-deputyship, the Bastard exposed the world of politics as 'a racket'.[1] The thought implicit in the making of that speech has the same quality of deep political penetration that emerges from the conflict of serious and comic in *Henry IV*—and in *Coriolanus* and *Antony and Cleopatra*. That speech shows the same ambivalence, but simpler; for Falconbridge is a noble fighting humorist as well as a critical wit. He is not, like Falstaff, a Universal Humorist; but some of the undermining intellectual clear-sightedness of the later Histories is there.

Throughout the Histories it is in the implications of the Comic that shrewd, realistic thinking about men in politics—in office—in war—in plot—is exposed: realistic apprehension outrunning the medieval frame. Because the Tudor myth system of Order, Degree, etc. was too rigid, too black-and-white, too doctrinaire and narrowly moral for Shakespeare's mind: it falsified his fuller experience of men. Consequently, while employing it as FRAME, he had to undermine it, to qualify it with equivocations: to vex its applications with sly or subtle ambiguities: to cast doubts on its ultimate human validity, even in situations where its principles seemed most completely applicable. His intuition told him it was *morally* inadequate.

Hence the unhappy feelings which generous-minded critics have displayed about the Rejection of Falstaff. That some of

[1] This was put too crudely. I would add now: Shakespeare wrote in an unstable equilibrium between a 'World' or 'Universe-of-thought' of faith in God-ordainedness, and another World: the Inverted World of belief only in Power. The 'Inverted World' symbol is familiar in Breugel's pictures, as an orb with its cross downwards. The 'upsidedownness' notion is in *Measure for Measure* and elsewhere. The pictorial emblem itself appears in Quarles (e.g. *Emblems* i. 15).

them have *overdone* it is neither here nor there. It is well enough for Dr. Tillyard or Professor Dover Wilson to tell us that the Prince *had* to cast off Sir John. We know that. We know what Kingship meant to textbook Tudors (far better than the Globe audiences knew, I dare say). Yet I still feel that as Shakespeare *was* Shakespeare—the man who made Hermione and Hamlet, drew Kate Percy as war-widow (a traitor's wife by the Code), drew Katherine as the fallen majesty of England—he must have known, *and felt*, the lack of humanity (of generosity, high-mindedness, true magnanimity) in his Hal in that scene. And again, I think, in Henry's treatment of the conspirators at Southampton; where the King is so obviously playing a publicity propaganda part, as Justice, iron-visaged, pitiless. . . . As obviously as he said he was in that first of unprincely soliloquies, 'I know you all. . . .' (*1 Henry IV*, I. ii. end.)

Is there not a resemblant quality in his father: the 'silent king', Bolingbroke, in the mirror-episode in *Richard II*? A separateness from the feeling world, which makes the actor in public affairs assume a predetermined part, like a *play*-actor, only with all his directives outside and none of his? One of those 'who, moving others, are themselves as stone', as the sonnet phrases it: 'the lords and owners of their faces'? And thus again a resemblant quality in John of Lancaster's treachery to the northern rebels? Oh, I know it can be argued that, to the Elizabethans, no ill treatment or trickery towards rebels could be unjustified. But can we assume that Shakespeare's sensibilities were so crass as not to know meanness as meanness, perfidy as perfidy, when it could be said to have profited the State? I say no more than, 'I think not'. And if you agree on any of these points I've hung on to the Rejection of Falstaff, doesn't it follow that you are made to *feel* (not merely 'see', notionally) how the frame of Order, the coherent rigid medieval system accepted by some of our most reputed modern scholars, is outrun by that mind which Jonson (who 'knew the man . . . etc.') considered to be 'not for an age but for all time'?

It follows, if I have taken you along with me, that we cannot dissect-out, stain and fix the system of Shakespeare's reflexion on History. A rigid political-moral good-and-evil system is there; but as the events and the people speak into our inner mind, we find that Shakespeare is shifting subtly from key to key, as if by what musicians call 'enharmonic changes': using ambiguous note-sequences till contradiction is itself confounded, and yields a precise evocation of the paradox of human experience.

Thomas Mann has explored this musical symbolism to the limit in his vast, amazing, fascinatingly wearisome novel *Doktor Faustus*. When his damned musical genius, Adrian Leverkühn, makes his first experiments with notes, the narrator (Serenus Zeitblom Ph.D.) records a comment which seems to be saying a lot about what I find in the ambivalences of Shakespeare. 'Relationship is everything', said Leverkühn. 'And if you want to give it a more precise name, it is Ambiguity . . .' And again, later, 'You know what I find?—That music turns the equivocal into a system' (pp. 47 f. of the American translation approved by Mann. Knopf, 1947).

What is more, Leverkühn finds something amenable to his music in Shakespeare. He takes *Love's Labour's Lost* as a theme to treat. On this Zeitblom reports, 'He spoke with enthusiasm of the theme, which gave opportunity to set the lout and the 'natural' alongside the comic sublime, and make both ridiculous in each other.' Mann is not explicit, but it is clear enough that he means the three lover-nobles by 'comic sublime', placed *vis-à-vis* Costard as 'the natural'. Zeitblom Ph.D. is unhappy about it: 'I have always been rather unhappy at the mockery of humanistic extravagances; it ends by making Humanism itself a subject for mirth' (p. 164). That would be a good text for setting out to explore the entire subject of so-called 'Comic Relief' in Shakespeare.[1] I must keep within my limits, come back to Histories.

'Music turns the equivocal into a system.' That is why I used the phrase 'The Dialectic of the Histories' in my—admittedly alarming—title (for which I now apologize). The Order-code-system of Tudor theory approaches History with the kind of

[1] See pp. 274-292.

argument that Plato called *eristic*: that is, argument aimed at the extinction of an opposite and 'bad' system of beliefs. The code is moral, but in the narrow sense: too much so for Shakespeare's contemplation of mankind; too narrow and bounded for his human insight, from which he derived a *political* wisdom. As Hazlitt once observed:

> Shakespeare was in one sense the least moral of all writers; for morality (commonly so called) is made up of antipathies; and his talent consisted in sympathy with human nature in all its shapes, degrees, depressions and elevations.

I shan't examine that for its shortcomings, beyond saying that it is *morally* acuter than Raleigh—as witness the distinction 'morality commonly so called'. Taking it as it stands, then, I say: Therefore, Shakespeare's intuitive way of thinking about History (which we cannot formulate as an abstracted notional system) is *dialectical*. The old eristic-argumentative system which he used is static, changeless; but *his* thought is dynamic, alterative, not tied to its age. It has that extra degree-of-freedom which is given only by what I called a constant 'Doubleness': a thoroughly English empiricism which recognizes the coextancy and juxtaposition of opposites, without submitting to urges (philosophical, moral, etc.) to obliterate or annihilate the one in the theoretic interests of the other. That is what I tried to express by the figure of 'two-eyedness'.

His awareness of the 'soul of goodness in things evil' is not less than his sense of the spirit of seriousness (or significance) in things base—or foolish—or farcical—or indecent. To laugh at Hotspurious honour is as good as to think. To laugh at Shallow, or at Falstaff with Doll Tearsheet, is the substance of some wry or wringing thinking. But no less funny for that. And thus it is that the serio-comic dialectic of the Histories leads on to the Tragedies, where you have (as in the Histories you have not, I consider) Coleridge's 'collation of the Great and the Little *in the presence of the Infinite*'. In none of the Tragedies is the Order-system the friend of human greatness; rather the enemy.

If you have difficulty in refusing the critics' directions to see Henry V as Shakespeare's Ideal; if you cannot quite accept what I've said about the constant Doubleness of the Shakespearian vision in the Histories; then let me ask you to face a straight question: 'WHO, in the later, greater plays, are the heirs and successors of those Order-symbols Henry V and Henry Tudor (the triumphant Richmond of the end of *Richard III*)? The men who are, to the State-order system, 'goods': unifying nuclei of the organism, whether a People or the mind itself: the beings on whom the political heaven smiles. Who are they?' I should reply, 'The Fortinbrasses, the Octavii, Lodovicos, Macduffs, the Edgars and Albanies. On whose heroic qualities Bradley is, for once, entirely adequate.'

But why is 'the other side', the reverse to the kingly, historic, patriotic obverse, the Comic? Is it not partly this? In History Shakespeare felt that men were constrained to be much less than their full selves. He knew the burden of princehood: the Ceremony lines alone would proclaim it. All the Lancasters are less than full men. None is himself; only what he wills to be for the time only. By and by he will 'be more himself'. Hal says it: Father says it. None does it. Richard does try to be himself, full kingly length. He finds a shadow in a mirror. Only the other Richard—Gloucester—can say, 'I am myself alone'. And *he* is the Devil, spinning the orb on his thumb. Now Comedy is the field of human shortcoming; and therefore Shakespeare's History, at its greatest, *had* to be comic. What isn't Comic History in the Histories is what I can only call 'Obscure tragedy'.

At the very end of his career, back here at New Place, collaborating with young bright immoral John Fletcher in his last history-play (or so I think; and others more eminent do not)—he brought the same elements into *Henry VIII*. The man of forty-eight had not changed his mind. That was 1612; in 1616 he was dead. I hope that he was ending in something like the mind of those lines of Yeats:

No longer in Lethean foliage caught
Begin the preparation for your death
And from the fortieth winter by that thought
Test every work of intellect or faith,
And everything that your own hands have wrought;
And call those works extravagance of breath
That are not suited for such men as come
Proud, open-eyed, and laughing to the tomb.

Note. In preparing this lecture for print, I have made no attempt to convert it to a literary 'essay', nor, indeed, to do more than fill in the breaks and gaps of my lecture-notes with words to the same effect as those I used at the time. Similarly, with only one or two exceptions (mere topical asides) I have left in those parenthetical turns which a speaking voice can make much easier for hearers than they usually are for a reader. The style of the whole was intended for public delivery, and in my own manner of lecturing. To print it as anything other than a very close transcript of the actual lecture would have meant a complete rewriting; and for that I had neither the leisure nor the taste.—A.P.R.

4

Much Ado About Nothing

THE PLAY'S date (1598 seems secure)[1] invites one of two general approaches to interpretation. *Either* this is all trivial, however clever: the author is totally disengaged throughout, and we are foolish to look for anything in any way deep, ourselves solemnly making ado about nothing; *or* it is a brilliantly superficial and deliberately *limited* 'Italian' love-fantasia on the theme of deception by appearances (all sorts of deceptions, by several sorts of appearances): and we remember that seeming and being will provide plots in very different tones from this, in the plays that Shakespeare goes on to write in 1599 and later.

In 1923 (*Much Ado*: *New Cambridge* edn.) Dover Wilson advanced the hypothesis of an Old Play in verse, put through 'prose revision' which left loose tags and oddments that no longer had meaning, as well as 'verse fossils'. This revision made the most of the Benedick-Beatrice sub-plot; less of Hero and Claudio; and reduced the original Borachio-Margaret 'sub-sub-plot' (on the parallel loves of the serving-man and maid pattern) to next to nothing. Undeniably there are some discrepancies in the text which this hypothesis explains away nicely.[2] But on one important point I have my objections. In

[1] Because (*a*) Meres would have mentioned it, had it been acted by 1597; and he does not. (*b*) In Q (1600) Dogberry and Verges are described in speech-headings as Kempe and Cowley; and Kempe left the Company during 1599 (*c*) Jonson's *Everyman in his Humour* (performed 1598) had popularized the humour of Humours; and the uses of it in *Much Ado*, though the word was not at all new, certainly sound like easy allusions to a newly fashionable interest in it.

[2] [Detailed discussion of these has been omitted. See Dover Wilson's Note on the Copy, *Much Ado* (*New Cambridge* edn., 1923); and, for criticism of it, E. K Chambers, *William Shakespeare*, 1930, i, pp. 385–7; and W. W. Greg, *The Editorial Problem in Shakespeare*, 1942, pp. 121–3.]

II. ii. Borachio, sketching the defamation-scheme, says that 'instances' will be offered: he is to be seen at Hero's window, and they are to 'hear me call Margaret Hero, hear Margaret term me Claudio'.[1] On pp. 105–7 of 'The Note on the Copy', Dover Wilson makes this 'slip' the one certain evidence for the existence of a Borachio-Margaret sub-plot in 'the unrevised text', which Shakespeare here repeated accidentally: aware only that in the old play 'Margaret was deceived as well as the Prince and Claudio',[2] when vanity would make her dress as Hero, and welcoming 'Borachio' would look like Hero's being faithless with him. Theobald substituted 'Borachio' for 'Claudio': the original Cambridge editors were not satisfied. Theobald wanted to know how it could displease Claudio to hear his mistress using *his* name tenderly; and the Cambridge editors commented that 'Hero's supposed offence would not be enhanced by calling one lover by the name of another'. With respect, I find both attitudes obtuse. It *would* offend Claudio to hear his name misused (and to a servant); and while adultery-in-advance is a severe offence to any bridegroom, it *is* made more offensive if the morrow's marriage is mocked in the meeting of the guilty lovers. The Cambridge editors went on to suggest that Shakespeare may have meant Borachio to persuade Margaret to play, 'as children say, at being Hero and Claudio'; but they did not see that this was a *sufficient* explanation, which it surely is. The use of Hero's name would have convinced the onlookers that what they saw was not just her dress; and that of Claudio's would have the most powerful effect on those who knew the real Claudio was with them. It would seem the acme of jadishness. Indeed, all Borachio need do is to deliver the names in a mocking tone of soupy infatuation.

If this convinces, the difficulty vanishes; and the best evidence for the Borachio-Margaret sub-plot with it. Shakespeare had a reasonably clear idea of how he *could* present the scene (which he never did); and it is not significant enough, as Dover Wilson

[1] Alexander follows Theobald's emendation, 'Borachio' for 'Claudio'.
[2] As Pryene is in *The Faerie Queene*, Book II, Canto iv., the Claribell tale.

claims,[1] that 'we are not informed' of the 'detail' of 'Margaret in Hero's garments' till v. i. 232. It shows what was in Shakespeare's mind: if he *had* written the scene to be played out, then we do not need informing of what we *see* (for Margaret must, obviously, have appeared in whatever Hero had worn before: probably the ball-dress from II. i.).

This weakens the Old Play hypothesis: although it remains possible that the 1598 composition may have been from an earlier draft (perhaps a mere sketch); and true that writing of distinguishably different sorts is juxtaposed in it, together with the uncertainties and dead-ends which result from quick composition. Detective-story consistency, and the elimination of all redundancies and contradictions, are not to be expected of an Elizabethan and especially not of a dramatist.[2] In short, the slight internal contradictions seen on reading do not signify (if Shakespeare saw them); and do not matter much, if we do. The 'old' matter (if it was old) suited certain contrasts which Shakespeare wanted to draw around 1598, and gave the 'main' plot the right lack of emphasis for the task in hand. There is no reason to doubt that the emphasis on Benedick and Beatrice is deliberate, whether he worked from a draft, a sketch, or in some other way. Nor, I think, can we fail to observe that in the 'main' plot *some* passages of a tone too disturbed or disturbing for the 'Old Play', or for early work, 'arrived' in the course of writing out, because there were already in his mind feelings and reflections on, say, 'what men daily do, not knowing what they do': feelings which were, after 1598, to lead his work towards tragicomedy (of a sort that this play is *not*).

Deception by appearances in *love* is patently what most of *Much Ado* is 'about'. As Hero puts it:

[1] Note on the Copy, op. cit., p. 107.

[2] The question, for example, of how Beatrice came not to sleep with Hero on the fatal pre-marital night, is simply improper in terms of stage-convention. Dramatists would emphasize seeming guilt in such ways, without realizing that another convention would want to have the answers to 'Why?', 'Where was she?', etc.

Of this matter
Is little Cupid's crafty arrow made,
That only wounds by hearsay . . . (III. i. 21–3)

Cupid is not responsible for calumny; but 'hearsay' is a main force in both love-plots: each is about its effects on proud, self-willed, self-centred and self-admiring creatures, whose comedy is at bottom that of imperfect self-knowledge, which leads them on to fool themselves. Is it exaggeration to bring even Dogberry into this pattern? to point to his manifest self-admiration ('a fellow that hath had losses; and one that hath two gowns, and everything handsome about him'), and to hint that the little arrow that wounds *him* 'by hearsay' is magnificent language and 'wit'? Are not words and wisdom his Cupids? No doubt that stretches 'love' too far. But self-love is a common term to all three of the splendid comedians of the piece.

The play's wit has been justly praised and is worth some examination in detail. It is of several distinguishable sorts: the simpler important only in so far as contributing to the cumulative effect, one of impetuous exuberance, a kind of competitive vitality, expressing itself in quick manipulations of language. The Messinans have dancing minds, and make words dance or caper to their unpremeditated tunes. At its simplest level, it is mere quibble: where A has used a word capable of two meanings in different contexts, and B shows his awareness of both, by displacing it. This may be no more than a conventional game, 'comic wit degenerating into clenches';[1] and though editors explain them, 'the mind', as Johnson says, 'is refrigerated by interruption'. *Much Ado* suffers but little from this. It may, again, be an elaboration of that: when A and B are the same person, as when Beatrice 'takes herself up' on Claudio: 'The Count is neither sad, nor sick, nor merry, nor well; but civil count—civil as an orange, and something of that jealous complexion.' (II. i. 262–4.) That is exactly at the point where mere verbal cleverness, non-significant quibble, passes over into relevant wit: evocative here either of Beatrice's vitality (the 'character'

[1] Dryden: *Essay of Dramatic Poesy*.

view), or of the exuberant quality of lively minds which strike fire by scoring off each other: the quality I called *competitive* vitality, as of a 'college of wit-crackers'.

In the wit-game Benedick and Beatrice rightly regard themselves as 'seeded' players. Beatrice makes this clear in the scene in Hero's apartment before the wedding (III. iv.), when Margaret scores off her for once. Shown Hero's new gloves, she is not interested (her mind is bothered with Benedick), and unguardedly pretends to have a cold:

> I am stuff'd, cousin, I cannot smell.
>
> *Margaret:* A maid and stuff'd! There's goodly catching of cold.
>
> *Beatrice:* O, God help me! God help me! How long have you profess'd apprehension?

('Since when have you been a wit-cracker in this line?'—which Beatrice regards, with good reason, as her own.) Beatrice gets more of her own medicine later, over the prescription of 'Carduus Benedictus': here the wit is both verbal and something more—we might call it the wit of situation. No precise *double-entendre* is made; but Beatrice's state of mind is such that she feels (like Benedick before her) 'there's a double meaning in that'; and she lays herself open to another laugh by again using the wrong word:

> Benedictus! why Benedictus? You have some moral in this 'Benedictus'.
>
> *Margaret:* Moral? No, by my troth, I have no moral meaning.

It is a notable point in Shakespeare's contrivance that he gives both wits their off-day, as soon as love has disturbed their freedom.

As a rule, bawdy quibble outlives its contemporaries—simply because of 'human nature'; or because the fundamental situation is practically constant. In this play, jesting about sex is apposite: its subjects are sex-opposition, wooing, wedding, wiving (with due attention to the dangers of the last in making sport of a man). The audience certainly laughed at Benedick's

F

'Well, a horn for my money, when all's done' (II. iii. 56), the *second* time they saw the play. It becomes comic dramatic irony, if you read Elizabethanly. Yet, quite often, I see no great gain by doing so. There is something pathetic in the detailed scholarship which laboriously strives to conjure from its grave every ghost of an expired laugh.[1] 'Lighthearted bawdry' has its point in *Much Ado* (as in Mercutio); but only the best of points can stand heavy-handed annotation. Much of it turns on obsolete phrases: the fuse of the whole firework has to be replaced with a dry note; and the verbal transaction, by losing all its speed, loses nearly all its crack. Quibble in slow-motion ceases to be witty. None the less, by noticing or examining the dexterities of verbal switch required, we are speeded up to a better awareness of the Elizabethan manipulations of language; and, at the same time, made more conscious of the vitality evoked individually by characters, and cumulatively by quibble, pun and jest together.

Shakespeare's wit in devising the linguistic mishaps and semantic excesses of Dogberry is the other side to the flat and despised 'mere quibble'. Dogberry exaggerates, by accident and in self-satisfied ignorance, the processes by which the true wits divert the meanings of words deliberately, knowingly, and with pride in their craft. But the one is the antithesis to the other; and both sides could be told, 'Thou hast frighted the word out of his right sense, so forcible is thy wit' (Benedick to Beatrice, v. ii. 48). Wit and nitwit share a common obsessive delight in the wonders of words. This is largely what makes Dogberry the apposite farce-fool for a play in which all three plots turn on understandings and misunderstandings: quite apart from his being a marvel of the official numbskull's capacity to make extreme ado about genuine nothing.

But has the 'Malaprop' had its day? It took the stage in *Woodstock* (? 1594), was cornered by Sheridan, survived to

[1] The smutty puns, for example, humourlessly expounded by Kökeritz in *Shakespeare's Pronunciation*, are often so far-fetched as to be linguistically dubious and not worth the carriage.

Dickens. It is perhaps funniest in hierarchical societies, where clever and witty management (or mismanagement) of language distinguishes the *élite*; and aping this makes the linguistic lower orders flatteringly absurd. My impression is that Malaprops are only comic nowadays to over-language-conscious schoolmasters; or, of course, when bawdily Dogburian: when the right idea comes out in very much the wrong word. But, unless I mistake, Dogberry's skids are never improper. Impropriety in this play is the privilege of the educated.

The wit that does *not* turn on word-play is best shown by examples. Essentially it is the exuberance which leaps beyond expectation in 'improving the occasion'. Not only Benedick and Beatrice have this hyperbolic comic inventiveness: the former his strokes of Falstaffian invention, the latter her alarming opportunism (she is likely to score suddenly off anyone, at any time). The qualities of swiftness and unexpectedness are just as neatly shown by old Leonato's perfectly timed shot at Benedick. Don Pedro asks if Hero is Leonato's daughter. 'Her mother hath many times told me so', is the conventional formula in reply. 'Were you in doubt, sir, that you ask'd her?' asks Benedick. 'Signior Benedick, no; for then were you a child' (a palpable hit). They appear equally in Beatrice's magnificent impertinence to Don Pedro. She must cry 'Heigh ho for a husband!'—

Don Pedro: Lady Beatrice, I will get you one.
Beatrice: I would rather have one of your father's getting. . . .

And the quality of 'comic inventiveness' is shown immediately after, when he teasingly offers himself, and she says she will not have him unless she can have another for working-days: he is so costly she would have to keep him for best.

Both quickness of repartee and comic inventiveness (hyperbolic feats of exaggeration and elaboration) are intrinsic to the attitudes of self-dramatization upon which the comedy of character depends. Energy is delight and accomplished dexterity a pleasure to watch. Benedick and Beatrice have both: all the more because they are playing a part before themselves, and playing it high in an infectious sort of daring: figures of pride, which is at once humanly splendid, and 'goes before a fall'. There is no need to repeat what others have said of their proud hearts as a source of misogamy, because marriage means submission and commonplaceness. Benedick shows a more delicately amusing self-conceit than this in, for example, the admirable lines (v. ii. 63 ff.), where the two mock-solemnly agree (*a*) that they are too wise to woo peaceably, and (*b*) that not one wise man among twenty will praise himself. Benedick then hits the high note impeccably with 'Therefore is it most expedient for the wise, if Don Worm, his conscience, find no impediment to the contrary, to be the trumpet of his own virtues, as I am to myself'—a pause, to let the conceit of it shock all modest minds; then he goes one better—'So much for praising myself, who, I myself will bear witness, is praiseworthy.' Here he is playing the Falstaffian game of carrying outrageousness as far as it will go. The *other* side of this self-conceit is in II. iii. 200 ff., his solemn resolutions to profit morally by what he has overheard on his character: 'I must not seem proud; happy are they that hear their detractions and can put them to mending'; and the heroic resolve to make the supreme sacrifice: 'No; the world must be peopled.' There, he is magnificently *absurd*, and totally unaware of himself. I stress the point to bring out the unappreciated fact that the common distinction between persons we laugh *at* and those we laugh *with* is too naïve and crude, at any rate for Shakespeare. Benedick's subsequent efforts to extract a double meaning from two snubbing sentences of Beatrice's repeat this vista of ingenious absurdity. Besides being excellent comedy of mistaken meanings, the last speech in II. iii. is a perfect miniature sample of the love-humour racing a man past himself: 'I will go get her picture.' (*Exit*)

It may seem a wantonly paradoxical view, in so verbally brilliant a piece, but I would contend that some of the wittiest work is to be found in the interrelations and inter-inanimations of the plots. Of the three, the one that takes attention foremost is technically a sub-plot. We hardly notice that it gets going before the 'main' plot, but Beatrice is 'at' Benedick before Claudio appears; and this sex-antagonism in a fencing match between experts with sharp words is musically 'the first subject'. The comedy of this Benedick and Beatrice plot is not the simple, sentimental indulgence of the 'boy meets girl' pattern, although that is included; rather it lies in the entertaining, good-natured, critically aware contemplation of the bents in human nature shown in (*a*) their antagonism (their incapacity to leave one another alone); (*b*) their deception by contrived intrigue; (*c*) the revelations which spring from this, under the pressure of circumstances (that arise from the main plot): leading to (*d*) reversal of all their first positions. The audience is always in a slightly superior position, *not* identifying itself with either of them, though sympathetic. When all the analysers have anatomized, and perhaps reconstructed Benedick and Beatrice, they remain 'just representations of general nature', and hence, as Johnson says, 'please many and please long'.

If I were to answer in a word what the Benedick and Beatrice plot turns on, I should say *misprision*. Benedick and Beatrice misapprehend both each other *and* themselves: each misprizes the other sex, and misapprehends the possibility of a complete agreement between them, as individuals, on what causes that misprision: love of freedom and a superior conceit of themselves as 'wise' where others are fools; as 'free' and untied; and as having a right to enjoy kicking over other people's traces. They fancy they are quite different *from*, and quite indifferent *to* each other. Indifferent they are not; and the audience is 'superior' in seeing their humours *as* humours; and in being aware that the opposite to love (as passionate, obsessive interest) is not hate (another passionate interest), but cool or unnoting indifference. How little Beatrice's 'disdain' for Benedick is truly disdainful is shown in her immediately thinking of him as a measure for Don John (II. i. 6 ff.).

Because the mind of each runs on the other, they can both be simply gulled by hearsay; provided that it is overheard and includes the sort of freedom of comment we all use on absent friends: mildly malicious in tone, unspiteful in intent, and near enough true on their recognizable oddities and shortcomings. The overhearers, for all their sharpness of wit, know that the *comments* have some truth, and naturally accept the rest as also true.[1] Thus the introduction of love-thoughts into both results from a species of misapprehension. They take the *sense* of the words, but totally fail to apprehend their *intention*. The two gulling scenes belong to the comedy of advertisement. Even the advertisers' nice touches of flattery are not lacking. The criticism is spiced with proper appreciation, as when Don Pedro hints—a very subtle inducement—that he would quite like to have Beatrice himself.

That the 'main' plot of Hero and Claudio turns on misapprehension leading to the misprision of violent disprizing, is too obvious to need commentary: but much of the play's total effect hangs on the structural mainness of this plot being displaced. As in Mannerist pictures sometimes, the emphasis is made to fall on what appears structurally to be a corner. This displaced emphasis helps to maintain the sense that the 'Ado' is about 'Nothing' (it is only through the distortion that reading gives, that much attention is given to the 'character' of Claudio).

But though the misapprehension from judging by appearances is quite obvious, it is easy to overlook the incidental touches by which the theme of false report, misunderstanding and jumping to conclusions is strengthened. Not logically strengthened: the 'incidents' are not necessary to the *story*; but the whole sub-episode of the proxy wooing does chime in cleverly with what is to follow. Don Pedro agrees to woo Hero; *immediately* Leonato's 'good sharp fellow' overhears and misreports (I. ii. 5 ff.); the correct report gets into the wrong ears, Borachio's; he tells Don John, who straightaway uses it maliciously on Claudio (pretending to think him Benedick behind the masque-vizor). And Claudio at once anticipates his

[1] cf. Aristotle on lying, *Poetics*, 24. 9: 'Homer more than any other has taught the rest of us the art of telling lies in the right way. I mean the use of a fallacy', *et seq*.

later violent and self-regarding impetuosity by assuming that Don Pedro *has* cheated him of Hero. Call this 'atmosphere', if you like; say, perhaps, that Messina is no place to trust any man's word; whatever you say, it strengthens the theme; and the ready *and perhaps drastic* misapprehensions of quick and apprehensive minds appear as of major importance in the play, as a play and not as a merely logical story.

I say 'perhaps drastic' to suggest how the matter of this part is balanced neatly on a tonal frontier: not between comedy and tragedy, but between comedy and tragi-comedy. Hence the 'limited' of my description of the play at the beginning: the drastic possibilities are so lightly touched that there is a sense of withholding—as if the author, in another mood, could give these incidents quite another tone: but not now; not yet. This feeling is most evident in the Church-scene, which is *not* tragic. T. W. Craik's line[1] here is mainly sound; and his interpretation that *all* the passions are presented to be viewed with comic detachment is preferable to the conventional explanation, that 'the audience is throughout in the know', etc.[2]

Without striving to make too much of it, the dance in II. i. is beautifully apposite. The couples walk their round, two by two, all masked; and all are using words to back the disguise of false faces with trivial deceit. The play-acted defamation of Hero, by means of a false dress on the wrong woman and names used falsely, is exactly parallel. In both, the truth is *behind* the looks and words. The *bal masqué* is only a game of seeming; yet it is a most apt symbol of the whole. The vizor is half deceit, half no deceit: you can never be sure. Believe it, and you make ado about what is nothing. And in the social order and shared delight of the dance—all moving to the controlling rhythm, in their appointed patterns—there is too the emblem of the harmony in which all will conclude: as the play does, with another dance, all the vizors laid aside. The real play is not ended with 'Strike up, pipers'. The very movement of II. i.,

[1] In *Scrutiny*, xix (1953).
[2] So is the audience in *Othello*, for what that is worth!

where all the main misapprehensions started, is repeated and completed; and even the professed misogamists are dancing to the same tune. It is as neat and pretty as 'Sigh no more, ladies, sigh no more'.

The third plot—Dogberry, Verges, the Watch—though mainly Dogberry, is not a mere farcical variety-turn: there *is* a thread of connected episode. The Watch overhear Borachio's scheme and hear it correctly enough (their invention of a thief named 'Deformed' is a nice touch: he has arrived at official constabulary existence by the end). They only overhear because they carry out Dogberry's ridiculous orders and make the policeman's lot a not-unhappy one by, as far as possible, doing nothing whatever. Despite their superb stupidity they do disentangle the plot: though only because, Don John having fled, Borachio tells everything, and gives them the game hands down. This is very natural and well-managed. For had Borachio set out to bluff, the Watch would have been utterly bamboozled in no time. *Superb* stupidity, however, belongs more rightly to Dogberry alone. One side of him is his art of 'comprehending vagrom' *words*: there a more 'senseless and fit man' could not be found. But this is not the whole of him; though a part entirely harmonious with the whole. Dogberry is a perfect instance of the comic mirth which Plato explained in *Philebus*: 'mirth', he says, 'is generally evoked by the sight of self-ignorance or self-conceit, as when a man fancies himself richer, more handsome, more virtuous or wiser than he really is; and this mirth must be present in one who is powerless to inflict hurt on others, otherwise he would cease to be a source of mirth and become a source of danger instead'.[1] As a *real* official Dogberry would be a terror. Conceited ignorance and vast self-importance in local government officers is—and was, in the time of Elizabeth—as good a joke in fiction as a very bad joke in fact.

But misprision and misapprehension are present here too, in a different guise. The incomprehension of the stupid ass is a limiting case of failure to apprehend; and over and above his

[1] *Philebus*, 48–9 (summarized).

miscomprehensions of language, Dogberry's own view of Dogberry is a vast misprision. To himself a superb creature, a wise fellow, as pretty a piece of flesh as any in Messina, he is superbly asinine in the Messina of wit and word-play. Yet, while apparently an *opposite* to the wit-crackers, he is also a parallel: in that pride of self-opinion and a nice appreciation of one's own wisdom and cleverness is as much theirs as his. There is no caustic correction of self-love in Benedick or Beatrice. But the parallel gives another common term, showing on analysis how the three plots have their implicit correspondences, how they genuinely belong together.

'Nothing can permanently please, which does not contain in itself the reason why it is so, and not otherwise.' I have been trying to probe down to the nervous system of those interrelations which *Much Ado* contains within itself, and which give it, as comedy, the poetic unity Coleridge there demands. I find a complex harmony of interdependent themes, some parallels, some direct oppositions; and it seems to me that misapprehensions, misprisions, misunderstandings, misinterpretations and misapplications are the best names for what the comedy *as a whole* is 'about'. The misapprehensions of language are one side of the play; those of human beings and states of affairs the other. At root the two are one; and both you can regard with Dogberry's formula for obdurate drunks: 'You may say they are not the men you took them for.' A step or stage beyond this, and what a different pattern of seemings might result: where neither looks nor words are to be trusted, but everything distrusted. . . . But *Much Ado* touches that for only a moment, and that unsymptomatic of the whole: for a few lines of Claudio's in the Church-scene. They only point to what *might* be thought and felt: in the real tragi-comedies it *will* be. Yet even in *Much Ado*, all appearances *are* equivocal.

Before leaving the plots, mark how deftly they are intertwined. Benedick and Beatrice misapprehend themselves and misprize each other. Claudio's contrived misprision of Hero, the result of intrigue, is finally dissipated by the *coup* of the

Watch, which reduces all the ado to nothing. But at its zenith this same disprizing is the catalyst which liquidates the mutual misprisions of Benedick and Beatrice in the Church-scene. But the reactions to that scene (the confessions of love and Beatrice's implicit admission that she needs a man—to 'kill Claudio') only occur because Benedick and Beatrice have been prepared to 'apprehend': prepared by intrigue, which, like Don John's, is dependent on hearsay and overhearing, taking appearances at their face-value, and being led or misled by words.[1]

Words I must stress, because Dogberry is no essential part of this intertwining as I have summarized it. I suppose you could formulate it all again by saying that the controlling theme might be styled 'mistaken identities'; for, in their pride or conceit, all the principals in some degree mistake themselves: as they mistake or wrongly take situations, and mistake or wrongly take words, on purpose and wittily or accidentally and absurdly. Leonato and Antonio, the two old men lashing themselves back into a youthful fury, and threatening duels, equally mistake themselves: they are pathetic and laughable at once. And, in a way, they reflect on Benedick's sternly assuming the role of truculent executioner to Claudio—and having a comical difficulty in maintaining the part. This is a good example of Shakespeare's detachment in this play: of the amused distance at which his creations should be held, if we are to take *Much Ado* as an artistic whole.

Despite Coleridge's too often quoted comment, 'The interest in the plot is always in fact on account of the characters, not vice versa, as in almost all other writers; the plot is a mere canvas and no more',[2] I still think that plot (in a deeper sense than 'story') is here even more important. His implied contention that the 'interest' in the main plot is 'on account of the characters' (Hero and Claudio, chiefly; and I suppose Don John) seems to me simply untrue. Against Coleridge and his echoers we might set Jonson, putting Aristotelian principle in his own

[1] cf. the fusing of plot with plot in *The Miller's Tale*.
[2] *Lectures on Shakespeare*, 1818.

words, and answering the question 'What is a Poet?': 'A poet ... is a maker, or a feigner: his art, an art of imitation or feigning; expressing the life of man in fit measure, numbers, and harmony. ... Hence he is called a poet, not he which writeth in measure only, but that feigneth and formeth a fable, and writes things like the truth. For the fable and fiction is, as it were, the form and soul of any poetical work or poem.'[2] In a later note, 'the very fiction itself', he says, is 'the reason or form of the work' (cxxx). 'Reason' and 'form' are abstractions from the apprehended, 'felt' interrelations between distinguishable parts of a whole. Such interrelations I have made the central matter of my examination, attempting to resolve the theme to which the three 'plots' are subservient.

Much Ado is not a 'serious' play: it is 'limited' in managing potentially serious matters with a deft nonchalance which passes by the possibility of some being sharp things that might cut. At the same time, it is a play full of themes which are to have sufficiently serious explorations and consequences in Shakespeare's later work. Othello's situation, for example, is a variant of Claudio's; just as Claudio's behaviour to Hero is a sketch of Bertram's (hurt pride turned spiteful: providing we do not see Claudio as only 'mechanical'). Deceit by words (especially words of great meaning) is a constant in the tragi-comedies; and the comedy or farce of crediting too much of what is heard, or thought to be heard, is only the other side to 'O love's best habit is in seeming trust', and the self-imposed deception by seeming and fair words which are found in the Sonnets.

Seeming and being in the later plays have a quite different seriousness. But such a theme exists here, as it does in *1 Henry IV*; and if we say that the one is on *love* (and sex), the other on *honour*, then, looking ahead, the change in Shakespeare's playwriting is partially represented by *Much Ado* leading to *Measure for Measure*; and *1 Henry IV* leading to *Troilus and Cressida*. By this I suggest that potentially serious and distressing human situations (involving love and honour) are in *Much Ado* and

[2] *Timber, or Discoveries*, cxxviii.

1 Henry IV handled 'lightly', as we say: contrived so as to keep them amusing, diverting, stimulating; but also so as to hold them more or less insulated from the deeper and more trenchant inquisitions into values of the tragi-comedies.

The place where we can hardly not notice little *points* of contact with the tragi-comedy outlook is the Church-scene. 'Seeming' is harshly emphasized; Claudio seems on the edge of playing a part that would make it quite another *sort* of play; and the Friar's moral lines on lost affections—sad, uncomfortable thoughts—are echoed by the King in *All's Well*. But those points mark the real insulation of *Much Ado*. The disturbed feeling of *Measure for Measure*—its troubled thinking—is not here. We can hardly speak of 'lack of feeling' in so bright, lively, glittering a piece: but is there not a certain *hard* quality, as with the bright colours of some Italian painting?

It is a *Decameron*-like story (barring the Watch), with some of the *Decameron* qualities of volatility in the persons, no wasting of sympathy on victims of jests, and the expectation of swift, unreflecting volte-faces of attitudes and emotions at the call of Fortune's pipe. That usually leaves an impression of shallowness, of a lack of *depth* of emotion, in northern European minds. The people seem rather heartless, while not in the least 'cold'; and the stories are apt to leave us thinking more about 'Now what did X really feel when . . . ?' than we know we *should*. In *Much Ado*, the brushing aside of the tone of calamity, the expectations of volatile changes of feeling in Claudio, the jocular (for so it is) 'Think not on him till to-morrow. I'll devise thee brave punishments for him. Strike up, pipers', only catch up a bright hardness (the result of a *deliberate* limitation of sympathies in the author?) which runs through the play.

Much Ado is a fantasy of equivocal appearances in a glittering world of amiable fools of all sorts. As naturally as Italians talk Italian, the Messinans talk 'equivocal'; but their 'double tongues' are as harmless as those of the 'spotted snakes' in *A Midsummer Night's Dream*. This equivocal quality, moreover, is deftly restricted to appearances: there are only the slightest touches of suggestion of any intrinsic equivocation in things themselves (in love, for example). Ambivalence is not a term to apply here.

These qualities urge me to 'place' the play in the course of Shakespeare's writing as follows. In the breaking down of sensitive endurance, and of mental resistance to the revelation of the unfairness of human nature, there is a point where a sense of humour *fails*; where to see life and the world in humorous proportions is no longer possible: it cannot be assumed by an act of will, or, if so, the assumption cannot be maintained. At this point distresses distress, and cannot be accepted tolerantly as the world's way, muffled by an easy 'they soon get over it' and by the cant of time. (I think of John Keats, of course; but without 'Keatsifying' Shakespeare. In the *later* plays the 'miseries of the world/ Are misery'; but not here in *Much Ado*). Immediately *before* that point, the besieged mind and invaded heart may defend themselves by the assumption of a certain hardness: assume the *Decameron virtu*—the trappings and the suits of *joy*—though they have it not within. They may also find a certain high-flown gaiety—not hysterical, but making the best, and most, of the farce of human misunderstanding, deception, misprision—in the comedy of language (devised, so one may suppose, to communicate: but often used for just the reverse, either in game or in earnest). It is as if the sensitive mind and heart sought to persuade themselves by demonstration that life is a jest, and that the wider the comic net the likelier it is to resolve all the unmentioned but implied and subjective troubles in one great humorous or laughable plan, in which Fortune favours the laughers. This is the point at which great clowns who are melancholic—Chaplin, Raimu, Jouvet, Fernandel—stand and abide. One step from that strange equilibrium may turn to 'cynicism' (especially in England): the cynicism where the attitudes I called 'hardness' (self-defensive) and 'farce' (offensive, debunking) combine to 'place' love, honour, truth, only to devalue them. *Much Ado* stands in the Shakespearian canon just at that point.

5

All's Well That Ends Well

THE 'STORY' of *All's Well* comes from Boccaccio: the ninth story on the third day, told by the Queen, accessible in 1566 in William Paynter's *Palace of Pleasure* (which Shakespeare read, even if as a crib only). Quiller-Couch, in the Introduction to the *New Cambridge* edition, says he 'retells it unmistakably, albeit with certain variations and additions well worth studying; so that, for once in a way, a detailed examination of one of Shakespeare's "sources" definitely advances the critic in his business' (p. xii). This 'detailed examination' 'Q' never makes. He says nothing about 'variations', condemns three 'additions' (Lafeu, the Clown and Parolles), drops a good word for a fourth (the Countess)—and that is all. Since I believe that source-study *does*—here—'advance the critic', I shall attack the play from this angle.

The story of Beltramo and Giletta is simple enough. The two are brought up together as young Count-to-be and the Count's physician's daughter who 'fervently fell in love with Beltramo, more than was meet for a maiden of her age' (Paynter). (The later translation of 1620–25 only calls it 'admirable'). Beltramo's father dead, he became a ward of the King and went to Paris; the King's fistula gave Giletta the chance to cure his sickness (and her own); and when the King offered her a husband, if she succeeded, she insisted on making her own choice. As she was prepared to burn if she did not marry on these terms, the King was so impressed with her confidence that he gave her both her points. He was cured, she chose Beltramo; and though 'the King was very lothe to graunte hym unto her' and Beltramo even more loath to have 'a physicion to wife', the King explained that he must keep faith. Beltramo's 'I assure you I shall never be contented with that marriage' he meets by persuasion: by telling him that the girl was 'fair and wise' and loved him 'most intirely', and that in his royal opinion he would 'leade a more joyfull life with her' than with someone of higher rank. Therewith Beltramo held his peace and was married.

Instead of going home to Rossiglione, the Count went to Florence to the local war. Countess Giletta went to Rossiglione and managed the estates with expected efficiency. When they were all in order, she wrote to tell him she would leave if he wished it; and to this he sent a churlish letter with the well-known conditions: he would live with her only when she got a ring he never took off and a son of his body.

Giletta announced her departure on perpetual pilgrimage, left bewept by all, and went incognita to Florence. There she found Beltramo wickedly pursuing the daughter of an impoverished gentlewoman; had herself substituted for the young lady; obtained the ring; got herself with child; and (not being a woman for half measures) had twins in due time. With this evidence she appeared at home (where Beltramo had returned—the 'seduced' daughter having been removed); fell at his feet, showed her tokens, and begged him to keep his word. This he did, full of 'admiracion' and perceiving 'her constaunt minde and good witte', and 'abjecting his obstinate rigour', loved and honoured her 'as his dere spouse and wife'.

Shakespeare's 'additions' to this simple story of impossible bargain improbably fulfilled are of many different kinds. To begin at the beginning, he invents the dowager Countess: a gentle aristocrat declined into the vale of years, experienced, understanding and with the tenderest and most capacious sympathy for youth in love; yet with no weakness whatever towards a son who falls short of the standards of his noble family. A calm moral beauty shines out from her, which I can only try to express with Donne's

> No *Spring*, nor *Summer* Beauty hath such grace,
> As I have seen in one *Autumnall* face. (*Elegie IX*)

Beside her, Shakespeare places the old lord Lafeu: experienced too, shrewd, a sharp-tongued humorist who, when provoked, adopts the role of a Peacockian Mr. Sarcastic who means to give offence to whatever offends him, and does it with a blandness which is imperturbable.

He is at his best in dealing with Parolles (an 'addition' who must come in here a little out of turn): a pompous, pretentious military braggart and hanger-on of Bertram's, whom Lafeu sees through like a window of lattice and treats with a caustic witty badinage, paying not the slightest attention to the victim's military bridlings at his bland insults. He diagnoses the bluffing coward, hand on sword, infallibly: the cock that ruffles its feathers, but will not fight. All Parolles can do is to be 'hurt' with an absurd attempt to keep his dignity:

Parolles: My lord, you give me most egregious indignity.
Lafeu: Ay, with all my heart; and thou art worthy of it.
(II. iii. 213–14)

Lafeu is throughout a commentator, keeping a watchful semi-paternal eye on Bertram (and perhaps on 'unbaked and doughy youth' at large). His warnings that Parolles is a 'light nut'—Captain, but with no kernel—pass unheeded; and it is only at the wars that the French Lords' pincer-movement extracts the nut's rottenness—at an important turn in the main plot.

Shakespeare made Parolles on the standard classical comedy pattern of the *miles gloriosus*, *il Capitano* of the *commedia dell' arte*, the blowsy braggart who exists to be pricked; but he added some contemporary material from the bogus military-looking rascals who hung about St. Paul's: 'apocryphal captains', like Jonson's Face in one of his metamorphoses. Prima facie he is just a uniformed windbag; but his significance is implicit in his name: because '*Paroles*' is *words*, not deeds. His fine feathers do not make a fine bird, and Shakespeare hatched him for the plucking. He had decided to add to his source-story a comic exposure: of the coward, liar, sham and traducer. I think, too, that Parolles belongs to the pattern which contrasts ageing or elderly people who are noble with younger ones who are not. He is young, I am sure. Those who think him old are misled by the false stuffing in him.

The King is an 'alteration' rather than an 'addition'. The character and moral weight Shakespeare gives him strengthen the effects of the Countess and Lafeu as types of old nobility: surviving exemplars of a generation, or a world, which is passing away. He is a sadly nostalgic figure, conscientious, burdened ('I fill a place, I know't'), a little weary. You can see a Jacobean Matthew Arnold in him:

> Or do I wait, to hear some grey-hair'd king
> Unravel all his many-colour'd lore;
> Whose mind hath known all arts of governing,
> Mused much, loved life a little, loathed it more?[1]

He is there to speak a mind full of reflections on honour, virtue, the values of life under the threat and march of 'Th' inaudible and noiseless foot of Time' (v. iii. 41). But he is not merely a victim of 'haggish age' which 'steals on' and 'wears us out of act', as he says at his first appearance, talking of Bertram's father. Those solemn and moving lines of tribute to his old friend are good and clear evidence that a contrast between generations is intended; between a fine *old* world and a *new*; between age and crabbed *youth*. But I do not see what Dr. Tillyard calls Shakespeare's 'evident dislike of the younger generation'.[2] I see the phenomena, but interpret them as valuations of man: aspects of his being, not intrusions of something personal from a *laudator temporis acti*. In Boccaccio or Paynter the father was simply 'Isnardo, the Counte of Rossiglione, who bicause he was sickly and diseased, kepte alwaies in his house a phisicion'. That is all. Shakespeare is not content to make the King a realized human creature, as distinct from the piece of plot-machinery he found him; he shows the play's moral pattern by making him speak to Bertram thus:

[1] *To a Gipsy Child by the Sea-shore.*
[2] *Shakespeare's Problem Plays*, p. 106.

It much repairs me
To talk of your good father. In his youth
He had the wit which I can well observe
To-day in our young lords; but they may jest
Till their own scorn return to them unnoted
Ere they can hide their levity in honour. (I. ii. 30–5)

The last two lines may be ambiguous, but the sense—'they can make scornful jests till their contemptuous manners make them contemptible without their noticing it'—seems more compelling than Dover Wilson's 'they can jest till their own jokes are so stale that they fail to recognise them . . . on another's lips'. And the accusation that 'they lack the honourable (respected) qualities to counterbalance their flippancy or frivolity' is firmly stressed later in the passage (I. ii. 55–63), where Bertram's father is quoted to the effect that these young men care only for fashion, their judgements are exercised on their clothes, and they have even less constancy than their fashions. The misplacement of the moral qualities—'judgement' and 'constancy'—upon *dress*, and the stressing of a trivial concern with appearances, give these difficult lines more point and weight.

There is, in the same speech of the King, an explicit measuring of the younger generation against 'the Courtier' (*Il Cortegiano*):

So like a courtier, contempt nor bitterness
Were in his pride or sharpness; if they were,
His equal had awak'd them . . .
. . . .   Who were below him
He us'd as creatures of another place;[1]
And bow'd his eminent top to their low ranks,
Making them proud of his humility
In their poor praise he humbled. Such a man
Might be a copy to these younger times;
Which, followed well, would demonstrate them now
But goers backward. (I. ii. 36 f.)

On re-reading, we cannot fail to apply these lines to Bertram

[1] The *Cambridge New Shakespeare* editors conjecture *a neyer (nigher) place*, i.e. a place nearer himself.

himself: on the stage, they prepare us for what he is ***not***. Contempt is the immediate response of his pride when Helena chooses him as her husband: 'A poor physician's daughter my wife!'; and he is as incapable of bowing his eminent top as of restraining his bitterness. As Helena reads his letter, she repeats the words: ' "Till I have no wife, I have nothing in France." 'Tis bitter.' (III. ii. 72.) The King's reminiscences of Rousillon Senior not only 'characterize' Bertram *per contra*: they add to the contrasted schemes of two worlds, two types of men. One is that of courtesy, traditional virtues; the other that of Bertram and Parolles (the latter in this connection a type of vanity and emptiness, camouflaged in aggressive military dressiness: see the 'clothes' image at I. ii. 60–3). Up to a point, these two are birds of a feather. 'Handsome is as handsome does *not*' goes for them both. Both are 'seemers'. Grant this, and the whole sub-plot of the exposure of 'Mr. Words' has its place and point: Parolles is there to be stripped; and stripped at just the very moment when Bertram's fortunes reach their apogee (in his suppositious conquest of Diana) and begin to turn retrograde—towards his own exposure before the King, the Countess and Lafeu.

Before the King: I repeat that, because one major alteration which Shakespeare has made is to convert the dénouement into a species of *Trial-scene*. The King is there because he has stood apart from the action throughout, as a kind of judge of his people and the times: a figure of superior insight and wisdom, in whose mouth the recurrent themes of true virtue and seeming, of rank and merit, are not inappropriate. In Boccaccio the ending is entirely different. Beltramo is judge in his own and Giletta's case, and all that is 'exposed' is the wit, determination, ingenuity and indefatigably constant love of the woman he had utterly underestimated. No detail is given, but it seems that he told the whole story without shame or undue embarrassment, recognizing that his 'obstinate rigour' was wrong, and that he had made a pretty good bargain in the dark. As he had. Shakespeare makes a thoroughly uncomfortable affair of it; and this is one of the easiest places to examine the 'Problem play' or 'tragi-comic' quality of the piece: so I shall enlarge a little.

One obvious but most important difference between Beltramo and Bertram is that the latter is a character, the former is not. Beltramo is only a couple of opposite *attitudes*: first dead-set against Giletta and the marriage; and then all *for*: converted by her constancy and wit—and her pretty brace of Beltraminetti. In Bertram Shakespeare produced something more psychologically plausible, more complicated—and disagreeable. He weights the dice very expertly against those who want this to be a straightforward 'fairy-tale' sort of comedy—with a Beauty-and-the-Beast young hero who is only a rough diamond—which will come out all right in the end. When Bertram objects to being married off (as a postscript to the King's prescription)—even in his rejection of Helena—he *could* be regarded as a 'young cub' and 'unlicked': a spoilt boy who turns boorish and spiteful because he *is* 'an unseasoned courtier' (his mother's phrase in I. i. 63) *and* an 'ass' (as Lafeu has just remarked). 'But', we may tell ourselves, 'he has had some provocation: no matter what scholars may tell us to think about wards of Court, their having no option over brides, the supreme authority of the monarch, and so on'. Yet even there, he has been largely insulated against sympathy: (1) by the King's 'placing' speech (just examined); and (2) by the effective stage-device of paving the way to his disgusted discovery that Helena wants *him*, with her gentle, courteous, even *affectionate* rejections of the three or four young lords, each of whom would be only too delighted to have *her*. Immediately after the wedding, the unfavourable light in which he is seen is intensified by two telling touches: his sullen, boorish word for Helena: 'Here comes my clog'; and his cruel snubbing of her when she begs a kiss (II. v. 82–5: expunged by Dr. Bowdler; I hope, because of the cruelty). The effect is to put Bertram in a *frame*. That is one of the characteristics of the 'Problem plays' or tragi-comedies.

In them, 'realistic' human types are isolated like 'heroes', but in a frame which emphasizes their lack of heroic, noble, gracious or even respectable qualities. A limited understanding in us (never quite sympathy) is set in conflict with ethical condemnation: and the outcome is all those various and complicated states of mixed feelings which are the heart of the 'experiences' of the Problem plays; and equally the explanation of the variety of assessments which critics have, and will, put on them. But this all starts with the isolation of a mind or sensibility, caught in a trap of circumstance which is cruel but also somehow petty; and the cool detachment of Shakespeare's presentation holds us to, at most, half-sympathies as we uncomfortably watch the exposures of human shortcoming, human stupidity, selfishness, blindness and limitation. *All's Well* is the slightest of these plays. But it contains one phrase which hits off exactly what I have in mind. When Parolles is un-blindfolded and sees his whole disgrace in a flash, what is his comment? 'Who cannot be crush'd with a plot?' It is a final comment on human nature as these 'unpleasant plays' reveal, or rather, expose it.

With that digression into generalities, let me return to Bertram. The plotting in Acts IV. and V. has a remarkable forward-and-back movement. It is the backward swing that obstructs the straight-comedy happy ending. We would like to find a Bertram who is not unworthy of Helena's devotion; instead, his disagreeableness is made most emphatic in Act V.: just before he is 'dismissed to happiness' (in Johnson's apt, disgusted phrase).

Source-study here is a useful guide. It shows how Shakespeare went well out of his way to complicate the plot, adding much intrigue that the dramatization of the *novella* assuredly did not require. It must be presumed that he had some motive in doing this. Let me summarize: not so much the 'action' as its effects. The main business of Act IV. is the stripping of Parolles, in which the explicit purpose of the two Lords (the Dumain brothers) is to open Bertram's eyes:

> I would gladly have him see his company anatomiz'd, that he might take a measure of his own judgments, wherein so curiously he had set this counterfeit. (1st Lord at IV. iii. 30–3)

Before this, however, Bertram has received his mother's letter:

'there is something in't that stings his nature; for on the reading it he chang'd almost into another man' (IV. iii. 2–4). The obloquy which Bertram has incurred is also stressed. All these pointers look like straws in a rising wind of self-knowledge and potential reformation (though the seduction of Diana is being pursued, and Bertram is only expected to be glad at the news of Helena's death). The effect on him of the grilling of Parolles cannot be judged. Evidently he is not amused, and we can think what we please of his surly state. Since this is 'All's Well that Ends Well', we may all well be pleased to think that a better Bertram is in the brewing.

At Rousillon (in v. iii.) this 'forward' movement is developed. Everything is prepared for the reception of the reforming wife-beater, all are ready to think the best they can of him. King, Countess and Lafeu share a party-line; his recently offended Majesty will receive him as 'a stranger, no offender'. To go several better than letting bygones be bygones, Shakespeare abruptly invents a daughter for Lafeu to provide this deserving 'widower' with a new bride.[1] What is more, this unheard-of, spontaneously generated daughter is offered by Bertram as his excuse for his inability to love Helena. Fair Maudlin had his heart, and 'contempt' accordingly 'warp'd the line of every other favour'. He loved Helena too—when she was gone; the King gives us our cue with 'Well excus'd'; and, with some solemn and ritualistic moral lines of lost opportunity in the sphere of the affections,[2] dust is left to close Helena's eyes. 'And now forget her,' says the King.

This is impossible. We know that Helena is alive, even if we have to wait for the chaste, but outspoken Diana to tell us that by now 'she feels her young one kick' (v. iii. 296). Before we know how to take this grave charade, Bertram's ring (sent as token to fetch Maudlin) springs the trap on him; and in a very little time he is in a 'frame' indeed: under strong suspicion of

[1] See *New Cambridge* edn., p. xxxii, for 'Q's' indignation at the fatuity of this 5th Act device.

[2] v. iii. 57–60.

being Helena's murderer. A second inquisition follows, with Diana and the other ring: Bertram's lies get deeper and dirtier, his bluffs are called one after another, and, as the unkindest cut of all, Parolles is brought as evidence against him and made a witness of *his* exposure. The backward movement is complete. Bertram is silent until Helena arrives, when all he is given is four words and a very lame couplet.

I hope I have not been tedious in tracing this deliberate reversal of any 'straight comedy' expectations. Shakespeare insists on the degradation of Bertram: insists on a naked, shameful exposure of commonplace, ignoble *man*. There is surely nothing excessive in 'Q's' comment on this: 'Confronted with Diana, he forgets all obligation of honour and seeks to protect himself by lying against her as basely as ever did any farm lout in a bastardy case . . .' But, if you say that, you cannot write off Shakespeare's Bertram as 'a stage puppet' (as 'Q' does). The upsetting thing about him in the 'trial' is that his behaviour does *not* conform to stage-expectations, and the traits he reveals are *not* those of a puppet-hero about to live happily ever after; but those of a weak, cowardly, mean-spirited, false, and ill-natured human being.

They are exactly the unlovely qualities which have been displayed in Parolles. The parallel of main plot and sub-plot revelations seems to me incontestable. Running a comic or farcical action in parallel with a serious one (which it may parody) was a symphonic device Shakespeare had mastered triumphantly by the time of *1 Henry IV*, seven years back. Again, in *Measure for Measure*, the main themes of sex and justice are farcically keyed down in the low-life accompaniment. The exposure of Bertram is not farcical, of course. The situation is potentially satirical-comical; indeed Jonsonian: for no sympathy is stirred for Bertram in his humiliations. This Jonsonian situation is, however, brushed away with an invitation to regard the sordid comedy of the woman-chaser caught in a man-trap as the prelude to happy marriage. Bertram's vices are buried hugger-mugger, and most of the critics want to say that Shakespeare has 'done but greenly', rushed their funeral, etc. Even those critics who do their very best to accept the happy ending are slightly uneasy; and not, I think, only because they are afraid of catching Dr. Johnson's eye ('I cannot reconcile myself to Bertram', which has the finality of 'Sir, the woman's a whore, and there's an end on't'). The usual line of the 'acceptors' follows Karl Elze's dictum: 'Nicht nur am Könige, sondern auch an Bertram vollbringt sie eine glückliche Heilung'.[1] Dowden develops Elze, Dr. Tillyard condenses Dowden. But neither Englishman is quite easy about it: and their uneasiness comes out indirectly in half-asides about the character of Helena.

Uneasiness I consider one real quality of the play (as it is of the endings of *Troilus and Cressida* and *Measure for Measure*). We know we should not look 'conventional' comedy-ending gift-marriages in the mouth: that there is a tide in the affairs of fifth Acts that pairs males and females off mechanically, into which further inquiry is inapposite. But the disagreeable qualities of this male have been so convincingly built up, the Beast made so unbeautifully beastly, that the effect is to shake to its fairy-tale foundations the very convention we are expected to accept. To invert Coleridge's too hackneyed formula: instead of 'a willing suspension of disbelief', we are in danger of 'a reluctant commotion of disbelief' in the theatrical formula we are offered. The realistic quality in Bertram is at odds with his theatrical redemption: put in another way, the sentiments generated by his psychology are at odds with the sentimentality of the convention. Here we have to choose between (1) saying Shakespeare is inept: he might have given us a convertible Bertram, and he has not; (2) saying Shakespeare is cynical about his audience: he relies on their being crass or unreflective; and (3) supposing that he was aware of what he had done, even if it was the best he could do with it.

Now there are 'ineptitudes' in this play: indeed, in all the

[1] 'Helena accomplishes a happy recovery not only for the King but for Bertram also.' *Shakespeare Jahrbuch*, vii., 1882, p. 222.

Problem plays. In *All's Well* there is an intermittent 'muddiness' —a failure or confusion in the stream where, here and there, you seem to glimpse the ideas that were in the writer's mind, only to be left guessing at their exact outlines, or their relevant place in the turbid flow.[1] The plotting, however, is so deliberate, its effect so firm, that it is too easy a way out to say that it was composed on a succession of Shakespearian off-days. Rather, I would call it an 'off-play': a piece in which the writer was aware of the off-notes, by which I mean the discords. The whole body is more than the tail-end, and there *are* off-notes throughout. In particular, though, I mean by the phrase those discords produced by playing off a harsh, disturbing human reality against conventional story-book or play-book sentimental expectations (as Shakespeare did in *Troilus and Cressida*, where nearly all the conventional *heroic* expectations are cheated, and poetic justice too: over Cressida, for instance, who is stripped and then dropped). It would be going too far to suggest any close resemblance to such modern dramatists as Sartre (who has an axe to grind) or Anouilh. They are much more self-conscious. Yet there is a likeness, in the way that, in the handling of 'traditional', already-known stories, the myth and the modernity run counter to each other. The stock plots seem to be repeated; but the result comes out disquietingly different.

If the exposure of Parolles is examined, we find discords—off-notes—there too. There is no surprise about the undermining and blowing up of the Braggart. Lafeu has 'tipped him off' for us, and it is plain that the Dumains' scheme will go like clockwork. So it does. But the moral commentary of these unexpectedly serious-minded young practical-jokers is *not* 'stock'. It strikes deeper notes, which are out of key. When Parolles is thinking aloud how to get out of the drum-venture, what self-inflicted wounds will look convincing, one eavesdropper whispers to the other: 'Is it possible he should know what he is, and be that he is?' (IV. i. 41–2). The answer to that question in the tragi-comic 'problem' world is Yes. The joke of the unsuspect-

[1] I enlarge on this later (pp. 100–105).

ing gull surveyed is broken into by the sudden straight look down into degradation. Momentarily we see into rats' alley.

In the exposure-scene we may seem to be back in a mild repetition of the Gadshill show-down, in which cowardice and lying are broad fun to watch. Indeed, when Parolles betters expectation by giving slanderous sketches of the Dumains and Bertram, one of them can say, 'I begin to love him for this.' But when the braggart is unblindfolded—confronted with his own nakedness—there is no Falstaff about him. Unexpectedly, discomfortingly, 'the Clown has a heart'. The stock stage-situation does not allow clowns these human inconveniences. No, '*Pagliaccio non sono*' is embarrassing, perturbing, in this context. The *miles gloriosus* should burst when pricked, and not upset us with feelings. But Shakespeare insists on the shame. 'Who cannot be crush'd with a plot?' is too wide and deep a question for comfort. It catches up the note of the exchange between the two Dumains apropos of Bertram's seduction of Diana: 'Now, God delay our rebellion! As we are ourselves, what things are we!' 'Merely our own traitors . . .';[1] and the first brother goes on to predict exactly what is to happen to Bertram—*and* to Parolles: each 'in his proper stream, o'erflows himself' (i.e., if we translate the disorder imagery, 'becomes a disordered chaos by flooding from his own appetencies'). The conclusion of the stripping-scene turns the thorn in the proud flesh as the skunk recognizes his stink and accommodates his ambitions to it:

> If my heart were great,
> 'Twould burst at this. Captain I'll be no more;
> But I will eat, and drink, and sleep as soft
> As captain shall. Simply the thing I am
> Shall make me live. (IV. iii. 307–11)

Those are thoughts from the theatre of life, clashing with the stuff of conventional Theatre. There is room in the world for rats, and to be degraded is a qualification in itself.

That this is not an isolated notion, which I have picked out

[1] IV. iii. 18-20.

and overstressed, is shown by an earlier speech of Helena's about Parolles:

> And yet I know him a notorious liar,
> Think him a great way fool, solely a coward;
> Yet these fix'd evils sit so fit in him
> That they take place when virtue's steely bones
> Looks bleak i' th' cold wind; withal, full oft we see
> Cold wisdom waiting on superfluous folly. (I. i. 94–9)

The central idea here, a point the commentators seem to have missed, is from Juvenal: 'Virtus laudatur, et alget' (Virtue is praised, and perishes (with cold).) The last line, 'Cold (naked) wisdom waiting on superfluous (overdressed) folly', too exactly echoes the thought of *Sonnet 66* to be passed lightly by:

> Tir'd with all these, for restful death I cry:
> As, to behold desert a beggar born,
> And needy nothing trimm'd in jollity . . .

A variant on 'wisdom *waiting on* folly' follows. 'And folly, doctor-like, controlling skill. . . .' *All's Well* has the sense of *ill* in it, but none of the ache of that sonnet. Shakespeare may have been 'tir'd with' *some of* these, but it was in the sense of finding them tiresome. For 'captive good attending captain ill' he made Bertram too little good (and far too uncaptivating); and the influence of Captain Parolles too inconspicuous.

I fail to see why Dr. Tillyard[1] says that 'the Morality role of the tempter protrudes' from Parolles. True, there is one speech (II. i. 48–55) where Bertram is enjoined to play the fulsome flatterer to the French Lords: it is not far from Lord Chesterfield, advising his son to make farewells *avec onction et une espèce d'attendrissement*; and surely not very immoral. Apart from that, Parolles offers no temptations whatever. It is only natural that when the Countess and Lafeu positively *need* to make every allowance for Bertram, they suggest that he has been misled (III. ii. 85–7 and IV. v. 1–6). So kindly elders always do with their near-relations. No doubt Parolles is 'a very tainted fellow',

[1] *Shakespeare's Problem Plays*, p. 109.

but if it comes to 'full of wickedness', no: Bertram is fuller, and needs little 'inducement' (III. ii. 87). The relation between the two is not that of misleader and misled, for all that Bertram is taken in by the military camouflage, the 'scarfs' and 'snipt-taffeta' of the 'red-tail'd humble-bee'. References to Prince Hal and Falstaff are beside the point. None the less, Parolles is important: not an irrelevant sideshow, nor an 'inept business' ('Q'). Charles I was a sound judge when he wrote 'Monsieur Parolles' as sub-title in his Second Folio (still preserved at Windsor).[1]

The play's structure can now be described. The Parolles ('Words, words, words') sub-plot of the seemer unmasked parallels and reflects a yellow[2] light on Bertram, the bed-trick and the unmasking 'Trial-scene'. In the bed part, Bertram's deeds are as false as *paroles* (words); in the trial his words come drastically into line with them. Parolles is exposed as coward, liar, sham and slanderer—farcically (with an unfunny edge to it); Bertram on trial comes out as dupe, liar (a word insufferable to the Elizabethan gentleman), twister ('boggler') and traducer of his own lady-love's good name: beside which, being 'a foolish idle boy, but for all that very ruttish' and 'a whale to virginity', are less serious charges in a sixteenth/seventeenth-century gentleman of non-English nationality. It is a tragi-comedy structure, in which 'Honour is the subject of my story' (military or gentlemanly) and seeming the unifying conception. This is a main theme of *Troilus and Cressida* and *Measure for Measure* too, although the treatment here is not comparable with the different severities of either.

A further tragi-comic trait—one which marks it off from its next-of-kin among the 'great Comedies' (*Much Ado*, for example)—is the moral reflectiveness which so far I have only remarked in the two French Lords. All the minor characters are minor moralists. The play is peppered with abstract ethical comments, which seem pointed in their context (although we

[1] See Peter Alexander, *Shakespeare's Life and Art*, p. 192.
[2] Lafeu at IV. v. 2 refers to Parolles' 'vilainous saffron'.

are not always sure how far we are meant to take the ideas they put into our minds); and their effect is cumulative. It tends to establish an attitude. The minor characters stand by like observers, presumably on the watch for virtue. The Countess, naturally enough, has a half-anxious eye on her son; Lafeu watches too; so does the King. At the wars the two Dumains take up the observational role; even the Clown has his own vulgarly cynical comments to offer. In a very different way from Hamlet, Bertram is 'the observed of all observers'. The questioning attitude that is set up by all this is one of the play's characteristics: although admittedly not all the reflections are clear. Some are tiresomely obscure; others suggest that they may have been current worries in Shakespeare's head, during the composition of a play that would not quite carry them.

The word 'virtue' is recurrent. The Countess moralizes from Helena's innate 'dispositions' to the deceptive effects of 'virtuous qualities' in 'an unclean mind': 'they are virtues and traitors too'. We wonder if the 'virtues' of rank (in Bertram) are included; but the lines are obscure. She also speaks of 'blood and virtue' contending for empire in him: where 'blood' cannot mean 'noble blood', and must therefore be 'pride, lustiness, energy'. Helena moralizes from Parolles' worldly-successful vices to 'virtue's steely bones' and their lack of success. The King's analysis of the courtly virtues in Bertram's father points the lack of courtesy in the younger generation, and, by implication, in Bertram. The theme of virtue comes boldly to the fore when the King lectures Bertram on the difference between 'title' (meaning rank) and 'virtue', and almost echoes the Countess with:

> Where great additions swell 's, and virtue none,
> It is a dropsied honour. (II. iii. 125–6)

Immediately after this, the major moral theme of the play is stated: the axle of the whole, if we want to make it *inclusively* 'a kind of Morality':

That is honour's scorn
Which challenges itself as honour's born
And is not like the sire. Honours thrive
When rather from our acts we them derive
Than our fore-goers . . . (II. iii. 131–5)

The continuity of such reflections in Shakespeare's mind is shown by what follows about the word Honour being 'a slave/ Debauch'd on every tomb ... a lying trophy': notions perilously close to the opinions of Falstaff, done into moralizing couplets.

Whether we apply all this to Bertram or not—and I think we must—it calls attention to *one* dominant ethical problem in the play, and one that undoubtedly existed for both the Elizabethans and Jacobeans. It is a problem which is not in the Boccaccio story. Shakespeare may have come upon it in Montaigne, who seems to be responsible for several of the deeper reflective passages in the play. In his essay, *Upon some Verses of* Virgil (Book III, ch. v.), there is a digression about the mistakenness of those 'who to doe vertue a favour, holde, that nobilitie is no other thing then Vertue.' That would, of course, be the traditional Elizabethan assumption: in a good world, a world in order, the nobles *are* noble: rank is merited, *is* merit. But Montaigne says: 'Indeed these things have affinitie; but therewithall great difference: their names and titles should not thus be commixt: both are wronged so to be confounded. *Nobilitie is a worthy, goodly quality, and introduced with good reason, but in as much as it dependeth on others, and may fall to the share of my vicious and worthlesse fellowe, it is in estimation farre shorte of vertue.*' He elaborates on this with witty comparisons, then contrasts 'nobilitie' with qualities which 'fall within compasse of commerce and communication': that is to say, qualities which are efficacious in the lives of others. The thought is very near to the Duke's in *Measure for Measure* at I. i. 33–6:

Heaven doth with us as we with torches do,
Not light them for themselves; for if our virtues
Did not go forth of us, 'twere all alike
As if we had them not;

especially when we notice how Montaigne says that nobility 'consumeth it selfe in it selfe, of no employment for the service of others'. (cf. the Duke's speech above, 30–2). Helena's virtues may not be of the brightest; but they do 'go forth'. She is effectual in action; and, in a little-virtued world, that is not nothing.

It is at least a strange coincidence that Montaigne digressed to 'virtue and nobility' from the subject of *marriage*. What is more, he was writing against love-matches:

> *I see no mariages faile sooner, or more troubled, then such as are concluded for beauties sake, and hudled up for amorous desires.* There are required more solide foundations, and more constant grounds, and a more warie marching to it: this earnest youthly heate serveth to no purpose.

The digression starts with his arguing that those who equate love and marriageability are as mistaken as those who equate nobility and virtue. If this coincidence means anything, then all one can say is that the 'marriage' question is never worked into Shakespeare's play. What *is* worked in is the 'problem' (not at all intriguing to us, who are democrats and egalitatians) of rank and merit, form and virtue: the question that was answered by Chaucer's Wyf of Bathe (taking her authority from Seneca) with her usual decidedness:

'That he is gentil that dooth gentil dedis.' (*Tale*, 1170)

Unhappily, the questioning is much more definite and definable than the answering. It is easy to say what virtues Bertram has *not* (soldiership is all he has; and his own mother has said, at III. ii. 92, 'his sword can never win/ The honour that he loses', although she forgets it by and by). It is easy to see that Jill is as good as her master, indeed several times better; but the question 'Is she, then, Virtue itself?' is unanswerable. Or rather, to borrow from Falstaff, it is a question not to be asked. That is why I have given Helena no attention in this lecture. I take her for granted, which is the right way with her. Analysis only results in confusion;[1] for if you analyse her, you find that her

[1] See Note on pp. 106–7.

only *noble* qualities are courage and the Stoical reserve which can take a blow with dignity and few words.[1] The rest of her qualities are: a possessive passion for her man; an unconquerable determination (which one man will ennoble as 'constancy', and the next call 'will to get her own way'); an accomplished opportunism or a good head for scheming; and the purely pragmatic virtue of success in action. The sum total of all this as 'virtue' is not ethically satisfying.

That is why I spoke of 'a question not to be asked'. This conclusion results only from asking it. Helena is (mainly) a fairy-tale, 'traditional' story-book female, who is 'good'; and we should no more inquire into the details than into those of her honeymoon (whenever we suppose that to occur!)[2] The problematic element remains, because this sentimental fairy-tale 'Good One' is conjoined with a realistic, real-life 'Bad 'Un'; and the two particles in this mysterious, alleged unity exist in not merely different orbits, but orbits in different systems. This produces a state of mixed feelings, in which the fairy-tale solution we might like to believe in (and are adjured to by the title, and by the 'historical method' interpreters) is in conflict with the realistic, psychological exposure—which is very much more convincing.

This state of mixed feelings corresponds with the *ambiguity* of some of the writing. The styles used are very mixed, and generalization is extremely difficult. In some places the author labouredly complicates what is less profound and difficult than it looks; in others he is forcefully tense and quite his middle-period self; in others again his lines have profounder and more

[1] Without reaching the clarity of Meredith's

> 'O have a care of natures that are mute,
> They punish you in acts; their steps are brief . . .'
>
> (*Modern Love*)

[2] It is an undeniable fault of the play that the urge to think too precisely on that event exists; and that Shakespeare has done something to put it in our minds (see IV. iv. 21 f.). It is not merely an imported 'modern' thought that whatever marriage (togetherness, and all that that implies) means in the 'happy ending', hangs on that night of lust in the dark: Helena and Shakespeare *tell* us that much.

far-reaching meanings or undertones than their contexts warrant. It is only these last that I can examine a little.

The best example of a profound and perturbing ambiguity is in those lines of Helena's where, for once, once only, Shakespeare does allow some legitimate thinking about the 'bed-trick'. Helena has achieved her consummation. Suddenly, in the middle of her thanks to the conniving Widow, a totally un-fairy-tale feeling erupts:

> But, O strange men!
> That can such sweet use make of what they hate,
> When saucy trusting of the cozen'd thoughts
> Defiles the pitchy night. So lust doth play
> With what it loathes, for that which is away.
> But more of this hereafter. . . . (IV. iv. 21–6)

(Alas, there is no 'more of this' hereafter, nor heretofore!) This is the utterance of a woman with a heart *and* a mind. But is the mind Helena's—or that of the writer of *Sonnet 129*? The lines hold a moral generalization about lust ('Th' expense of spirit in a waste of shame'); but the specificity of the reference diverts attention to that lust which slakes in the arms of a prostitute the desire for the unattainable love. 'So lust doth play/ With what it loathes' goes beyond the Sonnet's

> Enjoy'd no sooner but despised straight;
> Past reason hunted, and, no sooner had,
> Past reason hated, as a swallowed bait,
> On purpose laid to make the taker mad . . .
> . . . A bliss in proof, and prov'd, a very woe;
> Before, a joy propos'd; behind, a dream . . . ,

because in Helena's lines the loathing is assumed *present*; the degradation is insisted on in '*cozen'd* thoughts' and '*defiles* the pitchy night'. The Sonnet was about what 'All . . . the world well knows'; but these terrible lines purport to be about what only Helena can know: and if this is what winning his true bride in darkness means, then Bertram's marriage is dark indeed. The woman is left feeling prostituted (a thing lent for gain, not for love of the man), knowing that the man can only take her on debasing, defiling terms. Clearly we are not intended to think this, by the end. In giving us a depth of experience we have been waiting for from Helena, Shakespeare's writing has overrun itself. The painful, distressing thought is apposite enough; but to this sexual-substitution situation in a quite different play: in a genuinely unpleasant comedy, which this is not.

A not dissimilar ambiguity of tone, with a comparable uncertainty of precise reference, can be felt in Lafeu's prose-speech about miracles at the opening of II. iii. The idea appears to be that 'in this modern world we have our scientists who give rational, common-sense, commonplace explanations of what old-fashioned traditional thought found supernatural. But this is all wrong: we reduce terrifying mysteries to trivialities, and set ourselves up in an illusory knowledge, when we should "submit ourselves" to the unknownness of things (and ourselves) in a fear which itself transcends exact knowledge'. The thought seems to be from Montaigne; but, although not inapposite to the King's cure, the lines strike too deep a note; and, moreover, leave us guessing whether they do or do not belong to an inchoate contrast between the two worlds of people in the play: the traditionalists, who have a due and proper regard for the pieties; and the moderns, who lack respect and piety and have lost the true quality of human life. We can see, on reflection, how this *could* have become an organic part of the play; as they stand, those resonant lines are unconnected, presumably representing an idea that moved Shakespeare, but which could not flow into the substance of his play.

If the part of Lavache, the Clown, is examined, we find uncertainty everywhere; and also various ambiguous insinuations which suggest, if vaguely, that he was intended to be a cynical commentator on the major themes of the play. On the face of it, he is a rather tired comedian: a jester with a professionally lugubrious manner, but past his best. The Countess says, 'he has no pace, but runs where he will' (IV. v. 60): it sounds like

Shakespeare's apology for the dimmest of his clowns, who almost seems to live in fear of his employer's asking, 'Do you know that you are paid to be funny?'—and grinds it out laboriously. As a result, he comes down to the lowest common multiple of humour, and is rather dismally bawdy than bawdily dismal. Sir Robert Walpole always talked bawdy at table: everybody could join it. But Lavache's sallies have too little thrust: about his own unfortunately libidinous nature, which cries out for marriage; about Isbel's case; and then about finding new fish in the seas of the Court, which ruins his appetite for Isbel. He is, as the Countess calls him at I. iii. 53, 'a foul-mouth'd and calumnious knave'; Lafeu says 'a shrewd knave, and an unhappy' (IV. v. 56); and I think it plain that Shakespeare's *intention* was to provide a comic cynic whose lowness and coarseness make a glancing contact with the main substance of the drama.

He is, for example, 'unsavoury' (as W. W. Lawrence puts it) about marriage, just before the Countess learns of Helena's love and her designs on Bertram. She packs him off after his song (about Helen of Troy) and his cynical remarks on the improbability of one good woman in ten; and he exits with the scandalized comment 'That man should be at woman's command, and yet no hurt done!' (I. iii. 87), which sounds like an oblique shot at the main plot. An ambiguous insinuation appears in IV. v. 41 ff., his speech about the Devil (the Black Prince) as lord of this world's court, whereas he, he avers, is 'for the house with the narrow gate, which I take to be too little for pomp to enter'. The others ('the many') will be 'for the flow'ry way that leads to the broad gate and the great fire'. Here his profane biblical allusion, delivered with a derisory parsonical smugness, hits off an aspect of the Bertram theme (pride and virtue); but it is a touch and gone, rather than a hit. Such ambiguous glancings are more interesting than Lavache himself, of whom the reader—like Lafeu, but earlier—is inclined to say, 'Go thy ways, I begin to be aweary of thee' (IV. v. 50).

The uncertainties about the Clown, and his apparent inability or refusal to take things far enough, can perhaps be diagnosed too in the chatter of Parolles about virginity at I. i. 104 ff. Divers critics have taken foolish offence at it, because *their* Helen's chaste ears would never submit to such indecency. The lines are undoubtedly Shakespearian (as Dr. Tillyard shows well). The proper objection to them, if any, is that they stir up a problem to which there is absolutely no answer. Virginity as a barren virtue, turned to good in action (by losing it) could, very possibly, have been made a relevant part of a play about virtue, action and sex. As things are, we can only guess at what might have been in Shakespeare's head.[1]

All's Well does not end very well (it would have given Shaw another chance for a re-finish!) The themes of the whole are those of a Shakespearian *tragi-comedy*: about the unmasking of seemers; about pride of rank, as a hollow sort of honour; about sex (less unpleasant here than in the other Problem plays); about 'the web of life' as 'a mingled yarn, good and ill together' (First Lord at IV. iii. 67–8, taken probably from Montaigne); and, finally, about virtue which succeeds in action, and leads to a conversion, at any rate 'in principle'. We have no sanction for taking the title as 'cynical', or for putting into the mouths of the happy pair those tempting lines from the Third Citizen in *Richard III*:

> All may be well; but, if God sort it so,
> 'Tis more than we deserve or I expect. (II. iii. 36–7)

The dissatisfying thing is that the attitudes set up by Parolles and Bertram—questioning, detached, superior, contemptuous-amused, or sarcastic—insist on wanting to attach themselves to Helena too: to make her suspect as a half-unsympathetic figure, an image of will (of *virtu* rather than virtue), or 'a mere humour of predatory monogamy' (Tillyard's admirable phrase),[2] with the excellently-drawn old Countess as foil. The text gives no warrant for this; yet the 'feel' of the play is uneasy, even if read as a Jacobean moral allegory of Virtue.

[1] The treatment is curiously like Montaigne's of nobility, which 'consumeth it selfe in it selfe' (*Upon some Verses of* Virgil). See p. 98 above.

[2] *Shakespeare's Problem Plays*, p. 112.

Our feelings in the whole 'experience' of *All's Well* are shot with *arrière-pensées*; and if these go on to the bitter-sweet end, Shakespeare is certainly the main cause. It was unhelpful of him to make the King's final couplet ambiguous:

> All yet seems well; and if it end so meet,
> The bitter past, more welcome is the sweet.

(Change the emphasis, and what 'cynic'-critic could ask for more?)

'When a poet's mind is perfectly equipped for its work, it is constantly amalgamating disparate experience; the ordinary man's experience is chaotic, irregular, fragmentary', says T. S. Eliot in *The Metaphysical Poets.*[1] In *All's Well* there are 'disparities of experience' (thought and feeling) which fail to reach 'amalgamation'. The play came from an unresolved creative mind, in which sentimentality tried to balance the scepticism, and deliberately not seeing far enough (the fairy-tale element), tried to write off the results of seeing too far through (the 'realist' or tragi-comic inquiry into mankind). The King's epilogue, with its feeble attempt to suggest 'This is like Cophetua and the Beggar-maid: only here, the gentleman is the poor beggar', seems to be saying, 'After all, it is only a play.'

There are signs and touches of weariness throughout: that subtle weariness of the creative mind that cannot check the intellect and will (which plan the plot), and yet inhibits the unifying flow, leaving the work marked or marred with 'irregularities' and 'fragmentariness'. I do not suggest that His Majesty of the Globe, William Shakespeare, was thinking of himself when he made the King quote Bertram's father:

> —'Let me not live' quoth he
> 'After my flame lacks oil, to be the snuff
> Of younger spirits' . . . (I. ii. 58–60)

only that all lecturers, writers and critics of Shakespeare can take those lines to heart; that this is a wearying play to labour

[1] *Selected Essays*, p. 287,

at; and that (dubious as I must be whether *anything* 'ends well'), here is one with good reason to remember the King remembering his old friend in his 'good melancholy . . ./ On the catastrophe and heel of pastime':

> I, after him, do after him wish too,
> Since I nor wax nor honey can bring home,
> I quickly were dissolved from my hive,
> To give some labourers room. (I. ii. 64–7)

A Note on Helena

Analysis of Helena's character only results in confusion, because her love-speech ('I know I love in vain . . .': I. iii. 192 ff.) gives the character-critics the passionate woman, but all the latter part supplants this with what I have flippantly called a heroine in the Shavian Life-guards: a creature of *will* who gets her way, and has (except on one occasion) no feelings to mention. Out of this 'inconsistency' arise such misgivings—from a certain uneasy *arrière-pensée* about her 'sort'—as underlie

1. Dowden's remark that, in calling her 'the loveliest of Shakespeare's characters', Coleridge was only recognizing the quality which, in either of his Saras, would have made a coherent man of him:[1] i.e. Dowden seems vaguely to sense something less than 'lovely' in her.

2. The view of Quiller-Couch who, contrariwise, thought that her pushful, calculating, not-over-scrupulous qualities, and her ability to pursue passion and social advancement in double harness, all marked her as belonging to 'what we call the upper-middle class'—whereas all Shakespeare's other heroines are of noble blood.[2] (There is confusion here, because Shakespeare gives no hint of any such intention, which could easily have been expressed *via* Lavache.)

3. Tillyard's previously quoted remark, 'Not that Shake-

[1] *Shakespere: his Mind and Art*, p. 86.
[2] *All's Well* (*New Cambridge* edn.), p. xxxi.

speare makes her a mere humour of predatory monogamy', which shows that he too is holding something down—in his reader, at least. He means, 'It is easy to be left thinking that: but we mustn't.'

The allegorical interpretation tries to smooth all over by focusing on 'what Helena stands for' in an abstract pattern (exactly as with Isabella, who—in a totally different manner—has overmuch female life for her part).[1]

There is something unresolved in Shakespeare's mind in all this. The 'traditional' values condemned social upstarts, and nothing is given us that *clearly* meets this prejudice. Even a good surviving Elizabethan would surely have *some* mixed feelings about her? Reference to the Jacobean social context only makes her more difficult—not less. Moderns know what 'title' is worth.

[1] Dr. Tillyard flirts with this and wisely drops it (ibid., p. 108). See p. 123.

6

The Problem Plays

MY SUBJECT is 'The Problem Plays' and it is not entirely of my own choice. One can choose to talk about a single play; but over such a matter as the grouping of *Troilus and Cressida*, *Measure for Measure* and *All's Well*—their labelling in a separate category—a lecturer to-day is not a free man. His audience has certain expectations; and I am sure that (having had the temerity to come for such a title), you will be deeply disappointed if I do not contrive to send you away with heads full of glooms, disillusions, moral dilemmas and artistic perplexities, vexed questions of human psychology and behaviour; and, above all, if I fail to leave these plays as 'problematical' as either you or I found them, or more so.

Do not be uneasy: I have every hope of upsetting you (one way or another) before I have done. I cannot promise that each and all will emerge saying 'I am wrapp'd in dismal thinkings', as the King does in *All's Well*; but I shall do my best to catch at some of the qualities of this queer trio of middle-period pieces which we agree to bracket as 'Problems'.

But first: why put these three plays together—*The Tragedie of Troilus and Cressida* (as it is called on its three pages in the Folio; the Quartos call it *The famous Historie* . . .) and two comedies—and call them 'Problem Plays'? When my grandmother read them in Dr. Bowdler's *Family Shakespeare* ('in which . . . those words and expressions are omitted which cannot with propriety be read in a family'), there were no such things. Nor were there when my father read Dowden (1875). The title 'Problem-Plays' as applied to certain of the works of Shakespeare can in fact be dated very accurately. It was devised by

F. S. Boas in his *Shakspere and his Predecessors* (1896), but when it started it meant *four* plays—and the fourth was *Hamlet*. Boas considered that all were concerned with sophisticated, 'artificial' societies, rotten-ripe, in which 'abnormal' conditions of mind and feeling are expected, and 'intricate cases of conscience' demand 'unprecedented methods' of solution (the adjectives show that *Hamlet* came first in Boas's mind). He continued by saying 'we move along dim untrodden paths, and at the close our feeling is neither of simple joy nor pain; we are excited, fascinated, perplexed, for the issues raised preclude a completely satisfactory outcome'.[1] Then, having said that the fifth-act adjustments of *All's Well* and *Measure for Measure* are not solutions, and that in *Troilus and Cressida* and *Hamlet* there is no such 'partial settlement of difficulties . . . we are left to interpret their enigmas as best we may', he concluded thus: 'Dramas so singular in theme and temper cannot be strictly called comedies or tragedies. We may therefore borrow a convenient phrase from the theatre of to-day and class them together as Shakespere's problem-plays.'[2]

The date of Boas's book was 1896. 'The theatre of to-day' means the stage of the dramatic revival under the influence of Ibsen: the theatre of William Archer, Shaw and Pinero; and, later, of Granville Barker. The label 'Problem Plays' retains still *some* of its Ibsenite smell. The Ibsenite-Fabian slant comes out very nicely in Shaw's Preface to *Plays Pleasant and Unpleasant* (1898), where the assumption is that Shakespeare would have been an Ibsen if he had had the chance:

> 'Shakespear . . . has left us no intellectually coherent drama, and could not afford to pursue a genuinely scientific method in his studies of character and society, though in such unpopular plays as All's Well, Measure for Measure, and Troilus and Cressida, we find him ready and willing to start at the twentieth century if the seventeenth would only let him' (*Preface*, p. ix).

Clearly Shaw *thinks* of these as 'problem plays', though he does

[1] *Shakspere and his Predecessors*, p. 345. [2] ibid.

not use the term. In Sir Walter Raleigh's *Shakespeare*[1] they are 'later and darker comedies' (p. 162), though he scouts the idea of a Shakespeare who wrote them in a phase of despondency or pessimism. In 1910, in his article in the *Encyclopaedia Britannica*,[2] E. K. Chambers put all the weight of his authority behind quite a different view. They are 'the three bitter and cynical pseudo-comedies'. *All's Well* 'drags the honour of womanhood in the dust'; *Troilus and Cressida* confounds the ideals of heroism and romance; and in *Measure for Measure* 'the searchlight of irony is thrown upon the ways of Providence itself'.

I mention Chambers's article for two reasons. First, it tersely states one view of these plays (in an extreme form); and, secondly, it seems to have given the spur to Professor W. W. Lawrence, of Columbia University, whose *Shakespeare's Problem Comedies*, published in 1931, is mainly responsible for the currency of the label 'Problem'. Lawrence made it 'Comedies' to exclude *Hamlet*. None the less, the formula 'Problem Plays' established itself in the 1930s, and you may think that implies it is a bit 'dated'.

Since then—in the last twenty-five years—more has been written on these three plays than in the whole of the eighteenth and nineteenth centuries. Broadly speaking, there are two main groupings of critical opinion. One rejects the view of E. K. Chambers, and will have nothing to do with Shakespearian biography in connection with these plays; the other insists that these *are* 'bitter comedies', as they were called by Dr. Dover Wilson (*The Essential Shakespeare*, 1932, p. 119), from whom let me quote: 'The note of them all is disillusionment and cynicism, the air is cheerless and often unwholesome, the wit mirthless, the bad characters contemptible or detestable, the good ones unattractive' (p. 116). The centre of this group is still Sir E. K. Chambers, who wrote of *Measure for Measure* as a 'remorseless analysis which probes the inmost being of man and strips him naked before the spectators while he—

[1] In the 'English Men of Letters' series, 1907.
[2] 11th edn., Vol. xxiv, p. 785.

Plays such fantastic tricks before high heaven,
As make the angels weep,'

commenting 'It is the temper of the inquisitor; and you can but shudder as a soul is brought into the torture-chamber and shrivels to nothingness before some sharp test of circumstance.'[1]

The opposition to this point of view is harder to sketch without distortion. W. W. Lawrence's line was to argue that 'All's well that ended well for the Elizabethan audience'. His book adopts 'the historical method', and its main plank is that Shakespeare—like Kipling's 'Omer—was only staging traditional stories (some of vast antiquity).

When 'Omer smote 'is bloomin' lyre
'E'd 'eard men sing by land an' sea;
An' wot 'e thought 'e might require
'E went an' took . . . the same as me!

Lawrence's rejection of biography is uncompromising: 'there is no evidence that the problem comedies were composed . . . for the gratification of Shakespeare's aesthetic interests, or to give expression to his views on conduct and morality'.[2] 'They were written in the first place to entertain . . . and must in part be judged according to the immediate effects which they were designed to produce upon spectators.' That is an extreme point of view. It sounds all right until you reflect that we have not a single word of evidence about how the Elizabethan audience took any of these plays.[3]

The weakness of 'the historical method' stands out when Lawrence tells us we must 'base our primary conclusions upon definite and tangible evidence' (all right so far), 'discarding as far as possible the emotional and moral effect which the plays produce upon us today' (p. 13). There is, no doubt, much virtue in 'as far as possible'; but if we *do* succeed in 'discarding' the

[1] *Shakespeare, a Survey*, 1925, quoted by Dover Wilson, above, pp. 122–3.
[2] *Shakespeare's Problem Comedies*, p. 13.
[3] Unless we think that *The Phoenix* tells us how Middleton took *Measure for Measure*. The advertisement to the Quarto *Troilus and Cressida* says nothing much.

emotional effect of a play, I fail to see what we are left talking about. Of course, what he means is that it would be simply a blunder to ascribe to Bertram your or my feelings if we were suddenly imprisoned in wedlock for the duration of Her Majesty's pleasure; or to see in Helena the 'Unwomanly Woman' of *The Quintessence of Ibsenism*. There are many ways in which Elizabethan or Jacobean feelings and thoughts are demonstrably different from ours; and it is the business of scholars to tell us where these matter. But inasmuch as Shakespeare's plays have only 'lived' because his mind was *not* limited to that different world, the limiting-terms of Lawrence are a great deal *too* limiting.

One main conclusion he reaches is to throw doubt on the grouping of the three plays in a 'period', and therefore on what C. J. Sisson (in a British Academy lecture of 1934) called 'the Mythical Sorrows of Shakespeare'. In both critics you see the reaction against the nineteenth-century assumption that a man's personal experience can be read in his works, and his spiritual autobiography traced, as it can be in, say, *The Prelude*, or in Keats. In particular, the 'disillusion' of the Sonnets—the faithless friend, the inconstant mistress—cannot, Lawrence maintains, be held to have any real connection with the men and women of the Problem Comedies or with the mood of these plays (p. 229).[1]

The other turning-point of criticism was in 1937: R. W. Chambers's British Academy paper, *The Jacobean Shakespeare and Measure for Measure*.[2] On the one hand, it is a direct attack on Sir E. K. Chambers and Dover Wilson and their adherents. Lawrence and Sisson are brought into an alliance, the aims of which are:

(1) to cast doubt on the distressing and morally disturbing things which had been seen in the play;

(2) to question the irony which 'disillusioned' critics were

[1] Although that mood, as he says, is marked by 'preoccupation with the darker sides of life, serious and searching analysis of character and conduct, and drastic realism'. (p. 231).

[2] Reprinted in *Man's Unconquerable Mind*, 1939.

accused of having invented: especially over the 'cynical happy ending' (and that of *All's Well* also. See p. 92).[1] And

(3) to question (with Sisson) that there ever was any 'ferment of doubt and bitterness of disillusion' in Shakespeare's mind. Towards the end of it Chambers wrote, 'I realise how deeply fixed by generations of repetition, is the dogma of Shakespeare's disillusioned early Jacobean period, "in the Depths".' After mentioning Sisson and the 'Mythical Sorrows' he concluded: 'Shakespeare's career is that of an artist. Let us study his plays as the works of art which we know them to be, rather than weave baseless conjectures concerning details of a biography which we can never know' (p. 59).

The *positive* side of the paper was none the less actively concerned with what amounts to spiritual biography—of an 'optimist' and Christian cast. *Measure for Measure* emerges as 'a play of forgiveness' (anticipating the Last Plays), and Shakespeare's 'philosophy' of 1604 as 'more definitely Christian than that of *The Tempest*' (p. 54). Why should we not see his career as 'a continuous progress to the Heights?'. Why not, indeed? But that is as much biographical criticism as 'Never does Shakespeare seem more passionately to identify himself with any of his characters than he does with Isabel, as she pleads for mercy' (pp. 36–7). With 'Judge not . . .' on the same page, the official (British Academy) Christian Shakespeare was launched.

True, in 1910 E. K. Chambers had seen 'Providence' in *Measure for Measure* (under the searchlight of irony). Yet I think there is no doubt that R. W. Chambers had read Wilson Knight's *Wheel of Fire* (1930) and its essay on '*Measure for Measure and the Gospels*', though he never mentions it (in 1937 T. S. Eliot, who wrote the book an Introduction, was still a suspicious character). Whether you say, 'O Father Abraham, what these Christians are!' or not, it is certain that a cloud of Christian witnesses arises from Wilson Knight or R. W. Chambers, or both combined; and probable that you have only to wait for a complete Christian interpretation of all the 'Prob-

[1] This attacks an article in *The Times Literary Supplement* of October 1921.

lems'. Far be it from me to talk Shakespearian theology: but the Christianity of Dr. T. S. Eliot is not that of Dr. Billy Graham nor that of Dr. Donald Soper; and the Christian interpretations are as various as contradictory. I shall mention an extreme case by and by: Mr. Roy Battenhouse on *Measure for Measure* (1946). In the meantime, let me remark that it is perfectly possible to set to work on *Hamlet* with certain set prepossessions, and to show that it is about 'the misery of man without God' (Pascal), up to the time when Hamlet first recognizes that there *is* 'a divinity that shapes our ends'; and that this is followed by the full conversion implicit in 'there is a special providence in the fall of a sparrow' (cf. Matt. x. 29): the Prince's redemption being tactfully suggested by Horatio's farewell, 'And flights of angels sing thee to thy rest!' The bulk of the play can then be seen to be concerned with the pomps and vanities of this wretched world, and the ineluctable unhappiness of those who cannot look beyond it.

Forgive me if I seem only to scoff. I do not doubt that Jacobean England was 'a Christian society' in the sense that modern England is not; and that Christian commonplaces, allusions, images, biblical phrases and parallels lay all apt to Shakespeare's producing hand: as many of them did to my father's tongue (he was not a parson); and I have watched them dying out during my lifetime. But when I find up-to-date Shakespearian interpreters so emphatic, and so certain about significances which were totally missed by such great and discerning critics—*and* Christians—as Johnson and Coleridge, I take leave to lift an eyebrow. I do not doubt that William Shakespeare was a 'Christian', and when I say 'scepticism' in this lecture I never intend 'agnosticism'. Shakespeare was a Christian, yes; but so, beyond any shadow of doubt, was the great sceptic Montaigne.

To return to our Problems. There is a real division of opinion between those who find them 'bitter', 'disillusioned', '*navrant*', even 'cynical' (i.e. predominantly *negative*), and those who find them either undisturbing (as Lawrence does), or containing positives adequate to make it absurd to ascribe them to any phase or stage of 'disillusion', 'despondency' or the like.

Since some critics wedge off *Troilus and Cressida* from the rest (Dr. Leavis, for example, rejects any conjunction of it with *Measure for Measure*), the question immediately arises: 'How far can we justifiably make a separate group of these plays?' One thing we must not lose sight of is that they come from the period of Shakespeare's greatest versatility: a versatility unmatched by any other artist of any sort whatsoever. If you can imagine a being capable of producing within seven years *Cosi fan tutte* and the Fifth Symphony, Verdi's *Falstaff* and *Don Giovanni*, the Kreutzer Sonata and *La Belle Hélène*, then you are some way towards imagining what it meant to have written between 1597–8 and 1604 the twelve plays which include *2 Henry IV* and *Julius Caesar* and *Hamlet*, *Much Ado*, *As You Like It*, *Twelfth Night* and *The Merry Wives of Windsor*, our three 'Problem Comedies' and *Othello*. And all this by the time 'forty winters' had besieged his brow. In a genius of this prodigality, 'pouring (his) bounties forth/ With such a full and unwithdrawing hand', it is only human frailty that sets us looking for simple straight-line, step-by-step 'development'. 'Improvement makes straight roads,' said Blake; 'but the crooked roads without improvement are the roads of Genius'.

If these dozen plays are read 'without prejudice', we find, I believe, that we experience a certain uneasiness and a consequent uncertainty of interpretation in *2 Henry IV* (and not only about the rejection of Falstaff); and that while it is missing in the 'great comedies' (as in *1 Henry IV*), it is variously present in all three 'plays of the Hamlet period'—as they might be called—and not entirely absent from *Othello*. I shall not attempt to summarize what I have said on *2 Henry IV*;[1] but uncertainties about the nobility of Nobles and about the geniality of some of the humour are so evident in the criticisms of that play that I can say, 'Never mind about "ambivalence": there must be much ambiguity in the piece, or the qualified interpreters would not be so much at variance about it.' Exactly the same applies to

[1] See pp. 55–7.

Hamlet, where the Prince speaks a good deal of 'satire'; to the Problem Plays (where one main question is, 'How seriously do we take the "satirical" lights in which many, perhaps most, of the characters are placed?'); *and* to *Othello* (where Dr. Leavis's essay[1] convincingly brings out some things which leave an uneasiness in the mind and are missed entirely in Bradley).

I suggest that a label for the causes of these feelings might be *the tragi-comic view of man*: a view which splits the world today, and gives us the 'totalitarian' attitude *versus* the end-product of a European tradition which *was* chivalric and Christian. I mean by this any or all of the following, or any combination of these distinguishable attitudes:

1. A refusal or failure wholly to credit the dignity of man, and the significance that that gives the individual in tragedy.

2. An emphasis (comic, derisive, satiric) on human shortcoming, even when man is engaged in great affairs. There is a touch or more of this in Caesar: he is never *comic* (though you can see how he could be made so), but much the least *dignified* of Shakespeare's rulers.

3. Any trend towards suggesting that there is usually another side to all human affairs, and that the 'other side' to the serious, dignified, noble, famous and so forth, is comic. This implies a scepticism of man's worth, importance and value; and may range from the quizzical through the ironical to the cynical. Hamlet's commentaries on men and affairs run through the whole gamut. The pure comic of Shakespeare's comedy is never met in the 'comic relief' of the tragedies (contrast, for example, Jonson's *Catiline*): the comic relief of Shakespearian tragedy is 'tragi-comic', with many of the qualities found in the Problem Plays.

4. Any trend in the direction of expressing unhappiness, disappointment, resentfulness or bitterness about human life, by inverting these feelings and presenting the causes of them as matter for laughter or jest (which may mean 'mirthless laughter',

[1] 'Diabolic Intellect and the Noble Hero', *Scrutiny*, December 1937 (reprinted in *The Common Pursuit*, 1952, p. 136).

as in the indecent Sonnets): i.e. offering the comic, but giving it a grating quality which excludes geniality and ensures disturbing after-thoughts.

5. A corresponding attitude towards traditionally funny subjects which insinuates that in some way they are serious, or that the stock response to them by-passes pain at human shortcomings or wickedness; or that this stock response depends on a lack of sympathy or insight which an author can make us aware of *without* abolishing the comic situation.[1]

As the name suggests, there is something equivocal in the nature of the tragi-comic. I do not mean the simple or '*Much Ado About Nothing*' kind of dramatic tragi-comedy, in which a situation which has promised to be 'tragic' is switched to a happy ending (usually with some unconvincing *coup de théâtre*); although two of these plays operate on something like that pattern. I mean, rather, a kind of drama in which the contemplation of man is on the one hand held back from the 'admiration' and 'commiseration' (as Sidney put it) of tragedy; and on the other, denied the wholehearted (or heart-whole) enjoyments of human irrationality and human sentiment of comedy. Tragi-comedy is an art of inversion, deflation and paradox. Its subject is tragi-comic man; and my repetition is not tautology, because genuine tragi-comedy is marked by telling generalizations about the subject, *man*, of a seriousness which is unexpected in comedy and may seem incongruous with it.

Let me first give two examples of what is *not* tragi-comic. *Twelfth Night* is about human sentiment and irrationality, and what 'every wise man's son doth know'; and it is not very important to know that an Elizabethan proverb said 'The wise man has a Fool for his son'. Orsino is 'sentimentally' in love with Olivia. That is contrasted by juxtaposition and inter-

[1] cf. G. B. Shaw on stock jokes in *The Quintessence of Ibsenism*: 'The mask of laughter wears slowly off the shames and the evils; but men finally see them as they really are' (3rd edn., 1922, p. 176); and later: 'Falstaff develops into an enormous joke and an exquisitely mimicked human type. Only in the end the joke withers. The question comes to Shakespeare: *Is* this really a laughing matter? Of course there can be only one answer.' (p. 177).

weaved with Viola's being 'passionately' in love with Orsino. Sir Andrew 'imagines' he loves Olivia; and Malvolio is even more fancifully in love with her too, and can be fooled into believing his passion is reciprocated. Yet out of all this promising display of human gullibility (the irrationality of sentiment) *nothing whatsoever* is thrust at us by way of generalization about mankind. No sensitive spectator can identify himself with Malvolio or Sir Andrew; although this is not to say that there is *no* feeling for Malvolio—that he is only the comic gull. The play is not in the least tragi-comic; but parts of it are from a man who *could* write tragi-comedy, had probably written some already, was going to write more. Now consider *Much Ado* (1598). It *looks* like tragi-comedy, but we have only to read it beside *All's Well* to see the difference. The Hero-Claudio plot is potentially tragic, perhaps; but nearly all of it is soft-pedalled, 'shot' out of focus, in comparison with Beatrice and Benedick. It is about seeming and being in love, or, more comprehensively, about misunderstandings and delusions, most of them *verbal*. These misunderstandings, miscomprehensions and incomprehensions are 'serious' on the Hero side; 'high-comic' in the Beatrice-Benedict plot; and 'farcical' in Dogberry (but still the farce of misapprehension and non-comprehension. 'You shall comprehend all vagrom men', say the Standing Orders to the constabulary of Messina. Shakespeare carries out the instructions.) Considering the volte-face which Shakespeare demanded of our feelings at the end of *All's Well*, there might seem a possibility that, in the Church-scene, Claudio should plunge to the depths with Troilus—

> This Hero? No—this is Borachio's Hero!
> If beauty have a soul, this is not she. . . .

But the tone of the whole play forbids it. Claudio's outburst, 'Out on the seeming,[1] I will write against it' is theatrical hysteria, very different from the hysteria of Troilus. Yet *Much Ado* does give valuable help in attuning the ear and mind and heart

[1] Knight's conjecture, accepted by the Editors of the *New Cambridge* edn.

to the tragi-comic tone. From which of the Problem Comedies have I extracted these general comments on man?

> O, what men dare do! What men may do! What men daily do, not knowing what they do!

> O, what authority and show of truth
> Can cunning sin cover itself withal!

The second might well be Isabella in *Measure for Measure*; the first is exactly paralleled in *All's Well* (in Helena's lines on men's pursuit of lust and their after-hatred for the thing they 'love'). Both are from the Church-scene in *Much Ado* (IV. i. 18 and 34). They sound the tragi-comic note; momentarily, then gone. It is no tone of the play as a whole. We react perhaps like Leonato: 'Are these things spoken, or do I but dream?' (IV. i. 65). When we turn to the thoroughly tragi-comic plays, Don John's reply takes on its full weight: 'Sir, they are spoken, and these things are true.'

I hope I have clarified what I meant by 'telling generalizations about man', and tuned you in somewhat to their peculiar reverberant capacity. Beyond this I have no concern with *Much Ado*. A shift of tone—a deepening of Hero, more depth to Claudio—would shift it across a line that demarcates *All's Well*. But the tonal change would have to be general, and the implicit overall view of mankind very different indeed. 'Sir, they are spoken, and these things are true.' The implication is that they are disagreeable things. Suppose we take that to our three Problem Plays? No one will deny that they hold much that is unpleasant.

Troilus and Cressida is about the hollowness of the seeming glories of war, the hollowness of seeming heroes (Achilles, Ajax), and disillusion in romantic love. Troilus loves a woman who is 'unworthy', yet Cressida is so real a creature that he also looks 'an enthusiastic young fool' (Boas); and sympathy with him is drastically mitigated, even withered, by the dramatic context, in which the whole Trojan War is also about a woman who is unworthy. The theme of the play slowly emerges, on patient study, as the disorderly house of man (amorous and military), turned into chaos by the egoisms of pride and lust. The love-theme is debased by the sniggering 'humorist' Pandarus, the war filthily besmirched by the snarling clown Thersites. The last word is given to Pandarus, and is about procuring, brothels and venereal disease (of which he has advertised himself as a victim seven scenes from the end, when he delivers Cressida's letter). Ulysses speaks much wisdom, but it is true only negatively of the humans in the play; and his shrewdness is totally ineffectual in action. The whole is an acrid comedy of deflation, making a searching inquiry into manly honour, the illusions of sex and the deceiving power of women. There are the makings of tragic issues in Troilus betrayed, but the greatness of tragedy is nowhere. Hector is a great shadow. Ulysses would do well as a tragedy-commentator; but in the near-tragic Betrayal-scene he is present only to miss the true point of Troilus's agony. One effect of this is an irony like that of some of the more tormented Sonnets (e.g. 137, 141–2, 148), in which subjective and objective views of the Dark Lady's lust and treachery are counterpointed. The Time-theme of the Sonnets is also strongly present in the play. On the comic side Pandarus is droll, but debases what he touches; the 'comic relief' centring in Thersites is comedy without a sense of humour: a willing suspension of indignation or hurtness at human indignity, gullibility, meanness, lustfulness and folly. This 'two-clown pattern' is constant throughout the play.

Measure for Measure is about seeming justice in conflict with the rank reality of sex: about honour in the guise of 'the demigod Authority'. We are invited to 'see,/ If power change purpose, what our seemers be' (the Duke at I. iii. 53). As the Authority himself puts it, the virtuous-seeming Angelo:

> O place, O form,
> How often dost thou with thy case, thy habit,
> Wrench awe from fools, and tie the wiser souls
> To thy false seeming! (II. iv. 12–15)

Under the robes and furred gowns 'blood' is 'blood': that is, lust is lust. The main plot of the attempted moral rape of the nun-to-be by the seeming Justice is backed by an extensive revelation of the seething base vitality of the lower orders, mainly in the bawdy trade: observed with a kind of sardonic affection, and presented with great gusto of expression (frequently lewd, extensively indecent, occasionally brutally obscene). With the absconded Duke we are led to the exploration of a demoralized world, in which, as elsewhere in Shakespeare, rampant sexuality *means* disorder and chaos. The themes of justice and sex are twisted tight together by the Gilbertian law which makes the begetting of life (by Claudio on Julietta) the getting of death.[1] And, from the suburbs, Pompey the pimp has the humane sanity to imply that it *is* Gilbertian, with his innocent inquiry: 'Does your worship mean to geld and splay all the youth of the city?' (II. i. 218). Lucio, the loose-spoken gentleman-clown, takes much the same view.

That is the purpose of these humorists: one side of them stands for a world of vileness; the other exploits the Clown's function of switching a theme into a violently contrasted light.[2] The humanity of the base-born, the lack of it in the lofty, is one of the play's running paradoxes. Isabella, admirable in strength as she is, is not immune from Langland's 'Chastity without Charity is chained in hell.' Angelo (the name is patently ironical: he puns on it himself) is law or legalism, rather than justice. His hard, prim, precise ruling by the book is not felt to be just, because his rule makes all offences the same size; and to think of incontinence or fornication as if it were murder does violence to all normal human feelings. Again, once tempted, he is only seeming-justice and utterly vulnerable to the Biblical commonplace glanced at in the title: the exemplar of 'man, proud man,/Dress'd in a little brief authority' . . . playing the 'fantastic

[1] See pp. 154–5.

[2] As Pompey here switches it downwards:

Yonder man is carried to prison.

Mrs. Overdone: What has he done?

Pompey: A woman.

For Claudio, tragic calamity; but that is how the world sees it—a word and a jest (as Yeats said of Helen and *her* scandal).

trick' of condemning in others what is far worse in himself. There is further emphasis on the 'inequity' of the law, in that *legally* here, there is no difference between the incontinence of two agreed lovers and the forcing of a nun-to-be by blackmail.

Once conquered by lust and wilfulness, Angelo sinks deep into evil. Having enjoyed his sexual victory, as he thinks, he still executes the brother whose life was purchased with the sister's honour. A trick keeps the brother alive, but—since murder lies in the intention—Angelo the man is a murderer, even though Angelo the Authority is only carrying out the sentence of the law. The first half of the play is full of subtle casuistry like that. If there were nothing else to make this a 'play of the Hamlet period', there is the undeniable fact that, next to the Prince of Denmark, Isabella and Angelo are in a class by themselves as Shakespearian intellectuals—with Ulysses next on the list. I am only using 'character-approach' to bring out the quality of keen argumentative or speculative inquiry, especially into the nature of man. The Duke, disguised as Friar, generalizes with sombre finality on this in the strong set speech, 'Be absolute for death' (III. i. 5 f.): a speech packed with sceptic deflations of human pride and self-importance, doubts of human validity, and insistence on man's servitude to time and circumstance; and most un-Friarly lacking in the faintest whisper of a Christian hope, or even an urge towards penitence. (Presumably this is why the Christian interpreters give it so very little attention.) Those who want a 'pessimist' Shakespeare will make the most of this speech; and those who want to soft-pedal or mute the disturbing notes will do the opposite.[1]

Measure for Measure is tragi-comic in two distinguishable senses. In the first half it moves swiftly towards tragic calamity, twisting deeper and deeper into the quick; then the observer Duke turns *Deus ex machina*, and the puppet-master makes all dance to a happy ending, with a lot of creaking.[2] It seems need-

[1] W. W. Lawrence and E. M. W. Tillyard, for example, leave it undiscussed.

[2] In Act IV there is also a marked change of style, surprisingly unnoted by Dr. Leavis ('Measure for Measure': *The Common Pursuit*, p. 160): the only *competent* critic to be satisfied with the ending.

less to argue about this: particularly the abrupt conversion of Isabella and the deep damnation of her marrying-off to the Duke (as many worthy minds have found it; although others have as solemnly argued, 'she was not *really* a nun'). It is enough to say, This is the trick-switch type of tragi-comedy, in which a potentially tragic situation is knocked on the head with a *coup de théâtre* (which the Christian interpreters read as a *coup* by divine Grace).

I lack time to argue with them. But surely Dr. Tillyard is right in his objection to all the 'allegorical' interpretations of the play. Whether the Duke is Providence (Wilson Knight and R. W. Chambers); Rightful Authority conducting 'a controlled experiment' in moral education (F. R. Leavis); or a secular analogy of the Incarnation (Roy Battenhouse, in *P.M.L.A.*, 1946, 1029–59[1]): no matter what these special pleaders argue, Tillyard's objection remains:

> The simple and ineluctable fact is, that the tone in the first half . . . is frankly, acutely human, and quite hostile to the tone of allegory or symbol. And, however much the tone changes in the second half, nothing in the world can make an allegorical interpretation poetically valid throughout. (*Shakespeare's Problem Plays*, p. 123.)

It is true that in his study of *All's Well* Dr. Tillyard does consider *en passant* the hypothesis of a morality framework in which Bertram stands for Unregenerate Man and Helena for Heavenly Grace. But he very wisely does not press it, and even if he had, would never take it to the length of 'allegorical interpretation'. The inescapable objection to this would be that Helena speaks indeed of 'the great'st Grace lending Grace' apropos of curing the *King*, but is given not a syllable to suggest that she is furthermore intending the (moral) cure of Bertram. The allegorical interpreter must therefore slip in an undistributed middle term: Helena has her will with the King, who is restored

[1] Mr. Battenhouse is certain that, since Vincentio is the Duke's real name and Lodowick his assumed one, and the first means 'conqueror' and the second 'famous warrior', Shakespeare had in mind Isaiah, ch. ix. 6: 'and his name shall be called Wonderful, Counsellor, The mighty God, The everlasting Father, The Prince of Peace.'

to health. This is therapeutic. *Therefore* Helena stands for something miraculous. This cannot be found in the play, and must be imposed from outside. The difference between what Dr. Tillyard thinks possible and what allegorists offer is that Tillyard is concerned with what *may* have been in Shakespeare's mind (a sort of *Gestalt*); the others with what they must claim to have been communicated to Shakespeare's *audience*. The contrast is clear in *The Winter's Tale*: Leontes' repentance is duly sign-posted; but would anyone 'interpret' Paulina as 'Grace'—a Mrs. Julia Shuttlethwaite removed from *The Cocktail Party* to Sicilia?

The other sense in which the play is tragi-comedy depends on the parallel running of the same themes in two incongruous tones. The 'tragic' sex-plot of Angelo and Isabella is commingled with low-life comic stuff, involving Pompey, Mrs. Overdone and Lucio, not only in their bawdy or business relations, but also in connection with the operations of summary justice in the underworld—the sphere of operation of Constable Elbow, whose wife was (he avows) never 'respected' with man, woman or child. Sex, justice and mercy are the serious themes: with the comics, sex is seen only as bawdy and justice made the sport of buffoons. The crude jesting on venereal disease (which some have tried to reject as 'interpolation') seems to me to belong with this deflationary 'other side to the picture'. Here, as in *Troilus and Cressida*, lust is a major issue; and in the evaluation of lust (especially commercialized lust), this unpleasant fact of nature has its place. It also appears in *All's Well* and *Hamlet* ('pocky corpses') and in *2 Henry IV* ('A pox of this gout! or, a gout of this pox!' etc.): an interesting coincidence, if that is all it is?

However, the greatest scandal about *Measure for Measure*, one shared with *All's Well*, is irremovable. I mean 'the bed-trick': a term which has become current for a 'stagy' interlude in which a man beds with a lady in the dark, and commits himself to the very law he imagines he is breaking with impunity. He thinks he is committing fornication, while the lady (who is not the lady he took her for) knows that she is achieving consummation. Such is the final predicament of both Angelo (with Mariana) and Bertram (with Helena); and the two plays are certainly alike in making a tortuous trial-scene of the penultimate *exposé* by the conniving females. The exposure of the iniquity and meanness of both men is not 'tragic', yet it jars discordantly with the comedy-ending in marriage: in both cases not to the women of their choice. In *Measure for Measure* the 'low' comic key constantly erupts in the trial-scene (v. i.), in the witty but improper comments of Lucio. 'Know you this woman?' asks the Duke. 'Carnally, she says,' Lucio answers. This is comic inversion: the serious sex-situation of one 'plane' is a smart bawdy jest on another.

The difficulty about both bed-tricks and trick-endings is that the psychological realism, the complexity of shifting and sharply contrasted viewpoints, the *inquiringness* of so much of both plays, eggs us on to ask questions about the *minds* of the participants in these theatrical devices. We know we should not: enough critics have told us it is dramatically 'improper'; but curious and probing inquisition into human feelings and into the nature of man and woman is so much in the atmosphere that, in a sense, Shakespeare has set our wits to work making our own 'problems'. That these problems centre largely on sex has nothing to do with the changed viewpoint of the twentieth century. The exposures of Cressida, of Angelo, of Bertram (and, I might add, of Queen Gertrude by her son) suffice to show how strong the sex-theme is in these four plays. And *Othello* is to follow. Both tones on this subject—the serious and condemnatory *and* the bawdy or comic-derisive—are matched in the 'unpleasant' Dark Lady Sonnets (127–152: with possibly a sort of preview in 40–2), which our recent critics are showing signs of thinking much better of than their forbears could.[1]

I am *not* insinuating Shakespearian biography in making this connection; but lust, 'the expense of spirit', is central to all these plays. I must say 'lust', because there is in every one of them a, to my mind, pointed absence of *normal sexual love*: a self-

[1] Donne is largely the reason: the Donne who curiously and sceptically inquired into the patterns of love and lust.

fulfilling mutual enjoyment of man in woman (and woman in man) which is generative as much to mind and being as in body, and the very opposite of a frustration. 'You cannot call it love . . .', says Hamlet. No, indeed. But to turn 'sex' into a label in Shakespeare's 'Plays Unpleasant' is not adequate. They have other important terms or themes in common, and all have some echo or parallel in *Hamlet*.

1. They share a common evaluation of conventionally accepted 'nobilities': noble heroes in *Troilus and Cressida* (and the nobility of courtly love); Authority-in-ermine in *Measure for Measure*; a gentleman of family in *All's Well*. All are deflated; and with the deflations there runs concurrently the critical devaluation of man at large. Yet 'Man delights not me—no, nor woman neither' is again too simple a summing-up: even for its speaker, who readily admires man in Horatio, Fortinbras and Laertes, 'a very noble youth'.

2. Interpolated into the critical-analytical patterns we find 'ideal' figures who check our prattle of 'cynicism', 'satire' or 'misanthropy': Greek and Trojan chivalrically fraternizing; Hector; Ulysses in his Degree-speech, perhaps; the Duke in his quasi-regal moments; the Isabella who talks Christian charity so movingly; and in *All's Well* the King and the conjured spirit of Bertram's father. To these one might add Hamlet, son to the majesty of buried Denmark, the noble Prince: as contrasted with the other Hamlet, the bitter carping wit, the satirical rogue, the wag who brutally mocks Ophelia. I said 'interpolated'. All are as if inset or *montage* figures, so that in their context they appear out-of-phase; distanced, like Yeats's 'things that look/ Out of some old picture-book'; wish-fulfilments, perhaps, not realities. But that is not quite it either: rather they are counter-statements of 'what man might be' counterpoised with what he is, like the tragic and the comic tones of the play.

3. Surely it is needless to insist that these plays involve us in discoveries, always of a bad reality beneath the fair appearances of things: revelations, painful in the extreme—and we are *made to feel the pain*—of the distressing, disintegrating possibilities of

human meanness (ignobility and treachery, craft and selfishness) inflicted on Hamlet, Isabella, Troilus and, in a slighter way, Helena. *All's Well* hardly cuts deep enough to be called even potentially tragic; though perhaps it may be so to a woman. Yet all these have good reason to be 'cruelly disappointed in humanity', and this strikes home emotionally—more directly than reflective generalizations on man. We should not merely watch, but *wince* at the shock that Isabella meets when Angelo and Claudio fling the mire of masculinity in her cloistered-virtuous face. The wrenching emotional twists of *Othello* do not begin in *Julius Caesar*; rather, in the tragi-comedy of *Troilus*.

4. All the Problem Plays are profoundly concerned with seeming and being: and this can cover both sex and human worth (each claiming nobility). Combine this with what I have just said about 'disintegrating' discoveries, and, with a wider generalization, you can say that they share a quality which can be called *maskedness*: not only because 'unmasking' describes so many of the actions, but because the total effect of all three (or four) plays together is to present a world of appearances (very close to a realistically observed reality), capable of opening—like a masque-set transformation-scene—and disclosing something totally different. This maskedness brings doubt, mixed feelings, an 'edgy' curiosity, a kind of fear.

The fear is of the incalculable nature of man: or of the infinite incalculability of the answers to the question, 'What is man, *really*?' I do not pretend to know whether Shakespeare wrote these plays to bother our heads and make our hearts quaver: I do not even claim he may, in the writing of them, have been trying to un-perplex his own. I say only, 'They *do* bother us'. And I feel sure that the suave critics who smooth everything over are responding, like Lafeu's modern philosophers in *All's Well*, to 'an unknown fear': '. . . we have our philosophical persons to make modern and familiar things supernatural and causeless. Hence is it that we make trifles of terrors, ensconcing ourselves into seeming knowledge when we should submit ourselves to an unknown fear' (II. iii. 1–6).

'Terrors' is too strong a word, no doubt. But Doubt—the true Montaignian doubt (*Que sçay-je?*)—has its own 'unknown fear' when the scepticism is about the maskedness of man. For a final shot at the overall qualities of the Problem Plays, I throw out the term *shiftingness.* All the firm points of view or *points d'appui* fail one, or are felt to be fallible: in Ulysses, Isabella, Helena; even in Order, as represented by the Duke. Hence the 'problem'-quality, and the ease with which any critic who takes a firm line is cancelled out by another. To pursue this shiftingness I should have to explore at length the world of the 1590s: of Donne, of Chapman, Marston, Jonson and the young Middleton. But this much I can say: it was a world in which human experience, thought and feeling seemed only describable in terms of *paradox*: the greatest of all, man himself. Any of them might have said, with Donne: 'O to vex me Contraries meet in one', or

> This man, so great, that all that is, is his,
> Oh what a trifle, and poore thing he is!
> (*The first Anniversary*, ii. 169–70)

Either is a tragi-comic statement.

Like Donne's love-poems, these plays throw opposed or contrary views into the mind: only to leave the resulting equations without any settled or soothing solutions. They are all about '*Xs*' that do not work out. *Troilus and Cressida* gives us a 'tragedy-of-love' pattern that is not tragic (nor love?); *All's Well* a 'happy ending' that makes us neither happy nor comfortable; *Measure for Measure* a 'final solution' that simply does not answer the questions raised.

To catch the full range of Shakespeare's tragi-comic utterance, we must start with *Henry IV* (Part I gives the essential tragicomic *pattern*), and follow him through the ambiguities of *Troilus and Cressida* and *Measure for Measure*[1] to the uncertainties of *Othello*. We shall then no longer be content with an eternal triangle of three 'Problem Plays'.

[1] L. C. Knights' 'Troilus and Cressida Again' (*Scrutiny*, Autumn 1951, pp. 144–57) is a good guide here.

7

Troilus and Cressida

HOW DOES a man give a 'popular lecture' on a play undeniably unpopular; which is (with *Timon*) the least liked of Shakespeare's mature works; and which (unlike *Andronicus* and *1 Henry VI*) cannot even be said to have been 'a popular success in its own day'? How can you expect to interest a theatre-going audience in what even its admirers admit to be a bad stage-play: a play whose twenty-four scenes (in modern editions)—you can reduce them to fifteen or sixteen by imagining it in an Elizabethan theatre—include at most a mere *four* that can be called 'dramatic'?

We have reason to believe that *Troilus and Cressida* was written for a specific time and for a special audience:[1] the time, between *Henry V* and *Julius Caesar* (1599) and early 1601; the audience, young intellectuals, many of them law-students from the Inns of Court—young, critical, discontented minds who were attracted by the new poetry of Donne, the newish 'snarling-satire' of Hall, Donne and Marston: attracted by the challenge of deliberate and wanton obscurity—*and* obscenity, also

[1] The 'special audience' hypothesis of Peter Alexander has been questioned by A. Harbage, who says (in effect) that he has 'never heard of such a thing' (*Shakespeare and the Rival Traditions*, 1952, p. 116). Without arguing whether a thing cannot 'happen just once', you can still hedge your bet on Alexander by saying that *Troilus and Cressida* seems distinctly made *with a particular audience in mind* (and that, not the average Globe one). We do not know—are never likely to—what the Globe audience made of, e.g., *Satiromastix* (which was 'presented publikely, by the Right Honorable, the Lord Chamberlaine his Servants; and privately, by the Children of Paules'—1602 Title-page); nor how far those who saw it were aware of what the 'Children' were playing (*Cynthia; Poetaster*) in the 'Poetomachia' interlude.

It is very difficult to live in modern America or England—and not assume *either* a highbrow exclusive audience for *some* plays or a blessed homogeneity in the Elizabethan audience that is 'not in nature'.

deliberate and wanton: minds trained in logic and rhetoric, swift to grasp the general principles behind an argument and to distinguish the sound from the specious: trained and habituated to debate and therefore prepared to look beyond the mere immediate action (even of a stage-play and ostensibly about love), and to extract and consider the moral, ethical or legal points at issue—seeking to relate them to their own times, about which their late-Elizabethan heads were troubled.

They were troubled (by and large) because old traditional standards seemed to be failing; 'new Philosophy' put 'all in doubt'; the succession to the throne was unsettled, the Queen old, and her death might be the signal for a civil war; the country was weary of the wars with Spain, the rebels in Ireland; there were uneasy rumours about the ambitions of the Earl of Essex; and (to come nearest home) Donne and the satirists were demonstrating that neither life nor love was what it had been supposed to be.

The evidence for this is the play's style—the intellectual demands it makes; and, with that, the strange address to the reader attached to one of the two impressions of the 1609 quarto: where it is stressed that 'you have heere a new play neuer stal'd with the Stage, neuer clapper-clawd with the palmes of the vulger . . . not . . . sullied with the smoaky breath of the multitude'. It is patent that (whether from the seven books of Homer translated by Chapman in 1598 or from some other source) the audience is expected to know who everybody is; and even more obvious that a knowledge of Chaucer's story is assumed (e.g., Calchas in III. iii. 1 ff: never named till l. 31, at that). This knowledge makes a *kind* of Sophoclean irony possible; and, again, a particular sort of deflation of the heroic (the chivalric, *not* the Homeric of Homer: for Homer had no more heard of Troilus and Cressida than he had of Aristotle). It is *not* an assertion that the Homeric or heroic story was 'really only like that' (flat, unheroic, rather sordid or absurd). That is Shaw's method in *Caesar and Cleopatra* (a more amusing play, in that kind). The Troilus and Cressida story is medieval and chivalric, and it is this which is deflated. Much of the effect of the play depends on expecting what you do not get.

That is why there are only two proper costumes: either the 'modern dress' of 1600 or the modern dress of the 1938 Westminster production (when it achieved fame for the first time). *Troilus and Cressida* never was a play about Ancient Greeks, and it should not look like one; that only substitutes a banal, Samuel-Butler-like debunking for something more unsettling: the expectation of certain courtly and noble (chivalric) standards in war and love which are found not to apply to life as it 'really is' in these modern times. The names, so to speak, need to look a little *désorientés* in their dresses.

For one essence of this sort of Elizabethan play is that it invited a kind of 'application': i.e. evoked in the minds of the judicious stimulating and disturbing reflections, which revealed the world as it is—not *was*, more than several centuries B.C. At any rate, that is my basic assumption; as it would be with the Vienna of *Measure for Measure* and the *ancien régime* of *All's Well*: that all three are more about 'this-here' than any 'that-there'; and all 'modernist' plays full of vexing questions and perplexing riddles of the human mind, of feeling, conduct, *value*. That is how I shall examine *Troilus and Cressida*, which (*pace* W. W. Lawrence and Dr. E. M. W. Tillyard) is *not* 'chronicle-history' any more than *All's Well* is 'only a Fairy-Tale'. Its very appearance ought to have made the well-read Elizabethan ready for a neat pair of lines from Seneca: '*Hic Troia non est*' (Agamemnon to Cassandra); and the rejoinder, '*Ubi Helena est, Troiam puto*' (*Agamemnon*, 795).

If you consider only the main plot by itself and follow it to its climax (v. ii.), you feel that it belongs to a play with a false bottom. Another layer opens below the love-story, and if you see into it, you find Shakespeare 'importing' something different from what his title has declared. But even the opening of the play shows that anything in the nature of *Romeo and Juliet* would be a mistaken expectation. The Prologue leads off with military-heroical rhetoric, like that of the *Henry V* choruses, proclaiming an epic occasion. The first scene presents a languid, lovelorn young man, too amorous to fight; and to emphasize that hint of a let-down, all his poetically impassioned rhapsodizing is made somewhat absurd by the presence—and the comments—of a buffoonish old Pandarus who is simply a go-between, a mere broker of sexual stock. Chaucer (who invented the middle-aged Pandare) has been perverted: humorous sophistication has been turned to a trick of blatantly flat-footed comment—a knack of saying the wrong thing—which reminds me of Groucho Marx. Troilus's passionate hyperbole is jarred against by what turns the whole scene into a pattern of ridicule. We laugh at Pandarus, but the very aptness of his better ineptitudes makes the amorous-literary frenzies absurd. Throughout the love-scenes, Pandarus is never entirely out of the way. More than once he is utterly *in* it. An ambiguity of attitude towards Troilus's love is introduced before we even glimpse Cressida.

The second scene introduces her—mainly with Pandarus—and it is immediately plain that Troilus's idealized queen of courtly romance is not there. She is a chatty, vulgar little piece, and in the rhyming soliloquy at the end (where she speaks what she takes for her mind), the principles of the loftily chaste heroines of *amour courtois* are brought down exactly to the level of Mrs. Peachum's advice in *The Beggar's Opera*:

> O Polly, you might have toy'd and kissed,
> By keeping men off you keep them on;

and

> The wiles of men we should resist,
> Be wooed at length but never won.

'Things won are done; joy's soul lies in the doing.' This suggestion runs throughout the play. Sexual doings are soon over; and, as Ulysses tells Achilles, deeds in war soon forgotten. Up to a point, we all, doubtless, know that. Beyond that point, it becomes a principle of canny selfishness, and creates the woman who uses sexual attraction for power. The scene (III. ii.) where Cressida declares her love shows her still clinging to her mean ideal—and fearing to give herself: 'Let me go,' she says, 'my own company offends me.' 'You cannot shun yourself,' says Troilus. And she:

> Let me go and try.
> I have a kind of self resides with you;
> But an unkind self, that it self will leave
> To be another's fool . . . (III. ii. 143–6)

i.e. the 'self' which would give herself seems to her 'unkind' (unnatural), because it would put her entirely in his power. The character-item is important, for it explains her seduction by Diomedes in the crucial scene before Calchas's tent. Diomedes pretends to be walking out on her in a huff; only one thing will stop him quitting; and as she *must* have power and (as she thinks) make every man dance to her tune, he gets all he wants. As she is highly-sexed by nature, yielding is the easier; and, hiding from the betraying torch-light, Troilus mutters to Ulysses his horrified version of *Cosi fan tutte*:

> Let it not be believ'd for womanhood.
> Think, we had mothers . . . (V. ii. 127–8)

Ulysses does not in the least understand: the Cressida whom *he* has encountered, kissing the Greek generals all round as soon as she meets them, was one of the 'sluttish spoils of opportunity, And daughters of the game'. Shakespeare underlined that verdict with one of his wickedest puns. Ulysses has barely finished speaking when a flourish sounds from Troy (for Hector's entry); and all the Greek generals exclaim in chorus: 'The Troyans' trumpet'. A knavish piece of work. Despite this, the Ulyssean word on her is not final. Cressida is *not* simply a little harlot; and, though admittedly 'designing', is too frail to stick to her design. Her passion is quite genuine (so far as that goes); so is her grief at her separation from Troilus. Only nothing is deep-rooted in her. She drops short of all her intentions in a way that is common enough in this play of 'fools on both sides'. '*Vorrei e non vorrei*' labels her throughout, and she makes her final exit trying to say just that, through the obscurity of more Shakespearian verbiage (V. ii. 104–9). Thersites has the last word on her; but she is only the feminine of the rest of them. They *all* fancy or pretend they are being or doing one thing, whereas they are shown up as something quite different: something which egoism, or lack of moral insight, prevents their recognizing. This is true of Achilles and Ajax from the start: it is shown to be true of Hector and Troilus—even of Ulysses. It is the final verdict on the whole war, as I shall try to demonstrate when I deal with the other plots.

Pandarus is not present at the betrayal-scene before Calchas's tent. The harsh croak of Thersites is adequate comment on those who 'war for a placket'. Anyone who believes that the medieval story has not been degraded and defiled should pay attention to the residue of Pandarus. He appears twice more: to be cast off by Troilus (after lamenting various symptoms of disease which no Elizabethan could fail to identify), and to conclude with a lamentation for bawds in his thoroughly venereal Epilogue. I shall touch on this (discreetly) in a moment.

The splendid but difficult lines spoken by Troilus at the revelation of Cressida's faithlessness hold one of the springs of the play's 'double bottom'. On the face of it, the unhappy lover is trying to hold on to his illusion, to bully himself out of the evidence of his own eyes (as Thersites says). But in so doing, he repeats a movement of thought which is noticeable all through the play: the sudden shift from some particular question to an appeal to, or discussion of, the widest and most universal principles.

> This she? No; this is Diomed's Cressida.
> If beauty have a soul, this is not she;
> If souls guide vows, if vows be sanctimonies,
> If sanctimony be the gods' delight,
> If there be rule in unity itself,
> This was not she. O madness of discourse,
> That cause sets up with and against itself!
> Bifold authority! where reason can revolt
> Without perdition, and loss assume all reason
> Without revolt: this is, and is not, Cressid. (v. ii. 135–44)

The key is 'If there be rule in unity itself'. He is not simply saying, 'There ought to be one and one only Cressida, and she the image in my heart and mind' (though that is included in the sense). He is being made to think philosophically by Shakespeare, and his assumptions are those of Ulysses in his speech about 'Degree' in the Greek war-council in Act I. The assumption is that the universe *ought* to be an integral whole, in which everything has its proper status in a divinely-ordained hierarchical order, and therefore an absolute value, an absolute integrity. To recognize this ordered universe is right reason: its principle at the terrestrial level is Natural Law. But what Troilus has seen appears to him as the refutation of those principles. '*If* beauty have a soul . . . *if* souls guide vows, *if* vows be santimonies . . . this was *not* she.' Those *ifs* turn into negative propositions. For since this *is* she, there *is* no 'rule in unity itself', no principle of integrity. He can only try to think that he is insane. What seemed to him right reason in loving Cressid now seems madness, though he cannot believe he is mad; and the 'loss' of his reason (for loving) comes with all the sane authority of reason, though the result is rational insanity—alienation. 'Bifold authority', as he calls it, sets up 'cause' (a logical legal case) with and against the same propositions; and one apparently integral being, his love, 'a thing inseparate/Divides more wider than the sky and earth', though he can find no pin-point to mark off the one from the other of the irreconcilable contraries. He, certainly, is in the 'chaos, when degree is suffocate'; or, rather, he *is* it, it he.

If you like to look at it through twentieth-century eyes, this remarkable scene is a thoroughly Existentialist performance on Shakespeare's part. Troilus represents a mind which thinks in terms of the traditional (Platonic) absolute values, confronted with an *existence*: a phenomenon undeniably his, yet with all the sickening insolence of brute fact. For this is not 'Diomed's Cressida': the existence whose being agonizes him is solely his own. As if to invite this kind of examination, Shakespeare makes it utterly clear that for every participant in the scene there is a phenomenon called 'Cressida': Thersites' is no more Ulysses' (though both think her a mere flirt) than Diomed's is Troilus'; nor is Cressida's Cressida like any of these. In each, the individual consciousness spontaneously generates its own norms, and enjoys complete freedom in 'making its own existence'. But this is the same as showing that there are *no* norms, in the sense in which traditional philosophy assumes them. The absolutes are myths. The supposed 'rule in unity itself' is only a fallacious attempt to stifle my awareness that I am I, and (whichever I may be: Ulysses or Thersites or Troilus) that my 'her' is for me the only 'she'. This is the consciousness which Troilus struggles to evade. M. Sartre would tell him that his anguish was the index of awareness of existence come alive for the first time; and, simultaneously, a demonstration of his 'responsibility' for the Trojan War (which is about something called 'Helen').

Troilus has a mind incapable of irony. 'Irony', as Patrick Cruttwell puts it,[1] 'implies the ability to see and to feel more than one thing at once, and to feel one's own self as multiple. The single- and the simple-minded cannot achieve it.' He adds that this 'sense of a multiple and divided personality . . . is also a vital part, deep and widespread, of the new spirit of the age. Civil war—war inside the individual—is a favourite image' (used, e.g., by Shakespeare in *Sonnet 35*, 'Such civil war is in my love and hate'). *Sonnet 137*,[2] 'Thou blind fool, Love . . .', marks the essential difference between this consciousness and Troilus's character and cast of mind. Troilus is *in* an ironic situation, but its tortured victim, incapable of commanding it; the sonnet-writer is capable of the shrewdest ironies.

Before you dismiss all this as far-fetched, wait till I have gone back from this climax of the play to the other plot-threads which are nothing to do with the love-theme; or are only the

[1] *The Shakespearean Moment*, 1954, pp. 23–4. For a discussion of the ambiguities in the love-scene between Troilus and Cressida (III. ii.), see William Empson, *Seven Types of Ambiguity*, 2nd edn., 1947, pp. 178–80.

[2] Cressida's concluding lines on eyes and judgement, 'The error of our eye directs our mind . . .' (v. ii. 108 f.), show precisely the same antithesis as does *Sonnet 137*.

mechanisms which part the lovers (*via* the exchange of prisoners —Antenor for Cressida).

There are two other plots: one Greek, one Trojan. The Greek (I. iii, II. i, II. iii, etc.) is about the insubordinate and disorderly conduct of the proud Achilles and the plot hatched by Ulysses and old Nestor to give him a snub: by rigging the lottery so that Ajax becomes the champion for a single-combat with Hector. Achilles will then feel that he is no longer the Greeks' unquestioned supreme warrior, and he will come out and drive the Trojans all over the field. It is also about the general principle of order; for Achilles' example has infected the conceited and stupid Ajax, and the morale of the whole army is bad.

As a plot, the scheme is a fiasco. It generates two swollen-headed military nuisances instead of one; and though Achilles does come out and fight, it is only because his catamite Patroclus is killed: he then flies into a barbarous rage and has Hector slaughtered, unarmed and against odds, while he stands by like a gangster watching his gang do his work. Shakespeare did not invent this: it is in Lydgate's *Troy Book*.[1] It would be none the less shocking to Elizabethan standards of fair combat.

The treatment of Achilles is one of several points which prevent my agreeing with the American view—from J. S. P. Tatlock[2] and H. E. Rollins[3] through W. W. Lawrence to Alfred Harbage—that there is no deflation of the classical heroes here: that this is merely a 'chronicle-history'.[4] Another point is the transformation of Ajax. Steevens[5] pointed out that in Lydgate Ajax was one who 'learning did adore' and 'hated pride and flattery'. I fail to see how these American critics reconcile his treatment in the play with their contention that Shakespeare

1 [In Lydgate—and in Caxton's *Recuyell*—Achilles and his myrmidons thus murder Troilus.]

2 'The Siege of Troy in Elizabethan Literature, especially in Shakespeare and Heywood': *P.M.L.A.*, XXX, 1915.

3 'The Troilus-Cressida Story from Chaucer to Shakespeare': *P.M.L.A.*, XXXII, 1917.

4 See p. 111.

5 Steevens thought the Prologue to Harington's *The Metamorphosis of Ajax*, 1596, gave Shakespeare his idea. Ajax is there represented as 'strong, heddy, boysterous, and a terrible fighting fellow, but neither wise, learned, staid, nor Politicke'.

is merely keeping to the traditional lines of the story—as transmitted by the Middle Ages. Again, the treatment of Menelaus as the contemptible Cornuto is purely Elizabethan. Finally, the degradation of Pandarus, with the syphilitic emphasis (pox as a brutal joke), is totally different from the austere—and cruel—handling of the leprosy in Henryson. Nor is there any suggestion of a curse of disease on Cressida.[1]

Through the snub to Achilles, this plot throws up an excursus on *honour*: in a discussion between Achilles and Ulysses (III. iii). And the whole Greek plot is accompanied, as chorus, by the scurrilous abuse of Thersites, to whom warmongering and whoremongery are as indivisible as anything in the Athanasian Creed: therefore all deserve boils, blains, scabs, bone-aches and every other symptom which the Elizabethans associated with venereal disease. One cannot just dismiss this as 'nasty'. Caroline Spurgeon shows that the play has a dominant image of disease in the body-politic. Disease is the result of imbalance of 'humours'; and the humour in excess is here 'blood'—the essential principle at once of *lust* and *pride*. When I was a boy, country people still thought that boils and eruptions were caused by 'richness of the blood'.

There are, furthermore, *social* considerations about the Elizabethan realization of syphilis, into which I do not propose to enter. I believe, on Charles Sherrington's authority, that it was a 'new' disease (perhaps a mutant?), certainly generated in America and brought to Europe by Columbus. Its existence was one of the 'disturbing new ideas' of the later sixteenth century. Myxomatosis is not a good analogy; but if you imagine a thinking rabbit trying to order its notions of Nature, then you may go on to understand why certain parts of Jacobean thought are 'pathological'.

Now this Greek plot shows exactly that same shift of attention from particulars to wide generalities I have already called

[1] Harbage, *Shakespeare and the Rival Traditions*, 1952, has the desperate expedient of suggesting there was to be a Part II. The only evidence is that the American theories would require one!

your attention to. I assume that Ulysses's 'Degree' speech is familiar. It has been suggested that 'Commentators have been perhaps too much impressed by this piece of rhetoric.'[1] Maybe. But nothing hints we should not take it in earnest (though no one would question Professor Knights' view that Shakespeare is most deeply engaged at the *end*). It is a 'star' piece, yes; but quite untouched by the uncertainties one has about the exact degree of caricature in the orations of Agamemnon and Nestor. Both these certainly tend towards the comic: the first in pomposity (saying little, and that trite, as if it were much), the second in old politicians' prolixity. I am content myself to see both as *fully* intended caricatures of public men: or even as types of Mr. Huxley's third category of intelligence (as classified in the encyclopaedia—human, animal, military). But even on this extreme view, the proper dramatic effect is to produce a complete change of tone as soon as Ulysses speaks: i.e. to get the audience to attend by amusing them, and then to make use of that attention to carry them through a big, sweeping rhetorical unit, with an intensely important climax as its peroration.

In a weighty rhetorical address, meant to be followed with the concentration due to a legal argument, Ulysses shows how all order—in the heavens, the State, the human microcosm—depends on hierarchical subordination, or 'degree'. Observation of degree means that everything has its right place, and value is determined by that place. Thus when degree is 'vizarded,/ Th'unworthiest shows as fairly in the mask': i.e. 'seemings' cannot be distinguished from 'beings'—which is Troilus's dilemma over 'Cressid'. Later on, it is Achilles' problem about his value and Ajax's.

Ulysses goes on to speak of 'the unity and married calm of states', which is rent and deracinated by loss of order; and from that turns his argument to generalizations which apply with equal force to human society *and* to the individual man or mind:

[1] L. C. Knights, 'Troilus and Cressida Again', op. cit., p. 147.

Take but degree away, untune that string,
And hark what discord follows! . . .
Force should be right; or, rather, right and wrong—
Between whose endless jar justice resides—
Should lose their names, and so should justice too.
Then everything includes itself in power,
Power into will, will into appetite;
And appetite, an universal wolf,
So doubly seconded with will and power,
Must make perforce an universal prey,
And last eat up himself. Great Agamemnon,
This chaos, when degree is suffocate,
Follows the choking. (I. iii. 109–26)

With that he comes to the particular case: Achilles deriding the Supreme Command; and the next scene shows us Achilles and Ajax in—inaction (just as Cressida was shown to us, to follow Troilus's rhapsodies and the practicalities of Pandarus).

But I must pause there to call attention to two remarkable echoes of those closing lines. The first is in II. iii., when the Generals go to call on Achilles. Ulysses (having been in and seen him) returns to say that Achilles will not fight—makes no excuses—merely goes his own way

Without observance or respect of any,
In will peculiar and in self-admission.

Further:

possess'd he is with greatness,
. . . . Imagin'd worth
Holds in his blood such swol'n and hot discourse
That 'twixt his mental and his active parts
Kingdom'd Achilles in commotion rages,
And batters down himself. (II. iii. 160–1; 165–71)

The falling rhythm insistently recalls 'and last eat up himself', even if we do not realize that Achilles' wilful *pride* was the *point d'appui* of Ulysses' oration on degree. 'In will peculiar' and 'imagin'd worth' have echoes elsewhere, as you will see when I come to Troy and the other plot. This same phrase of Ulysses' comes a second time, quaintly echoed by Thersites during the battle. He has sought everywhere for 'the wenching rogues', Troilus and Diomed, cannot find them, and concludes they have eaten each other like the Kilkenny cats: 'I would laugh at that miracle. Yet, in a sort, lechery eats itself.' (v. iv. 34–6.)

I need hardly remind you that one meaning of the word *will* in Elizabethan English was 'lust', as is more than adequately shown by the surprising games Shakespeare plays with it in *Sonnet 135*:

> Whoever hath her wish, thou hast thy Will,
> And Will to boot, and Will in over-plus. . . .
> Wilt thou, whose will is large and spacious,
> Not once vouchsafe to hide my will in thine?
> Shall will in others seem right gracious,
> And in my will no fair acceptance shine?

With that borne in mind, I can leave the Achilles-Ajax or 'Pride' theme (one sort of 'imagin'd worth'), and turn to the third strand of plot-material: that about Troy and Hector.

This begins with the middle scene of Act II, where there is a council of war, and a debate, on the question of whether Helen shall be returned to the Greeks. Hector says 'Let Helen go'. Immediately Troilus shows his contempt for 'reason', arguing that honour demands that they do not so lower themselves. When Hector insists 'she is not worth what she doth cost the keeping', the discussion plunges abruptly downwards into the question of the nature of values. For Troilus the subjective is all: 'What's aught but as 'tis valued?' To this Hector replies:

> But value dwells not in particular will:
> It holds his estimate and dignity
> As well wherein 'tis precious of itself
> As in the prizer. . . . (II. ii. 53–6)

That is: 'The wilful inclination of an individual cannot of itself confer value: it depends on intrinsic merit, as well as on being precious to someone. " 'Tis mad idolatry/ To make the service greater than the god"; and the will which ascribes value to what attracts it (and infectiously) is a *doting* will, if it sees imaginary excellences in the object of its affection.' (I have paraphrased the whole of Hector's answer. The lines are extremely difficult, and a convincing example of the close critical attention that Shakespeare expected from his audience for this play—whoever they may have been).

The importance of the thought in this speech is evident as soon as we see that it draws a distinction which applies to all the main characters. 'Particular will' gives the valuation of the impassioned, wilful and egoistic man who is deaf to reason—and therefore blind to Natural Law. This point is made explicitly. Hector tells Paris and Troilus that they argue like youths incapable of moral philosophy (precisely following Ulysses' argument already quoted):

> The reasons you allege do more conduce
> To the hot passion of distemp'red blood
> Than to make up a free determination
> 'Twixt right and wrong. (II. ii. 168–71)

He follows this with a direct appeal to Natural Law, by which wife belongs to husband (Helen to Menelaus), thus making nonsense of Troilus's argument that you cannot take and marry a woman and then send her back like clothes on approval (any more than you can buy clothes and return them).

I remark again how Shakespeare seems to be writing for a legal-minded and acutely attentive audience. Troilus's argument was quite specious and self-deluding—rape confers no rights—but critics have been taken in by his 'chivalrous passion' and never noticed that his argument is nonsense, and *meant to be seen to be nonsense*. Carrying off Helen established no contract: the analogy of marriage is therefore totally spurious. Hector replies very justly: 'Statute law exists to curb wilful people who are as blind to right and wrong as you are.'

Now this obfuscation by 'particular will'—and the resulting self-delusion—explains the false estimates that Troilus makes of both Helen and Cressida. He 'idealizes' both: both are 'pearls';

but the idealization is not respectable (that alone totally marks off this love-story from *Romeo and Juliet*). Troilus is, indeed, equated with Paris—whose will to keep Helen is merely desire or lust. Helen is to Troy as Cressida is to Troilus; but the whole Trojan destruction is not women, but *will*.

Shakespeare conscientiously produces Helen in III. i., suitably accompanied by Pandarus (who accompanies himself with an obscene little song); and she is silly and empty, with some of Cressida's tricks of playing the men up prettily. To leave the true valuation in no doubt, he blasts her later through the mouth of Diomed:

> She's bitter to her country . . .
> For every false drop in her bawdy veins
> A Grecian's life hath sunk; for every scruple
> Of her contaminated carrion weight
> A Troyan hath been slain. (IV. i. 70–4)

The Trojans have good reason to fear 'bad success in a bad cause'; but at the end of this scene of close debate, Hector commits an inexplicable volte-face, and swings over to the side of Paris and Troilus against his own reasoning. That switch is his death-warrant. In V. iii. he rejects all the pleadings of Andromache and the inspired ravings of the prophetess Cassandra, goes out to fight because he has said he would and 'honour'[1] (he insists) demands that he keeps his word: and so meets his end, and Troy with him. Both are victims to Troilus's style of 'thinking'.

Such is the very sketchy and attenuated Trojan plot. But now clues can be carried back to the Greeks. 'Particular will' offers the same diagnosis as 'imagin'd worth'. Just as Troilus is infatuated with a false image of love, so is Achilles with an image of self-love. Ajax, when swollen with flattery, is at once a monstrous balloon of conceit *and* a caricature of Achilles. On a final analysis, the *love*-theme, the *pride*-themes, and the *fall-of-Troy*-

[1] This kind of 'honour' has been exposed before. Troilus argues that since they all agreed to carry off Helen, it must be honourable to keep her. You are left to see that this is thieves' honour.

theme (for Helen and honour), present a single core of thought. The play is a comedy of ideas, and coherent on no other assumption.

Its special technique (like that of *Henry IV*) is that the scenes and episodes cast changing lights on one another: as 'cutting' achieves in film-production. This can be shown by the long scene (III. iii.), where Achilles is slighted by the off-hand manner of the Generals, then left to be played on by Ulysses. As intrigue, it is only another attempt to persuade him to fight; but as thought, it belongs to the over-all debate on values. 'What is honour?' is Achilles' problem: 'Am I no longer what I was, because these men slight me?' To this wavering in 'imagin'd worth' Ulysses arrives with ready answers. The measure of worth is recognized effectiveness in the world of action:

> . . . no man is the lord of anything,
> Though in and of him there be much consisting,
> Till he communicate his parts to others;
> Nor doth he of himself know them for aught
> Till he behold them formed in th' applause
> Where th'are extended. (III. iii. 115–20)

He develops this in the famous lines about Time's wallet (in which good deeds are done and dropped and lost); and thus to

> Perseverance, dear my lord,
> Keeps honour bright. To have done is to hang
> Quite out of fashion, like a rusty mail
> In monumental mock'ry. (III. iii. 150–3)

Consequently:

> O, let not virtue seek
> Remuneration for the thing it was;
> For beauty, wit,
> High birth, vigour of bone, desert in service,
> Love, friendship, charity, are subjects all
> To envious and calumniating Time. (III. iii. 169–74)

'One touch of nature makes the whole world kin': that is, immediate and transitory appeal wins their praise (as Samuel Butler said, it might better be 'One touch of *ill*-nature').

Ulysses is disingenuous; but though I recognize his intention to fool Achilles into action, his real 'fooling' is much more serious. He has turned his back on all the absolute values implicit in his 'Degree' oration; is telling Achilles in effect that there are *no* absolute values: that 'honour' is the dividend in a ceaseless business of self-advertisement. Look critically at what he says, and how does the thought differ from the reflections of another experienced practical philosopher on the same subject?

> What is honour? A word. What is in that word? Honour. What is that honour? Air. A trim reckoning! Who hath it? He that died o' Wednesday. Doth he feel it? No. Doth he hear it? No. 'Tis insensible, then? Yea, to the dead. But will it not live with the living? No. Why? Detraction will not suffer it. Therefore I'll none of it. Honour is a mere scutcheon. And so ends my catechism.
>
> (1 *Hy. IV.* v. i. 132 ff.)

It sounds very different in blank verse and Greek costume. Yet the 'rusty mail in monumental mock'ry' *is* 'a mere scutcheon'. In practice, Ulysses shows nothing but a glib and oily art, and denies the 'estimate and dignity' of intrinsic merit. The 'Degree' thinking asserts universal, eternal values: this practical, 'realist' argument denies them. But the *motif* of *Time*, which from this point pervades the love-scenes, cannot be dismissed as a politician's cynicism. Time *is* love's remorseless enemy. Time is the theme of those tragic Sonnets which seem to have the closest connections with some of the deepest feelings in this play. In the agony of separation Troilus is made to catch up Ulysses' image of Time with a wallet; only now as the hurried burglar:

> Injurious time now with a robber's haste
> Crams his rich thievery up, he knows not how.
>
> (IV. iv. 41–2)

There is keener feeling in these time-references than in anything else; and, for all that, and simultaneously, the implied verdicts of time add their weight to the general riddling and exposure of seemings and appearances. It is not merely Cressida who is 'inconstant': inconstancy is the quality of everyone.[1]

There is no such thing as true honour (based on genuine values) on either side, Trojan or Greek. All the high thinking comes to nothing: ceases to apply the moment men have to act. It is *doing* that counts; and whether in war or love the effects are brief, soon over and forgotten. Moreover, it is passion that leads to the act; and the impassioned will (lustful or furious) is impervious to right reason. Achilles fights, not because order and integrity have been re-established, but from personal rage. Troilus also. I know that Dr. Tillyard[2] says Troilus has effected a 'self-cure', and found 'vent in action' for a new 'fierce and resolute temper'. But what Shakespeare shows me is that he has exchanged one mad passion for another: his rebuking Hector for his magnanimous habit of not striking men when they are down marks the chaos in his mind (if chivalry is old-fashioned folly and 'total war' laudable, what is wrong with Achilles' method of disposing of Hector?).

If the battle-scenes at the end *have* any intended meaning, it is that the whole universe of discourse has become chaotic. As Cassandra says,

> Behold distraction, frenzy, and amazement,
> Like witless antics, one another meet. (v. iii. 85–6)

Witness the whole battlefield croaked over by Thersites, like a moral vulture, feeding his mind's eye on carrion. But these later scenes are so incoherent—with so many undeveloped hints in them—that I am not at all sure that Shakespeare was not simply using stuff from some older play (cf. the hasty, ineffectual, careless ends of the two plays of 1599, *Henry V* and *Julius Caesar*).

I can now make an attempt to pull the results of my examination of the different plot-strands together. The play has been

[1] Barring Thersites perhaps: but is he not blown a new way every moment by the winds of his disgust?

[2] *Shakespeare's Problem Plays*, pp. 77, 82.

called 'a comedy of disillusion' (Dowden), 'a wry-mouthed comedy' (Ridley), a satire (Ulrici, Boas, O. J. Campbell), a piece of propaganda (Dover Wilson and G. B. Harrison), a morality, and (of course) a Problem play. I call it an '*inquisition*'. It has been forgotten that *c.* 1850 the German critic Gervinus made some very shrewd comments which seem apt for its appearance on the stage: 'It is very remarkable, but every reader will confess that this piece creates throughout no real effect on the mind' (the context shows he means no *emotional* or *sympathetic* effect. This is the final answer to those who would try to see the play as a tragedy).

> We feel throughout the play a wider bearing, a more remote object, and this alone prevents the immediate effect of the subject represented from appearing. The understanding is required to seek out this further aim of our comedy, and the sympathy of the heart is cooled. Here, as in Aristophanes, the action turns not upon the emotions of the soul, but upon the views of the understanding, and accordingly the personages acting occupy the mind as symbols rather than the heart.[1]

He also remarked that we feel no ready engagement with any of the characters, 'not even in the affair of Troilus and Cressida, which speaks to the heart more than any other incident'. He might have backed this strongly, if he had noticed how, from the very beginning, a romantic, indulging self-identification with Troilus is checked by the implicit derision of Pandarus's very existence. There is, again, that queer, totally unrealistic ending of III. ii. (where the lovers are brought together), when each in turn steps right out of character and speaks as if the end of the story were already known: as to the audience it *was*. Troilus says (in effect), 'Let "True as Troilus" become a proverb'; Cressida, 'If I am false, then let "False as Cressid" become one too'; and Pandarus, 'Good; and if that is so, all go-betweens shall be panders'. He ends with a bawdy joke directed at the audience—but never mind that. The important thing is that all

[1] G. G. Gervinus: *Shakespeare Commentaries*. Translated by F. E. Burnett, new edn., 1875, p. 685.

the genuine notes of passion come in the *next* scenes: and we (knowing our Chaucer) have been ironically inhibited from taking them at full face-value. At the same time, the verdict of *Time* has been thrust on us—underminingly.

This rather uncomfortable detachment characterizes the play. We see codes of conduct, standards of values, ethical principles and passions, all standing on trial; and the conclusion appears to be that while the system of thought expounded by Ulysses and relied on by Hector *ought* to be the measure of human conduct, the proper calculus of right and wrong, it simply does not apply to realistically observed human conduct in war or love or diplomacy. This is what has given some the impression of a 'disillusioned Shakespeare', a man embittered by the Sonnet-story, etc.; and others the impression of a satire (where everyone's conduct is measured against Medieval principle, and shown to be wrong—and contemptible).

I do not accept either alternative. I can see this as nothing but a Jacobean play, concerned with the questioning of values in the new and sceptical atmosphere generated from the decay of the worlds of Spenser and the Petrarchan sonneteers: a world in which the perplexities (rather than the triumphs) of Renaissance individualism occupy the attention; where the dismissing of the old stable Medieval universals leaves thoughtful minds with the distressing discovery that if every individual thinks freely for himself and follows his own will, then chaos results, in which all order is lost. Donne plotted the position on the map of the contemporary climate of opinion quite adequately. In *An Anatomie of the World* (1612), having sketched the current devolution-theory (that the world has been in steady decline since the Fall), he turns to his own times:

> And now the Springs and Sommers which we see,
> Like sonnes of women after fiftie bee.
> And new Philosophy calls all in doubt,
> The Element of fire is quite put out;
> The Sun is lost, and th'earth, and no mans wit
> Can well direct him where to looke for it.

And freely men confesse that this world's spent.
When in the Planets, and the Firmament
They seeke so many new; they see that this
Is crumbled out againe to his Atomies. (203–12)

So much, on the disturbing ideas generated by the 'new' Science. Then he turns to the changes in men's attitudes towards themselves:

'Tis all in peeces, all cohaerence gone;
All just supply, and all Relation:
Prince, Subject, Father, Sonne, are things forgot,
For every man alone thinkes he hath got
To be a Phoenix, and that then can bee
None of that kinde, of which he is, but hee. (213–18)

In *Troilus and Cressida* such Phoenixes are only too frequent.

You notice how Donne explicitly refers to 'Degree' in 'Prince, Subject, Father, Sonne', and contrasts that with a 'modern' attitude of self-assertion, self-centredness—'will peculiar and self-admission'. The 'will peculiar and self-admission' of Achilles, the 'particular will' of Troilus, the blatant selfishnesses of Cressida, Paris, Diomed, Ajax: all seem to belong to this world of 'all cohaerence gone'. So too do the three quite distinct cynicisms of the three commentators: Pandarus (who defames love), Ulysses (a Machiavellian puppet-master, as shrewd as unprincipled), and Thersites (who defiles everything).

This last is unmistakably the Jacobean malcontent: the self-advertising moral critic whose avid curiosity about life brings him only a raging misery at its meanness and meaninglessness, and a self-tormented rage which spits itself out in railing, contempt and abuse (the filthier the better). Whether or not this play had anything to do with the 'War of the theatres' (the Poetomachia, that stage-lampooning-match of 1599–1602, which was really Jonson *versus* the rest), there is much John Marston in Thersites. But despite that (quite irrelevant) 'character' of Ajax in I. ii. (Alexander to Cressida), which sounds like a caricature of Jonson, I cannot be convinced that this is the 'purge' which Shakespeare is said to have administered to him.[1] None the less, it has *resemblances* to the Poetomachia plays. It is a debating-piece, where the Greek and Trojan setting means no more than Rome in *The Poetaster* or Rufus's England in *Satiromastix*; and much of it is tuned to the carping notes which appealed to the active young discontents of the Court and the Inns of Court. As you know, Shakespeare never staged his own times: his settings are historic, exotic, fairy-tale; he never touched the 'realistic' modern-life, satirical-comedy field worked by Jonson, Chapman, Marston and Middleton. Maybe this is the nearest he came to it: a debating-play on moral and philosophical values, in which (as with Marston's *Antonio and Mellida*, etc. and Chapman's *Bussy D'Ambois*) the *ideas* mattered immeasurably more than the action. It can be called 'somewhat un-Shakespearian' in its refusal to engage our sympathies; yet there is a resembling aloofness about *All's Well* and, it seems to me, *Measure for Measure*, in which sexuality appears in an unlovely light and the old stable values have dissolved into a chaotic confusion of seemings.

Yet *Troilus and Cressida* shows even stronger Shakespearian continuities. It stands between the *Henry IV* plays (which are about honour and action, rule and order) and *Othello*, which I agree with Dr. Leavis in regarding as the tragedy not of perfect idealist love, but of the overwhelming of reason and self-knowledge by passion and self-love, in a self-glorifying egoist—'naturally jealous' (for all that Othello himself or Coleridge or Bradley may say). Human egocentricity and a wincing at human degradation mark, for me, these middle-period plays. The tone begins with *2 Henry IV*, and if I were compelled to illustrate it in a single phrase, it would be from the exchange of the two French Lords in *All's Well* on Bertram's seduction of Diana.[2]

[1] The authority is only a Cambridge undergraduates' play—a sort of topical revue—and it is always probable that Cambridge does not know as much about the London stage as it sometimes likes to pretend. Anyhow, the 'purge' ought to be as monstrous and ruthlessly comic as the vomitings of Crispinus-Marston in Jonson's *Poetaster*, who spews up specimens of Marston's bombastic and absurd vocabulary: and this it obviously is not.

[2] IV. iii. 18–20 (quoted on p. 94).

Beyond doubt, the exposure of self-treachery goes further in *Troilus and Cressida* than elsewhere. Go through the play, and who is there left unscathed? The old are old fools, the young either young fools or thriving young cads. All the high talk comes down to Troilus's contemptuous dismissal of Cressida's letter: 'Words, words, mere words, no matter from the heart.' It perplexes me that Shakespeare did not make an overt symbol of the 'one in sumptuous armour' whom Hector kills and strips (v. vi. and viii.); only to find him somehow disgustingly diseased—'Most putrified core so fair without . . .'

One character alone comes out of it without a scratch: Antenor. When I used to be told, long ago, to write essays on 'The character in Shakespeare (or fiction) you would most like to have met', I had never heard of Antenor. Now, he would be my man. But perhaps you have not noticed him? Never mind, you will next time you read the play. Five times he enters for certain (it may even be six), and five times he goes out as non-committally as he came. Pandarus sums him up at I. ii. 182f.: 'He has a shrewd wit, I can tell you; and he's a man good enough; he's one o' th' soundest judgments in Troy, whosoever, and a proper man of person.' But even when the exchange of prisoners is afoot, they speak of him as if he was not there and he does not mind. He never speaks a line; he never utters a word. I see in him the prophetic outline of the average man of good will involved in war: never knowing why he is there nor what is really going on: as muddled as Fabrizio at Waterloo in *La Chartreuse de Parme*, but less scandalized—and, most certainly, Shakespeare's one strong silent man.

8

Measure For Measure

Oh, wearisome condition of Humanity!
Born under one law, to another bound;
Vainly begot, and yet forbidden vanity;
Created sick, commanded to be sound;
What meaneth Nature by these diverse laws?
Passion and Reason, self-division's cause.

Is it the mark or majesty of power
To make offences that it may forgive?
Nature herself doth her own self deflower
To hate those errors she herself doth give.
But how should man think what he may not do,
If Nature did not fail, and punish too?

Tyrant to others, to herself unjust,
Only commands things difficult and hard.
Forbids us all things which it knows we lust,
Makes easy pains, impossible reward.
If Nature did not take delight in blood,
She would have made more easy ways to good.

We that are bound by vows and by promotion,
With pomp of holy sacrifice and rites,
To lead belief in good and still devotion,
To preach of heaven's wonders and delights;
Yet when each of us in his own heart looks,
He finds the God there far unlike his books.
(Fulke Greville, Lord Brooke)

Undershaft: You have learnt something. That always feels, at first, as if you had *lost* something.
(Bernard Shaw: *Major Barbara*)

I HAVE presented tragi-comedy[1] as an inquisition into human nature and humanism; and that implies an inquiry into what controls human nature: into 'institutions' such as the principles of order, the essences of honour or virtue, etc. I have insisted that these inquiries are 'sceptical', in the sense of relying

[1] See pp. 116–28.

on empirical observation, not on *a priori* hypotheses: in the same way that Donne's inquiries into love are empirical—and sceptical.

In drama, this means investigating (in the frame of a play) things as they are, as distinct from 'seemings'; and as deceit is human, this means the unmasking of Man. I have (I hope) firmly rejected the term 'cynical' for that. Cynics do not ask questions: they know the answers. 'Pessimistic' I refuse to argue about: beyond saying that to call the empirical observation of Man (or anything else) 'pessimistic' is only the emotive expression of a preference for some kind of delusion.

Tragi-comedy found this inquisitorial field through the critical use of the comic in 'serious' plots: 'serious' (rather than 'tragic'), because in them the sceptical contemplation of Man checks approach to tragic greatness, even if the pseudo-hero is not presented as too pinched by *circumstance* to have the necessary degree of freedom. In the pseudo-heroes Troilus and Bertram, a critical and intellectual detachment checks or denies sympathy; and that is what makes their plays inquisitions. Jonson's intellectual-critical comedies differ only in degree.

Expert inquisitors manipulate circumstances so that the truth is extracted from men undistorted. They do it by playing on weaknesses; and all men are weak before unknowns. In dramatic inquisitions, highly improbable circumstances are used (the Trojan War is a fantastic one, and Bertram's a fairy-tale marriage); but out of these 'possible improbabilities' are wrung implications about human fundamentals: about action, passion, pride, honour, love, justice. This gives the plays the air of being highly developed Moralities: with this difference, that the accepted *code* itself may be on trial. Order is, I think, in *Troilus and Cressida*; in *Measure for Measure* nobody questions that justice is on trial. In *All's Well* it is virtue, mainly examined as masculine honour. How all these intertwist is shown by a passage in Montaigne which Shakespeare used in *All's Well*:[1]

[1] 'The web of our life is of a mingled yarn, good and ill together . . .' (IV. iii. 67 ff.)

> We taste nothing purely. . . . When I religiously confess myself unto myself, I find the best good I have hath some vicious taint . . . if Plato in his purest virtue had listened to it . . . he would have heard therein some harsh tune, of human mixture, but an obscure tune, and only sensible to himself. . . . Man all in all is but a botching and party-coloured work. The very Laws of Justice, can not subsist without some commixture of Injustice. . . . (*Essays*, II. 20)

Now sex is a human fundamental: it is also a theme where the web of life is a highly mingled yarn, and man most plainly a 'botching and party-coloured work', if you look clear-sightedly and empirically at all the facts. But as it is a theme too on which human hypocrisy (self-defensive masking) is highly developed, the inquisitor needs ingenuity in manipulating his circumstances. It would be hard to devise a more shrewdly searching situation than one in which a nun and a pimp comment on an unwanted pregnancy; yet Shakespeare's ingenuity adds to the discussion-group a severely chaste male Puritan and a gentlemanly whore-monger, a good-natured worldly magistrate and the expectant father. That is only one aspect of *Measure for Measure*: yet one in which human nature must inevitably give itself away a lot, in the opinion that each of the six expresses. (There is something almost prophetic in staging the play in Freud's own city of Vienna.)

The situation is twisted tighter still by making the sex-mishap truly a matter of life and death: through a law which is completely Gilbertian. Like the 'wise Mikado (virtuous man)', the Duke is

> Resolved to try
> A plan whereby
> Young men might best be steadied.
> So he decreed, in words succinct,
> That all who flirted, leered or winked
> (Unless connubially linked),
> Should forthwith be beheaded.

—only, *he* has an old dead-letter law which can be recalled to operation. Angelo's task is to do this: to make men chaste by Act of Parliament; and this brings in not only the unchaste Claudio, but the brothel-world as well. To them too

> This stern decree, you'll understand
> Caused wide dismay . . .

The point of my analogy is that, unless the persons are presented very realistically, the Gilbertian absurdity will make the whole thing a fantasy; and that this kind of flippant badinage on sex *is* a normal (if also hypocritically denied) human attitude towards 'getting into trouble'. You may say 'not normal to *me*': I congratulate you. For others (who do not see life with that clear-eyed empiricism), I may add that such flippancy is partly a defence-reaction—'denying the importunity of the blood' by making sex a base jest—and partly the index of a potential or real hardness of sensibility. Lucio and his fellow-Gentlemen stand for both. They are a chorus of *je m'en fiche*, the voices of shallowness of mind and feeling; yet their jesting has a serious implication, since all turns on the incongruity of men's dignified pretensions and their animal behaviour; and on the latter's usual consequences: sexual scandal and venereal disease (as a kind of cruel practical joke which makes the sufferer ridiculous). Lucio is an entirely human being: if very low, he is also very funny. And though he 'stands for' sex intellectualized as witty smuttiness, stripped of emotion and therefore debased, he is a mingled yarn; for there are touches in him of good sense in a 'low' mind which is denied to his betters. 'Why, what a ruthless thing is this in him, for the rebellion of a codpiece to take away the life of a man!' (III. ii. 106); and (earlier in the same scene): 'but it is impossible to extirp it quite, friar, till eating and drinking be put down'. The humane (and respectable) Provost agrees: 'All sects, all ages, smack of this vice; and he/ To die for't!' (II. ii. 5).

The comic part of the play ('very natural and pleasing': Johnson!) acts as a commentary on the difficulty of applying *law* (a reasoned thing) to matters of *instinct*. It supports the serious part, which results in a damaging analysis of the shortcomings of law and justice as social institutions. It also has its own farcical sidelight to throw on law in the persons of its officers (Elbow *versus* Pompey). And it presents aspects of sex which reflect on the sexual side of the main plot: so that lust—like law—is subjected to an inquisitorial cross-questioning. The worlds of Mrs. Overdone and Pompey, of Claudio and Julietta, and of Isabella and Angelo,[1] all meet—in *prison*. One might say, 'In human bondage' (in the sense in which Somerset Maugham took the title from Spinoza).

Lust is *disorder* and *confusion* of good and bad. I consider that the Duke's absconding from office must be taken as symbolic shorthand for the abrogation of 'degree' and order. He is not a personification of the Gospel ethic (Wilson Knight[2]); nor a peripatetic Providence performing a 'controlled experiment' (F. R. Leavis[3]); much less 'the Incarnate Lord' in an allegory of the Atonement (R. W. Battenhouse[4]). He is not a character who moves in the same plane as the rest (the Arden editor went wildly astray here), and he does 'stand for' Government and 'the Prince's duty' (E. M. Pope) in the over-all pattern; though he is a shadowy figure, and his speech 'Be absolute for death' is apart from the rest.[5]

[1] Angelo's valuation of 'love' is no higher than that of the brothel-world: he thinks it can be gained by force; they, by sale and purchase.

[2] 'Measure for Measure and the Gospels' in *The Wheel of Fire* (1930).

[3] 'The Greatness of "Measure for Measure,"' *Scrutiny*, X (1942).

[4] 'Measure for Measure and the Christian Doctrine of the Atonement,' *P.M.L.A.*, 1946.

[5] Wilson Knight, in *The Wheel of Fire*, sees this and says so honestly: the other 'Christian' commentators take evasive action, or do not mention the speech at all. And Knight forgets about it by the end of his essay, where the Duke becomes a kind of Jesus-figure: a type 'standing for' idealistic anarchism—that of the Millennium.

Many of the critics remind one of the 'sanctimonious pirate', mentioned by Lucio at I. ii. 7 f. He 'went to sea with the Ten Commandments, but scrap'd one out of the table'. The Second Gentleman guesses right instantly: it was the inconvenient one about stealing. Commentators on *Measure for Measure* are no better. Sooner or later you find yourself saying: 'Ay, that he raz'd'; and you have but to read more commentary to find what X has scraped out restored by Y, and what Y enhanced and wrote *up*, dismissed or written *off* by Z. The more a critic has a cause to push, the more of a sanctimonious pirate he is seen to be, only by taking into consideration the opinions of others not discoverably less

What follows the Duke's abrogation of his office is the exposure of a corrupted world. 'What Tiresias *sees*, in fact, is the substance of the poem,' Eliot wrote of *The Waste Land*. What the Duke sees is *inversion*, topsyturveydom. The images in

> And liberty plucks justice by the nose;
> The baby beats the nurse, and quite athwart
> Goes all decorum (I. iii. 29–31)

are not only paralleled by Ulysses and by Timon: they belong to a European tradition—pictorial and literary—to the traditional figure of *Die Verkehrte Welt*, *Le Monde Renversé*, the Inverted World. (Breugel painted it in his 'Flemish Proverbs'. The *topoi* are traced by E. R. Curtius from Virgil, *Ecl.* viii. 53 f.; and Breugel's picture shows humanity doing the opposite of all that traditional wisdom—crystallized in *Proverbs*—says it should or should not do). I mention this, because (*a*) Peter Brook's production at Stratford in 1950 appositely dressed the 'low life' Flemishly and from Breugel: I. ii. really proclaimed the vices. (*b*) This inversion-figure does symbolize the essential clash or disharmony in *Measure for Measure*: that things and people, 'realistically' seen and staged, indeed are like that (odd as they look); but by all the rights of things, they should not be. For example, the vice beneath the Judge's robe; the humanity of the Overdones and Pompeys—a sanity which is pearls in mud. The inverted world is the subject of 'Tir'd with all these, for restful death I cry' (*Sonnet 66*). It is the subject too of the 'cryptic' sentences of the Duke at III. ii. 208 ff.:

Escalus: What news abroad i' th' world?

Duke: None, but that there is so great a fever on goodness that the dissolution of it must cure it. Novelty is only in request; and, as

sane. If nothing else refuted those who deny the 'problem' quality of the play, then this would; for the divergencies of opinion are hardly ever on the trifling or secondary points. Two obvious test-places—discussed later—are:

(*a*) 'Be absolute for death . . .',
(*b*) The ending and its meaning.

But (*b*) really implies also (*c*). Whether there is or is not an important change in the last 100 lines of III. i. (from l. 150), affecting all the serious main-plot matter from then on, through Acts IV. and V.

> it is, as dangerous to be aged in any kind of course as it is virtuous to be constant in any undertaking. . . . Much upon this riddle runs the wisdom of the world.

With the development of the Angelo plot, this 'disorder' theme enwraps the whole. The Puritan has been specifically appointed Deputy to clean up a very dirty city; but when Claudio's life is in his hands and his sister comes to plead for it, lust determines him to rape the Nun, by blackmail. The conflict of sex and law, which *is* Vienna, erupts in him too—and law or justice itself becomes a mask:

> O place, O form,
> How often dost thou with thy case, thy habit,
> Wrench awe from fools, and tie the wiser souls
> To thy false seeming! (II. iv. 12–15)

The Duke and Isabella express the same idea: 'the demigod Authority' is a *seeming* where

> Degree being vizarded,
> Th' unworthiest shows as fairly in the mask.
> (*Troilus and Cressida*, I. iii. 83–4)

It is not only his robe which masks Angelo. 'Ha! little honour to be much believ'd,' Isabella cries when he has revealed his 'most pernicious purpose'. 'Seeming, seeming!' But he meets her threat to expose him by showing her his other mask—his chilly reputation: 'my unsoil'd name, th' austereness of my life.' Hardness of that *will* which is lust defeats her: just as the other hardness of will—a narrow self-righteousness—had turned aside the appeal of the tolerant, worldly-wise Escalus:

> Ay, but yet
> Let us be keen, and rather cut a little
> Than fall and bruise to death. . . . (II. i. 5 f.)

But Isabella calls out for Christian charity, and truly speaks as 'a thing enskied and sainted':

> Why, all the souls that were were forfeit once;

> And He that might the vantage best have took
> Found out the remedy. How would you be
> If He, which is the top of judgment, should
> But judge you as you are? (II. ii. 73–7)
>
> Go to your bosom,
> Knock there, and ask your heart what it doth know
> That's like my brother's fault. (ibid., 136–8)

There is a terrible irony here: he could answer nothing at the very moment when her beauty, her impassioned sense, had struck home to his heart. The two scenes with Isabella are unlike anything else in Shakespeare: and few, few indeed retain such power on the modern stage.

But exactly there—at the end of Act II.—the difficulties begin: with the soliloquy which contains 'More than our brother is our chastity'. This and the subsequent hardness towards the terrified Claudio, who has come to see a dreadful ray of hope, turn some critical ink to gall at Isabella's expense. Other critics cling to her saintliness as if it were their own. Sir Arthur Quiller-Couch[1] calls the character inconsistent; Dr. Tillyard[2] brings in Whetstone to explain. L. C. Knights[3] calls it 'ambiguity'; and Dr. Leavis[4] says 'why assume it must be "either or"?'—'chaste serenity' or 'self-regarding puritanism'. These critical contradictions are quite needless if you can entertain the concept of *ambivalence*. Isabella is a dramatic parallel to Angelo untempted. In both, the higher nature (of a Christian kind: Pauline Christianity) is taken too high; and by being too far from instinctive sympathy, approaches the unnatural. Lucio's very remarkable 'fertility' speech (I. iv. 39–44) is 'implied criticism' (F. R. Leavis) of Christian tradition. The apparent intention was to show Isabella first as the nun-elect (Johnson); then as exemplifying Langland's 'Chastity without Charity is chained in hell'; and, finally, as released—by a real conversion

[1] Introduction to *New Cambridge* edn.
[2] *Shakespeare's Problem Plays*.
[3] 'The Ambiguity of "Measure For Measure",' *Scrutiny*, X (1942).
[4] op. cit.

—to magnanimity. But the graph we read in the play is quite incoherent; hence the commentators' interpolations. They call the process 'interpretative criticism': in Bradley they damn it as invention (which it often is).

But 'More than our brother is our chastity' need trouble no one. The line makes sense—whatever Quiller-Couch, Una Ellis-Fermor and others may say—if you see that Isabella is just as terrified as Claudio is, and with an analogous cry of the reluctant flesh. As he fears death, so she fears the unknown violence and violation of lust (' . . . and go we know not where;/ To lie . . . to rot . . . or to be worse than worst/ Of those that lawless and incertain thought/ Imagine howling.'[1]) Hence her hysteria as she screams at Claudio 'O you beast! O faithless coward! O dishonest wretch! . . . Die; perish.'[2] It makes 'More than our brother . . .' something very different from that tight-lipped, resolved, hard-principled, priggish utterance which the angry chastisers of Isabella apparently hear. Scared souls are small souls; and as she leaves Angelo, Isabella's soul is scared—to a tiny rod of iron principle which is all she can think. She is beyond despair. 'Who would believe me?' What irony there is in that line! There is not a soul in Vienna who would *not*, so far as we can judge: not even the eavesdropping Duke, who never for a moment believes what he tells Claudio—that it is only Angelo's 'practice' or a try-on to put her to the test, not meant. Again:

> . . . had he twenty heads to tender down
> On twenty bloody blocks, he'd yield them up
> Before his sister should her body stoop
> To such abhorr'd pollution.[3]

The hyperbole reveals her real doubts of Claudio: but she dare not think, dare not calculate; and so entertains the notion of this obliging hydra, rather than realize now a Claudio with only *one* head; for that way lies despair too.

[1] III. i. 119 f.
[2] III. i. 138 f.
[3] II. iv. 180–1.

Her fury at Claudio is the fury we feel at people made the centre of self-indulgent fantasy, when we find them mere humans. I am not 'against' Isabella: it is a very painful emotion. But brother and sister are of one family in lacking imagination (sympathetic insight); or their circumstances make them appear akin. And they are akin in selfishness; or in self-preservation, without insight into the cost—to another. Hence there is a hollowness in II. iv. 100 f., Isabella's avowal that she would 'strip myself to death as to a bed': she is too ready for the rhetorical sacrifice which has not been asked of her. 'I would sooner die' is rhetoric unless you achieve your aim by dying; and her aim is to save Claudio's life—to which her readiness to be stripped and whipped does not contribute. But, again, she is scared there; and to take the lines as a programme ('greater love hath no man . . .') is to misread them.

But Isabella does not *end* as 'small-souled'. Her plea for Angelo[1] has a sufficient magnanimity, though Shakespeare has not built up to it, and it can be taken several ways. (*a*) We can see her speech as consistent with 'More than our brother . . .': chastity has not been lost, and if Claudio has—well, 'My brother had but justice,' he deserved to die, and was the minor issue. On this view, Isabella is presumably a 'realist'? (*b*) 'Till he did look on me' opens awkward doors. 'I did all this wickedness for you' is a formula of seduction for a woman; and 'this man wanted *me*' is surely not a weak undermining—when there is no chance of his proceeding further? Is Isabella then mere woman? (*c*) She is—or ought to be—in love with the Friar-Duke; and therefore feels for Mariana. And what is the good of revenge *now*? (*d*) 'I partly think/ A due sincerity govern'd his deeds' marks her theoretical sympathy with the snow-broth frenzy. The official half of Angelo[2] is just such a hard man on lechery as she would admire, support, and aid ('There is a vice

[1] v. i. 442–52.

[2] Critics who say Angelo's actions were *tyranny* depart utterly from the text. To Escalus and the Provost, Claudio is simply 'a hard case'—not a case of illegality or wresting the law.

that most I do abhor . . .'[1]). She is still intellectually a Puritan.

Shakespeare's fault lies in giving Isabella no transitions. She ought to require some over-persuading before she permits Mariana to do rather more than Julietta had done by way of risking her soul. (Julietta is 'fast' Claudio's wife; Angelo has rejected Mariana—and might refuse to marry her. She would then be—casuistically, I suppose, and legally, without doubt—worse off than the seduced Isabella: for Isabella would have submitted to Angelo without consent of the will, and presumably without falling into desire—lust—at all. But what Shakespeare thought here is anybody's guess.) Again, her plea for Angelo comes too suddenly, too like a Beaumont and Fletcher switch-over—without *thought*. Yet she is a thinking woman: hence intellectuals fall for her—as Angelo did ('She speaks, and 'tis/ Such sense that my sense breeds with it': II. ii. 141–2). But though she twice needs to show hard thinking, and is entirely the woman for it, Shakespeare does not let her open her mind to us. This is worse than her silence for over eighty lines at the end of the play, before she declines coyly into the ex-Friar's bosom.

'Chastity' some critics call her: but what would St. Paul have to say to this? Chastity should be in no such inner combustion as to fly from fire even to ducal arms. And she does it with no dramatic preparation either, making it hard on both actress and critics. The 'conventional' comedy ending is a weak plea. There is no need for either Duke or cloistress to marry to end the play—unless we are being pushed up to an allegorical plane, which is 'unconformable' with the realism and psychology of Acts I.–III. Moreover, Shakespeare plots points on Isabella's curve which require a true conversion. At IV. iii. 131–3 the Friar offers her revenge on Angelo:

> And you shall have your bosom on this wretch,
> Grace of the Duke, revenges to your heart,
> And general honour.

[1] II. ii. 29 f.

Revenges do not go with the enskied and sainted object of the 'Christian' critics; and we equivocate much if, quoting Prospero or Scripture, we say that 'revenges' here means the opposite.

It is not only Isabella's character which is 'double'. The whole play is full of equivocal speeches, of a kind where there is no resolving the ambiguities, since both meanings 'belong' in the play-frame. Sometimes quite opposite value-judgements are involved:

Claudio: Fellow, why dost thou show me thus to th' world?
Bear me to prison, where I am committed . . . .
Thus can the demigod Authority
Make us pay down for our offence by weight
The words of heaven: on whom it will, it will;
On whom it will not, so; yet still 'tis just. (I. ii. 110 f.)

He alludes to Romans, ix. 18: 'Therefore hath he mercy on whom he will have mercy, and whom he will he hardeneth.' But 'yet still 'tis just' can equally be Claudio's bitter comment that Authority can order these needless shames once you are in its hands: and 'it is all called *just*'. No actor can play contrite resignation and angry bitterness at once.

This same quality appears in the oddly frequent use of *hendiadys* (seen in *Troilus and Cressida* and *Hamlet* too):[1] e.g., 'leaven'd and prepared choice' (I. i. 52); 'the fault and glimpse of newness' (I. ii. 151); 'a prone and speechless dialect' (I. ii. 176); 'rebate and blunt his natural edge' (I. iv. 60); 'nicety and prolixious blushes' (II. iv. 162); 'abominable and beastly touches' (III. ii. 21); 'lawless and incertain thought' (III. i. 128); 'stroke

[1] There are a few, but interesting occurrences in *All's Well*: 'on the catastrophe and heel of pastime' (I. ii. 57); 'captious and intenible sieve' (I. iii. 193: Dover Wilson would read 'inteemable', from French *intemible*); 'into the staggers and the careless lapse/Of youth and ignorance' (II. iii. 161–2); 'inaudible and noiseless foot of Time' (V. iii. 41). And a further and excellent example in *Othello*:

let her will
Have a free way: I therefore beg it not
To please the palate of my appetite,
Nor to comply with heat, the young affects
In my defunct and proper satisfaction,
But to be free and bounteous of her mind. (I. iii. 261–6. Q.1
Editors emend, and read *in me defunct*.)

and line of his great justice' (IV. ii. 76). It suggests a mind taken up with the complexity—and contradictoriness—of experience: trying to force as much as possible of it into double epithets or verbs with an abrupt change of aspect. And we find a remarkable falling-off in the use of this figure in the last two acts.

Something like doubleness of vision or aim is present in words, situations (Claudio's) and characters. And the ethical subtleties we are drawn into half *compel* a casuistic, fine-spinning attention which, despite ourselves, runs beyond the warrant of the text. Even Claudio's 'sin' and Angelo's application of the act are double.

Nearly all critics are agreed that there is a break in the play, and that 'the last two acts, showing obvious signs of haste, are little more than a drawing out and resolution of the plot' (L. C. Knights).[1] Dr. Leavis calls this view a 'casual and confident assumption', and says he finds it 'staggering'.[2] I find it staggering that he is staggered. It is to me quite evident that the texture of the writing—the tenseness of image and evocative quality—undergoes an abrupt change when the Duke begins talking prose in III. i.; and that this change applies more or less to all the *serious* matter thereafter. The commentators who are extracting or elaborating themes, of course, do not heed this: though it seems to me a quality that any *literary* critic *must* observe. But Dr. Leavis's terms are evasive, and give the impression that only *theme* is under consideration.

I agree with him that 'what one makes of the ending . . . depends on what one makes of the Duke'. But I do not quite know what to make of the Duke; and I am confident that it is not the case that he 'has been very adequately dealt with by Wilson Knight'.[3] Here is Wilson Knight[4] on the Duke: 'After rebuking Pompey the bawd very sternly but not unkindly, he concludes: "Go mend, go mend."' What is this 'not unkindly'?

[1] *Scrutiny*, X, p. 232.
[2] *Scrutiny*, X, p. 243
[3] ibid.
[4] *The Wheel of Fire*, p. 90.

Fie, sirrah, a bawd, a wicked bawd!
The evil that thou causest to be done,
That is thy means to live. Do thou but think
What 'tis to cram a maw or clothe a back
From such a filthy vice; say to thyself
'From their abominable and beastly touches
I drink, I eat, array myself, and live'.
Canst thou believe thy living is a life,
So stinkingly depending? Go mend, go mend.[1]

'His attitude', Knight continues, 'is that of Jesus to the woman taken in adultery: "Neither do I condemn thee: go, and sin no more." (John, viii. 11).' It is impossible to accept that comment as adequate.

The Jesus-figure of Wilson Knight breaks down in the final scene, where the Duke's treatment of *Lucio* is harsh and not far from spiteful. If you want a *charitable* attitude, read Montaigne, Bk. iii. ch. 5: '*Socrates* to one that told him he was railed upon and ill-spoken of; Tush (said he) There is no such thing in me. . . .' Montaigne comments: 'Likewise should any man call me traitour, theefe or drunkard, I would deeme myself but little wronged by him.' (*Upon Some Verses of* Virgil.) It is a poor business if a Jesus-figure, or even Dr. Leavis's 'Peripatetic Providence', must be sent to Montaigne to learn generosity of mind.

Finally, neither Wilson Knight nor the other interpreters of his group are adequate on the effect of the speech in III. I ('Be absolute for death') on the Duke seen as a total character. It is full of Montaigne, but it is not his scepticism: rather the record of its emotional effects on a mind which wants to believe in human magnificence and the nobleness of life—and cannot. It enwraps a death-wish far profounder than 'Tir'd with all these'; yet is never a cynical dismissal of life as sour grapes, nor a self-dramatizing welcome of death with heroic, histrionic gesture. There is no touch here of 'encounter darkness as a bride'. It takes away all Man's proud additions, honours, titles, claims—even his selfhood and integrity; and the soul and after-

[1] III. ii. 16–24.

life are not even dismissed as vain hopes. It cannot be the pseudo-Friar speaking Christian world-contempt: there is no redemption, no hint of immortality in the whole. The only certitudes are existence, uncertainty, disappointment, frustration, old age and death. It mentions values only as delusions. It determines an attitude of mind in which tragedy is quite impossible; in its sombre light all odds is gone. Man is a quintessence of dust: Pompey Bum no more nor less than Isabella, nor the Duke above Claudio or Angelo, nor better than Froth, the fool of Mrs. Overdone. Everything exists: nothing has value. We are in the Jacobean equivalent of E. M. Forster's Marabar Caves, of *A Passage to India*.

The Duke absconds from all this by the end of the play: returning as re-instated Justice (which, within this speech, is just another illusion). Meanwhile, Shakespeare has made us feel that there would perhaps be more humanity and kindliness in a world of Pompeys and Lucios, than in one of Isabellas and Dukes of dark corners. We do not know. In the complete and heart-aching doubt which is the world of that speech, the world (if it is a world) is one where the accommodated man is the magnificent and horrible *Barnadine*. He lies under sentence of death, and takes life as it comes—in prison ('Denmark's a prison')—content in his filthy straw, usually drunk, 'careless, reckless, and fearless, of what's past, present, or to come'.[1] His sentence means nothing to him, not even fear of the law. He leaps into greatness with his blunt, unshakeable refusal to be executed to suit anybody's plans: 'I swear I will not die today for any man's persuasion.' And back to his straw he goes, to sit in state like a judge and condescendingly listen to anything more they have to say.

In this world of tottering values and disordered will, Barnadine stands out as admirable. His will is single: mere will-to-live; and in him the will to be oneself, and to manage others in action by force of mind, reaches a limit. It is one which puts those other characters of action, Prince Henry, Ulysses,

[1] IV. ii. 136–7.

(?) Helena, and even Authority (the Duke) itself, in their right perspectives. I can but suppose he fascinated Shakespeare too; for at the end of the play, in flat defiance of justice and in shocking contrast to Lucio's harsh tit-for-tat treatment, Barnadine is let off scot-free:

> Sirrah, thou art said to have a stubborn soul,
> That apprehends no further than this world,
> And squar'st thy life according. . . . (v. i. 478 f.)

He is sent off to learn to live—from a Friar. Ridiculous. In the *Measure for Measure* world, he knows already. In the world of these Problem comedies, he is the one positive: man without a mask, entirely assured, unstrippable, 'complete'. All the rest are doubters and seemers. Develop Barnadine and the Duke's 'Be absolute for death', and you pass to Hobbes's picture of the world: where 'the nature of man is solitary, fearful, nasty, brutish and short'; a world where force and fraud are the only laws. Yet is not that exactly the world of Iago, that other Sirrah with 'a stubborn soul,/ That apprehends no further than this world', and squares his life according?

It is only one of the many continuities between the Problem plays and *Othello*: a play about sex, much of it obscene in a nastier sense than most of *Measure for Measure*; a play too of *masks* and criss-cross patterns of *seeming* (Desdemona has but little 'character', yet there are three of her: ideal, real, and Othello's fantasy of her as a whore). And—as I have remarked of the Problem plays—where love is concerned, there is no standing-ground between the ideal and noble, and the base and vile or horrible.

To return to the Duke—and the play's ending. The earlier critics (the Arden editor, for example) are wrong in 'character' lines of approach: or if they are not, then the Duke is 'consistently inconsistent'. Yet if we eschew these lines, and accept the 'symbolist/allegorical' interpretation, there is no integrating 'Be absolute for death' with the Duke of the end (nor that Duke with the one of earlier acts, such as offering Isabella 'revenges').

We cannot get out of the difficulty by saying 'He speaks in the role of Friar'; for to omit from Christianity 'the resurrection of the body and the life of the world to come' destroys the Christianity: at all events from any seventeenth-century viewpoint—and, I should have thought, from any normal twentieth-century one too.

The *allegorical* reading gives two Dukes at least: the ideal shadow of the end (flawed, for me, by lack of magnanimity) and the realist of a pessimistically-contemplated world-order: and in this mixture he is like the whole play, slipping or skidding from the one to the other. The view that he is, like Prospero, an image of Providence, operator of an apparatus for 'controlled experiments' to test souls before forgiveness, suffers in the same way. That is why its supporters side-step the 'Be absolute for death' speech, and overlook the lack of charity and forgiveness towards Lucio. To my mind, this interpretation very much depends on two things: (*a*) on reading Shakespeare's works backwards, beginning with twentieth-century interpretations of the Romances, especially *The Tempest* and *The Winter's Tale*; and (*b*) on this syllogism: God moves in a mysterious way: Duke Vincentio moves in a mysterious way: therefore the Duke is God. There is a piece missing in the syllogism: something missing in the play corresponds to it. Can we, moreover, import into a seventeenth-century play the notions of deity derived from the tormented Christianity of Kierkegaard? If we *can*, then the 'Be absolute' lines are a *temptation*—to despair; and Shakespeare ought to have made this clear to us. If what we make of the ending depends on what we make of the Duke, then all I can say is that the Duke (like everybody except Barnardine) is ambiguous: therefore the ending is ambiguous too: and L. C. Knights' essay[1] wins on points.

I believe that *Measure for Measure* was *intended* to finish as a play of a higher ethic, and that ethic 'Christian'. But this remains largely an aim: achievable by manipulation of the plot (which is why you can take out 'the moral fable' and talk about that),

[1] *Scrutiny*, op. cit.

but carried out neither by character-development, nor (more important) by the texture of the writing. It goes thin: the earlier tension and realized imagery are absent; and this quality marks a lack of inner conviction. It agrees with the *imposed* quality of the action. There is a solution there: but the 'problem' is on one plane, the 'solution' on quite another. It is like a wish-fulfilment; or like Ulysses's cosmic order. It ought to apply to existence absolutely: it does *not* apply to experience-as-observed.

> The old 'moralities' exemplified most often some rough and ready lesson. Here the very intricacy and subtlety of the moral world itself, the difficulty of seizing the true relations of so complex a material, the difficulty of just judgement, of judgement that shall not be unjust, are the lessons conveyed.

That is Pater on *Measure for Measure*.[1] I find it nearer to the theme of *justice* in Shakespeare's play than most modern interpretations get. Is it not perhaps odd that we had to wait for that singularly *Christian* century—our own—to see what Johnson and Coleridge never even noticed? But when I say that, remember that not even an Elizabethan 'atheist' could get his mind outside a 'Christian tradition'.

Last Tuesday—4 March [1952]—Charles Sherrington died. Who was he? The man who, asking himself what natural religion the twentieth-century man of science can retain, wrote this:

> Its view of the world and of itself is based upon the purview of what by its lights it can accept as true. In that way, for it, much that is comfortable in other religions lapses. If you will, Man's situation is left bleaker. One feature of that situation is that the human mind, such as it is, is left the crown of Mind to which human life in all its needs has direct access. Compared with a situation where the human mind beset with its perplexities had a Higher Mind and Higher Personality than itself to lean on and to seek counsel from, this other situation where it has no appeal and no resort for help beyond itself, has, we may think, an element of enhanced tragedy and pathos. To set against that, it is a situation which

[1] *Appreciations.*

transforms the human spirit's task, almost beyond recognition, to one of loftier responsibility. It elevates that spirit to the position of protagonist of a virility and dignity which otherwise the human figure could not possess. It raises the lowliest human being conjointly with the highest, Prometheus-like, to a rank of obligation and pathos which neither Moses in his lawgiving nor Job in all his suffering, could present. We have, because human, an inalienable prerogative of responsibility which we cannot devolve, no, not as once was thought, even upon the stars. We can share it only with each other. (*Man on His Nature*, 1941, p. 404 to end.)

We talk glibly in our literary courses 'and their background' of the human situation. We start our 'modern age' from the seventeenth century. Why shouldn't it (modernity, *our* human situation) begin with these plays I have ended with today?[1] 'We have, because human, an inalienable prerogative. . . .' If you follow what I have been saying, my doubts about 'Christian' solutions to *Measure for Measure* will be immediately intelligible.

I can imagine *Measure for Measure* being read, for its humanity, its keen and subtle inquisition into man's nature (into justice and truth, sex and love), by humans in a remote future to whom all the Gospel references belong to a bygone myth—'a local faith called Christianity'—no nearer to them than the gods in Euripides. And I can imagine it holding them none the less, as *we* can be held by the human tangles of the Greek problem-playwright.

[1] [This was the last play discussed in a course of lectures on Elizabethan and Jacobean Tragi-comedy.]

9

Hamlet

THOUGH nineteenth- and twentieth-century commentators differ stupendously, there is a consensus that there is something very 'personal' or 'subjective' in the play. The nineteenth century rejoiced at it, thinking that here was a key to Shakespeare's mind and heart. Since T. S. Eliot's essay of 1919, it has been fashionable to depreciate the play for very nearly the same reason: that it lacks impersonality, is full of something Shakespeare did not 'manipulate into art', and especially of feelings in excess of their objects (which, in some unexplained way, are made synonymous with the inexpressibly horrible). That revaluation is in key with the devaluation of the Romantics; but it is not, I think, a *necessary* consequence of it—unless *Hamlet* is only Hamlet misread by the descendants of Goethe and Coleridge.

I do not think Hamlet need be so misread. I propose nothing but a *view* of *Hamlet*, simplified but coherent; and the end I propose to take hold of it by is that strong element of the *subjective*: the element which makes Hazlitt say 'It is we who are Hamlet' (Coleridge concurring much later), and the biographers write as if 'This *must* be Shakespeare himself talking'. But by the 'subjective' I do not mean either of those things. Prince Hamlet is an *illusion*: not an historical figure, as Bradley would have it, nor William Shakespeare in self-revelation (Shakespeare's *Prelude* or *Excursion*, perhaps), but an illusion of a living mind's intense and immediate experience; and experience in a dilemma which is truly *universal* (as murderous uncles, incestuous mothers and feeble and treacherous—if well-meaning—sweethearts and male acquaintances are *not*). The dilemma is concerned with the mind's experiences of itself as a mind, supposed unitary, in contact with its experiences of a world perhaps also unitary, but certainly assumed to be other than the mind experiencing it. Is that obscure? Then consider Hamlet's second soliloquy, 'O, what a rogue and peasant slave am I!' (II. ii. 543 f.). It is only partly 'about' the story: much more about 'What is it that happens to me when I see an actor act and am moved?' And that is a very subjective theme indeed. It is not a psychological inquiry; but an *experience*, enacted in the words, and, by the turn given by the second and third parts of the speech ('Yet I,/ A dull and muddy-mettl'd rascal, peak', and 'Ha!/ 'Swounds, I should take it'), an intense experience of moral confusion: of self-awareness, but of the mind's own lack of togetherness and coherence. To that awareness, the piece of the external world presented—the actor—is less a man and a player than a symbol: symbolic of a coherence of spontaneous reaction which is not possible for Hamlet's psyche at all. The Player calls up 'a tragic story', the appropriate 'action' follows; Hamlet *has* a truly tragic story: there is no action—not even stage-action.

Because of this subjectivity, nearly everything in the play can be felt as 'happening to Hamlet': and this includes those scenes in which he is not on the stage nor even being talked about. If that seems absurd, call it just my way of putting it: a device for avoiding talking about what went on in the mind of Shakespeare (a subject with which experience has not made me familiar). What I mean is this. *Hamlet* is about a Mind, in the world of its mind (a distracted globe), and also the world *about* that mind, which is partly what that mind makes of the whirl. In Rilke's phrase, it is being '*verwirrt mit Wirklichkeit*': 'reeling amid reality', we might paraphrase it. We encounter the 'Hamlet-world' before we know anything of Hamlet: it is ghostly and unreal, with a brooding suggestion of something damnably wrong about the kingdom in which it erupts; and it is itself a portent of eruption. In the next scene—before Hamlet speaks—we have encountered the 'Elsinore-world', which seems a real world of courts, funerals, weddings. It is only after the fourth and fifth scenes (on the battlements) that a kind of reversal of values happens to that scene, and we become aware that, though the Court belongs to the 'factual' world of Elsinore, it is not *real*. It sugars o'er the devil himself. The reality of the 'Hamlet-world' was what *seemed* 'unreal' or a midnight fantasy of terror. Similarly, the world of Polonius and his family (I. iii.)—the private world of Elsinore—is but another aspect of unreality: of the *ordinariness* which can be disturbing (even frightful), because it looks so like the norm of normal life, and yet is only a distraction from the vile reality which is the truth. That vile reality *is* the '*Hamlet*-world'; though never the world of Hamlet himself, the sea of barely-graspable troubles into which his mind is drawn and thrust. Perhaps I exaggerate about the first Polonius scene; but about that much-discussed second one (II. i.), No. It does mark time; it does 'prepare' for more plotting; but, placed just there, it gives a different kind of insane, dreamlike unreality to the play by its very infusion of ordinariness. The fussy father keeping an eye on son and daughter and the attitude of 'what's up with young Hamlet?': it is all so wrong; and that going astray of the world-of-men about him and his mind *is* part of Hamlet's experience. Hence I feel the scene as 'happening to Hamlet'; though in the story, he gets only its unintelligible consequences: Ophelia's returning his gifts.

The Ghost-world was, as it happens, quite real. But these ordinary events that follow, as well as human weakness, make it nearly impossible to go on thinking so. The average, usual, commonplace is the enemy of the deep, the intense: makes it appear 'over-strained', if not quite insane. Anyone who has ever had a profound and utterly disturbing emotional experience—not merely a 'shock', but something finally significant—knows what I mean. It is because of this confusion of worlds and realities—with the real most unreal and the ordinary business of Courts a most extraordinary and poisonous charade—that the Players ('incarnation of the unreal', as Granville-Barker calls them) enter into the play's second movement, and 'playing' becomes a main theme in the third. Nor is it disharmonious irrelevance, or forced topicality, which makes these players the Lord Chamberlain's, troubled about little eyases; and themselves troubling William Shakespeare by periwig-pated earsplittings or clownish gagglings. It *is* disharmony, but relevant: since about illusion. And the play is lined throughout with relevant disharmonies and manipulated discords of tone (most of what is funny, for example, has a horribleness clinging to it, by the time it passes over to the level of notions at which Hamlet's thoughts hold our minds. Even Hamlet's baiting of Polonius goes beyond a joke).

It would be a drastic over-simplification to say that the play was 'about' *seeming* and *being*: although Hamlet the actor in his 'suit of solemn black' throws out that theme in his first unriddling lines (his fourth cue). Yet is it less of one to make the main theme Hamlet's *delay*? For this *is* a simplification of a genuine leading theme: that of *action* (willed, purposive and conscience-backed) and its springs in the set and felt edge of the tempered mind, with the emotional urges that determine and make that 'edge' (and make it something more than 'thought'). That this is thematic is shown by its recurrence. We hear it not only in Hamlet's own reflections on 'the native hue of resolution' and 'enterprises of great pitch and moment' being turned awry by coward-making 'conscience'. It is in the mouth of the Player-King:

> I do believe you think what now you speak;
> But what we do determine oft we break.
> Purpose is but the slave to memory,
> Of violent birth, but poor validity . . .
> What to ourselves in passion we propose,
> The passion ending, doth the purpose lose . . .
> Our thoughts are ours, their ends none of our own.
>
> (III. ii. 181 f.)

Claudius returns to the same theme too:

> That we would do,
> We should do when we would; for this 'would' changes,
> And hath abatements and delays as many
> As there are tongues, are hands, are accidents;
> And then this 'should' is like a spendthrift's sigh
> That hurts by easing. (IV. vii. 118–23)

'Action' and 'thought' misdescribe this; yet I labour for terms which do not. The focus on the sensibility of Hamlet perpetually forces on us the half-unreal conflict between 'mind-sense' (the sense of our own being, *in* the mind) and the 'self-sense' of ourselves as agents in a world of things outside the mind. These things, of course, are only effective in so far as they *do* have an existence within us: but one inanimate and so outside our control. Ultimately, I suppose, they are 'unknowns' in equations where we think we know the known: the mind, which is their opposite. We do not. And that is one plain reason why Hamlet is *not* Shakespeare. For Shakespeare knows that Hamlet often does not know Hamlet; and part of our deeper experience of the play is the awareness of that not-knowing.

To clarify this idea of the conflict between 'sense-of-mind' and 'mind-as-agent' (or cause of action), and also to show where Hamlet does not know his Hamlet, consider the third soliloquy.[1] It is distressingly hackneyed, and yet, I consider, a central knot. 'To be' means 'Is this act to be?'; and there are two acts: the first, nearest to mind, is suicide; the other is *action*, taking arms against the outside sea (and, presumably, opposing and ending the King). But 'to be or not to be' means also 'to exist or not to exist'; and thus 'not to be' is the same as 'to be' in the first sense, since one act that might be is self-extinction. And there is a third sense, only revealed when Hamlet reaches, first, the dream and then the dread, of 'something after death': to exist eternally, to be immortal. For if he can be assured that he is not immortal,

[1] III. i. 56 f. It came in II. ii. in Q.1, before the entry of the Players, and after Polonius has tried to show that Hamlet is love-crazy. In Q.2 it moves back (apparently with the elaboration of the opening lines), with more emphasis on 'suffering' or 'taking arms', and a resulting increase in complexity. The Q.1 version is nearly all on suicide, as against the thought of immortality.

then all this can have a final end: whether by suicide or death in attempted action.

Corresponding to these senses (none *separate* in the movement of his mind) are the variant meanings of 'suffer': to endure the pain and find it stoically ennobling; to bear it in the silence of would-be inanition; to 'take it', grunting and sweating under a weary life; to put up with it because afraid to do otherwise; and the meanings of the metaphors about weapons, arms and the sea. The main controlling sense hangs on the values attached to immortality: 'I fear to kill myself, since worse may follow . . .' That is the consideration (the 'respect') 'That makes *calamity* of so long life.' But 'enterprises of great pitch and moment' implies more than suicide, which belongs with 'the pale cast of thought', not 'the native hue of resolution'. Thus, once again, *action*—the aggressive antithesis to suicide—is back in the ring; while 'conscience' (though still the 'inner sense of right') is also 'consciousness', awareness of the mind within itself. And it is, above all, *awareness* that makes Hamlet, not a coward, but a mind so torn and dragged between the betrayal of action and the failure of non-action (a different betrayal) that he can call himself coward, 'John-a-dreams, unpregnant of my cause', and the rest. 'The human mind's awareness', he is saying, 'its sense of responsibility, perhaps to powers above, prevents *resolution* from taking on the clear hue of the uncomplex and active man, and leaves us pale, harassed, hag-ridden with strengthless notions; and, but for this awareness of immortal intimations in myself—even in the moment of doubting them—I would let all go, I would act, and kill myself. And all irresolution is like this: that is what makes our miseries last so long. Life is a burden, a bitter mortification of the spirit, and a long insult: we bear it because we do not ever certainly know what we are. In our sceptical moments we retain a wavering dream of eternal things; and in our faith, a dream that we are but burdened beasts that die and perish; and only fear persuades us not to act . . . So it is that our very awareness thwarts all our resolutions; the natural thrust of the active, healthy mind and will is parried; the current of blood is diverted;

and only impotent mind-stuff fills the mind: and to be, as existence, is another name for the being nothing, for the not-being of inaction: denied even the act that ends the need to act.'

In a way, Hamlet is observing that thoughts are infinite, all acts subject to limit; or that we cannot act without inhibition: so that any act must be a falsifying limitation of the mind, which can think and un-think all acts at will; but, having acted, must have 'chosen'—even if it had no choice.

This distance between 'resolution' and 'action', especially as seen by Hamlet as a contrast between the full-blooded sanguine temperament ('the native hue') and his own 'pale cast', is the recurrent theme of the play observed by everybody. But to make Hamlet the type that steadily has a thing in mind to do, and does not do it, is to vulgarize Shakespeare's idea. Hamlet often sees himself in this contemptible light—as a thing of bestial oblivion or craven scruple—but Hamlet's roundings on himself are not Hamlet any more than his roundings on Ophelia, or his making rings of wit round Polonius.

In *Of the Inconstancie of our Actions*,[1] Montaigne observed that 'irresolution is the most apparant and common vice of our nature'; and no Shakespeare was needed to write a tragedy to show how men come to grief through missed opportunities or that 'procrastination . . . , etc.' No. The true theme lies elsewhere: in Hamlet's feelings about his own discovered irresolution; in the *mystery* of his irresolution (of *all* irresolution: what becomes of our intentions when we cease to be conscious of them?); in the problem implicit in

> I do not know
> Why yet I live to say 'This thing's to do',
> Sith I have cause, and will, and strength, and means,
> To do't. . . . (IV. iv. 43–6)

Cause, will, strength, means: nothing is lacking. Yet since the thing remains undone, some or all of these must be illusory. But, says Montaigne, '*There is nothing I so hardly beleeve to be in*

[1] *Essays*, Bk. II. Ch. i. (Florio's transl.).

man, as constancie, and nothing so easie to be found in him, as inconstancy'.[1] The fact is, the Hamlet who reproaches himself only exists intermittently, produced by circumstance. So too does the Hamlet who is reproached.

Hamlet is not the tragedy of the man who 'thinks and cannot act'; nor 'the tragedy of a man who couldn't make up his mind', as the J. A. Rank film put it (the common mind, well satisfied with its power to act, and dubious—on very reasonable grounds—of its power to think, is flattered by a thought-bound inactive genius: hence some of the play's popularity); but much rather the tragedy of 'conscience': of self-awareness so acute that there is no self, but only selves—or perhaps no self that Hamlet can be aware of till after the event. In sudden emergencies a Hamlet springs into existence, unknown before and hardly perhaps credited afterwards: as with his following the Ghost; his boarding of the pirate-ship; the forged letter to England. Only then is he single in purpose: and it is in the light of this other being that Hamlet reproaches Hamlet. There he is the type and representative of everyone who ever wished to be more constantly that other, completer, intenser, braver self he knows he has once or sometimes been. But when the deep-revolving mind looks at that apparently consummate self, what does it find? (*a*) That impulse is as often wrong as right. Hamlet spares the King on impulse; stabs the King (so he imagines) behind the arras: both acts of fatal consequence. He leaps into Ophelia's grave, acting doubly like a fool; is impulsively generous in his apology to Laertes, to no effective end; is coarse and cruel to Ophelia, conduct neither worthy nor of any use. (*b*) That this apparently consummate self may be merely another denial of self-hood, another by-product of circumstance, no more valid than the coward-dreamer self Hamlet vilifies as a scolding bawd, a whore unpacking her heart, a stallion.[2]

> Our ordinary manner [says Montaigne] is to follow the inclination of our appetite, this way and that way; on the left, and on the right hand; upward and downe-ward, according as the winde of occa-

[1] ibid

[2] [Q2: here, male whore or courtesan.]

> sions doth transport us: we never thinke on what we would have, but at the instant we would have it: and change as that beast that takes the colour of the place wherein it is laid. What we even now purposed, we alter by and by, and presently returne to our former biase: all is but changing, motion, and inconstancy.[1]

But though Hamlet is like this, he does not, as Montaigne does, accept it cheerfully, nor agree that 'to embrace all the rules of our life into one, it is at all times to will, and not to will one same thing'. It is his situation—his circumstances, not his nature—which makes this impossible. So far as his nature is concerned, he could agree with all Montaigne so expressly and neatly offers us to apply to him: 'I have nothing to say entirely, simply, and with soliditie of my self, without confusion, disorder, blending, mingling; and in one word, *Distinguo* is the most universall part of my logike.'[2] *Distinguo* is the most universal part of Hamlet's logic too: he also resembles the chameleon, 'that takes the colour of the place wherein it is laid;' all with him is 'changing, motion, and inconstancy'. But he does not assume this to be so: Shakespeare knows it about him, but does not make Hamlet accept it about himself. This is where reference to Montaigne is of real importance; for where Montaigne's scepticism arrived at a total disbelief, for all human purposes, in absolute standards of value, Shakespeare's empiricism made him even more sceptical.

In Hamlet, Shakespeare presents a keen and philosophic mind innately inclined to believe in unchanging standards of good and evil, but placed in circumstances which result in his behaving as if nothing was absolute, everything relative, conditioned, accidental. Thus Hamlet, looking at his own actions and inaction, becomes, as everyone has noted, the type of 'modern' or post-Renaissance man: a man essentially divided within and against himself, and, as himself—a very uncertain quantity—necessarily at war with circumstance (the world about), or, seeing it another way, with the self or selves produced by uncontrollable circumstances. In other words, he is 'Faustian man':

[1] ibid. [2] ibid.

a being never fully 'in' any of his experiences, because always capable of being aware that there are other experiences; and therefore other selves *in posse*, including a self that is one with Mephistopheles ('*der Geist der stets verneint*'[1]). Hence everything is at once great and petty for him: great in respect to the absorption or emotion of the moment, petty in relation to the recognition that the moment is transient. Hence too he is 'saved' from Heaven and Hell, because nothing can bring forth and absorb his whole self: nothing commit him to '*Verweile doch* ...'[2]

It follows that Hamlet himself, like the world he inhabits, is at once great and trivial. His greatness is that of the spirit: 'nobility' the obvious word, a fineness and delicacy of *being*. But most of what we see of him in the action is controlled not by his fineness and nobility, but by accidental circumstance: by his mother's re-marriage; the Ghost's revelation of foul treachery; a stupid, loving girl's conventional behaviour when slighted; by his committing the wrong murder; showing his feelings (for Ophelia) in the wrong way, the wrong place; accepting the fencing-challenge not only against his 'gain-givings', but also contrary to his own shrewd calculation of his limited opportunity to plot against Claudius before the news from England arrives. Against the fineness of being, there is constantly clumsiness and sometimes ignobility of doing. Hamlet is, as we all recognize, so much too good for his fate. That is the central conflict of the play: the clash between what we feel for the intelligence, generosity, fineness of Hamlet, and the fortuitousness, meanness and clumsiness of the forces by which he is destroyed. 'It is no marvell (saith an old writer) that hazard hath such power over us, since wee live by hazard.'[3] Hamlet assuredly lives so, once he has spared the praying King. His speech about the special providence in the fall of a sparrow *sounds* pious enough; but is it more than a weary fatalism? The famous lines about the 'divinity that shapes our ends' follow his reflection

[1] 'The spirit that ever denies.' [2] 'Stay yet . . .'
[3] Montaigne, ibid.

that

> Our indiscretion sometimes serves us well,
> When our deep plots do pall (v. ii. 8–9);

yet, at that very moment, his indiscretion is trapping him, in the fencing-plot. What right has a man of his keen wit to find a shaping divinity in all he has seen in rotten Denmark?[1]

Hamlet is measured in two ways. First, in terms of *action*, where he is a failure, an utter failure: unless we reckon his life as worth the King's and write off both Gertrude and Ophelia as worthless, as well as Laertes. This failure is most evident in the *triviality* of his witty part in the graveyard and with Osric. In both scenes he is no better than a clever chatterer: highly intelligent, amusing, critical—except of the self that talks. The grave is that of one of his real, but unintentional victims. There is nobility shown in the final scene: generosity of mind, an aristocratic largeness that rises above personal injuries or slights. But the Laertes Hamlet shakes hands with is only another illusion. He sees his brother-gentleman: what is really there is a mean and treacherous murderer (though this is only temporary: for that Laertes is not permanent, nor even the *real* Laertes: only a pseudo-Laertes made savage by circumstance and the slavery of passion). But there is no nobility in the actual revenge: it comes about by occasion, and no steadfastness of mind directs it. In *action* Hamlet is first to last the creature of circumstance: neither good nor bad, because direction by pure eventuality excludes responsibility and leaves only a conditioned machine, a tortured automaton.

Nevertheless, we retain, unshakeably, a belief in Hamlet's nobility, just as we do in our own; and for the same reason: that we are our worse and feebler selves because of circumstance; because our innate goodness was unable to express itself in act. Shakespeare, then, unlike his creature Hamlet, rejects the

[1] The 'divinity' tag is popular, because it hits the spirit of all unmuscular Christians: let be, and hope for the best. It is the very voice of Hamlet's sloth that hands to Providence all he had 'cause, and will, and strength, and means/ To do'. '*No winde,*' says Montaigne, '*makes for him, that hath no intended port to saile unto*' (ibid.).

criterion of action. He applies it very honestly, and shows Hamlet's failure to be himself; but at the same time he makes a figure that appeals beyond the range of effectiveness in worldly action; appeals to standards his creator's plays make us feel to be valid, though every event in a long life should deny them. In *Hamlet*, Shakespeare is not, I think, at all assured of those 'higher' standards: he feels there may be much to say for Henry V (as Prince and King); much to say for Ulysses; perhaps he doubts the validity of the higher standards even in Hamlet. In the later tragedies that is not so: the criterion of worldly efficacy is never applied to Othello, Lear, Antony; the ability of Iago or Edmund to do everything next to holding the Fates fast bound is nothing to the final purpose. But in *Hamlet* Shakespeare seems to halt between two opinions: that in which he wrote *Troilus and Cressida* and that which is the heart of *King Lear*.

The essential difference is between the oppositions to the later heroes and the forces against Hamlet. Iago, Edmund, Regan, Goneril, and Macbeth as villain-hero, all have that extra dimension which makes them objects of wonder, if of horror. But Hamlet's opposite is either an efficient, worldly schemer *or* a world generally vile, and vile in mean ways: as the worlds of *Measure for Measure* and *Troilus and Cressida*, and perhaps some aspects of that of *2 Henry IV*, are vile, comical in a way that makes you wince, and, above all, base. This is the second way in which Hamlet is measured. The effect is chiefly to enhance his nobility, disinterestedness, penetration, his ironical genius (for the irony that springs from his never being entirely absorbed in the situation is a good quality in an evil or mean world); but it is also to make us dubious of the ultimate worth of his intelligence, his acute criticism: since it seems to result only in giving him less control of his life than the other creatures have, who are native to that greasy element. This is why people compare him with Brutus.

Denmark is diseased: we are never allowed to forget that. 'Things rank and gross in nature/ Possess it merely.' It is rotten with rankness of 'blood', with the lust and ambition of Claudius, with the lust of Gertrude. And one is Hamlet's mother, the other his father's brother. Hamlet flings it at Ophelia that 'virtue cannot inoculate our old stock'. He too—part of him—is 'an unweeded garden.' The impressive mystery of the night, the horror of the returning dead, suggest 'some strange eruption to our state', before Horatio lectures on portents or the Ghost reveals the full rottennness of Denmark. We can still catch at the sensation of foreboding and the unknown in that fine nervous opening scene, where even the watchword of the sentries—'*Long live the King!*'—is ironical (the true King is dead; and walks). The Elizabethan audience, more devoutly certain of immortality than we are, knew at first sight of the Ghost; but, since we all know the play, difference of creed makes far less difference than it seems to.

For us, detail is supplied by Hamlet. But apparently unconnected scenes support it. Denmark is a world where Polonius's lecture to Laertes on the way to get on is the substitute for virtue. 'Look after yourself,' he says; and lays the same gospel of self-interest before Ophelia. He sets a spy on his son at Paris, and teaches the man how to get at the improper truth with a little cunning and prevarication. Everything here is under-hand, meanly self-interested; nothing is frank or generous. It is also undignified, not *great* evil; and often ridiculous, as in Polonius, Rosencrantz and Guildenstern, and Osric. In Claudius's phrase, this is a world where deeds are hid, like harlots' cheeks, under most painted words; to Hamlet, a world where the innocent painted vanity of a girl who wants to look the fashionable lady says the same thing; where the animal that Ophelia does not recognize in herself becomes the sensual beast he loathes in Gertrude. The only people entirely at home in it are Rosencrantz, Guildenstern and Osric: creatures purely Darwinian, taking form solely from environment, and strong in their belief in the survival of the slickest. All these have a quality in common, 'slipperiness', the quality that Hamlet hits at in his mother's laying flattering unctions to her soul. In the others (Polonius,

Rosencrantz and Guildenstern, Ophelia) there is either nothing to appeal to, morally; or nothing to hit. He beats the infected air or, rather, thrusts it through and through with wit, doing as much damage as the vain blows of the sentinels could do to the Ghost. The 'malicious mockery' is his: this slipperiness is invulnerable.

Claudius is master of this world, through cunning, resource, a smooth and deceptive affability, and a complete severance of scruple from action. He has a conscience; he is once perfectly aware of the world of higher values:

> In the corrupted currents of this world
> Offence's gilded hand may shove by justice;
> And oft 'tis seen the wicked prize itself
> Buys out the law. But 'tis not so above:
> There is no shuffling; there the action lies
> In his true nature. . . . (III. iii. 57–62)

It denotes his intellect to see himself so clearly, but has no bearing whatever on his actions. There, he does what is necessary, heeding conscience not a whit. Resolution is never sicklied o'er with thought; and, as a result, he is master, for a time, of the 'real' world: playing on men's weaknesses to make them tools (in this, like Ulysses); and, with women, getting what he wants and keeping his own counsel. His is the moral deformity described in Plato's *Republic* as not merely ugly, but terrible, because it has power. It is a blunder to see him as a melodramatic villain, or as merely base; for he is a highly efficient king—a king of smiles, like Bolingbroke, a 'vile politician'—with all the strength that comes from concentration on a narrow pragmatic aim. Hamlet's abuse of him as his mother's lover—'a king of shreds and patches', a 'mildewed ear', etc.—is sexual commentary, the index of Hamlet's loathing, not fair comment on Claudius the man. You only weaken Hamlet by making Claudius less than a 'mighty opposite'.

Meanness, craft, exploitation succeed: that is the point. Generosity, freedom from 'all contriving', and intelligent disinterestedness fail, or are impotent. That is why Denmark is the world, and a prison: a prison of the spirit controlled by minds of practical efficacy, which can *use* the sensuality of Gertrude, the self-satisfied worldly-wisdom of Polonius, the affection of Ophelia, the toadishness of Rosencrantz and Guildenstern, the impetuosity and touchy sense of honour of Laertes. Claudius is never finer than when he faces the insurrection (every inch a King), and then twists Laertes deftly round against Hamlet. Nor is any passage more characteristic of the world that, as it were, draws Hamlet's noble nature *per contra*.

The central 'moral' theme of the play, then, appears to be this. To bring the 'native hue of resolution' to bear on life, and to make the deeper findings of 'pale thought' effective in the world of living men, the thinker must come down to that world. By coming down to that world, he accepts its terms, its ways of making things happen; accepts the necessity of managing affairs by making levers of men's weaknesses, and so necessarily tends to live in a world, not of men, but of machines.[1] Looking into himself, he believes intensely in the soul of man: 'how infinite in faculties! in form and moving, how express and admirable! in action, how like an angel! in apprehension, how like a god! the beauty of the world! the paragon of animals!...' 'And yet, to me, what is this quintessence of dust?' For, looking at men about him, and especially at those men who are effective in the corrupted currents of this world, he sees creatures not of spirit but of circumstance: circumstance which a clever, contriving mind can partially control, and so make men dance like puppets to his twitch. 'How like a god!' Yet that very power of insight denies, by implication, his own soul; for he too is a man: a thing of mind and mechanism, controlled as others are controlled; a mass, a chaos of selves, but having no self free from 'crass causality' and the pressure of aimless circumstance.

[1] Of the twenty thousand men who go to their graves as to beds, rightly great, because they *have* found quarrel in a straw: which they cannot see to be all 'for a phantasy and trick of fame.' They *believe* in what they are doing: i.e. they believe in doing, and that in what is *done* lies 'honour'. The nearness to Falstaff's analysis of battle-values is striking; but only the abstract idea is the same: the *tones* could not be more different.

In fact, Hamlet's profoundest intuitions of nobility, goodness, value, truth are without validity; are 'springes to catch woodcocks': obviously, since he can watch them doing it. The world of fact, in which things truly happen, shows them happening clean contrary to his inner sense of justice and right reason. Virtue must apologize for itself:

> Forgive me this my virtue;
> For in the fatness of these pursy times
> Virtue itself of vice must pardon beg . . . (III. iv. 152–4)

Yet Hamlet's fineness is noble, though all life confute its efficacy. And much life does. That is why the play is a tragedy, and symbolizes the conflict between two antinomies, the contradictions I have called 'circumstance' and 'inner values'. It is as alive today as ever it was in 1601, because the tragedy of that opposition is *man's* tragedy; and William Shakespeare was able to write it not merely because he was Shakespeare (which begs the question), but because of a historic accident, or rather, two.

Hamlet is the first modern man. 'Modern' means post-Renaissance, and 'Renaissance' there implies (*a*) belief in man as the measure of all things; (*b*) the resulting problem of power, and especially of the claim of power to be an end in itself, so that Truth and the Good are only of value as means to power; (*c*) scepticism: not merely about established religious dogma, but as a *method of doubt*, which calls every principle in question till empirical evidence, gained from observation of the outside world, proves it by test and trial (and thus proved, it *disproves* much that man holds dearest).

The first of these, the belief in man, or humanism, was the legacy of Greece: its valuation of man and his mind is the foundation of the civilization we claim we are fighting for. In 1600, anthropocentricity was a newish thing; but it was thirteen years old on the English stage, for it is the soul of *Tamberlaine the Great*. The second, the problem of power, associated with Machiavelli, was still newer. Claudius, a constructive Machiavel —like Prince Henry, Cassius and Ulysses before, and like Iago later—was Shakespeare's imaginative projection of the *novus homo*: the new species of man, with a new order of conscience-less getting and self-seeking, that seemed to threaten command of a world of weaker and more scrupulous men. The third, the most important in connection with *Hamlet*, was the scepticism of Montaigne, which by probing into the unsteadiness and varyingness of purely human standards, set men's minds to the discovery of what in this mutable world *was* enduring and stable and the same from generation to generation. Montaigne's method led to Descartes (born in 1596), whose method of doubt is the foundation of all our modern scientific theories about man. The answer, so far as there *is* one, to Renaissance scepticism is *science*: a system of the apparent certainties of circumstance—leaving the 'values' clean outside.

These three patterns of thought fell together in Shakespeare's mind as the result (mainly) of reading Montaigne, and of his horror at the utterly de-spiritualized world threatened by Machiavelli. The clash between the new vision of man as 'how like a god' and the sceptical, *real-politik* view (felt in the blood, not merely thought), which denied the worth of his best and finest visions, made the tragedy of Hamlet, Prince of Denmark.

The same clash, the same antinomies, make the world we inhabit: because new apprehensions, in minds of great imaginative power, can and do lead to their discovering symbols for emotional experience the ultimate grounds of which only centuries of intellectual investigation can explore. Intellectual and scientifically-tested information on man and his nature has developed vastly since 1600; but the most comprehensive view of man this twentieth century has produced does not leave the sweet Prince one whit less representative. The same superior, ironical, mocking voice, quickly turning sharp and contemptuous, as derided Rosencrantz and Guildenstern in the scene with the recorders (III. ii. 336 f.), is still there: to answer physiologist and priest, dictator and demagogue, philosopher and psychologist: 'Why, look you now, how unworthy a thing you make of me! You would play upon me; you would seem to know my stops; you would pluck out the heart of my mystery; you would sound me from my lowest note to the top of my compass; and there is much music, excellent voice, in this little organ, yet cannot you make it speak. 'Sblood, do you think I am easier to be play'd on than a pipe? Call me what instrument you will, though you can fret me, yet you cannot play upon me.'

'It is no part of a well grounded judgement, simply to judge our selves by our exteriour actions: A man must thorowly sound himselfe, and dive into his heart, and there see by what wards or springs the motions stirre. But forasmuch as it is a hazardous and high enterprise, I would not have so many to meddle with it as doe.'[1]

[1] Montaigne, ibid., final paragraph.

10

Othello: A Moral Essay

I AM aware that my comments on this play may seem eccentric and governed overmuch by a 'moral' angle of vision. This is because I place the play in a *continuum*, starting *c.* 1598 with *2 Henry IV*, and running through the Problem plays, with a special connection with *Troilus and Cressida*. The probing of human egocentricity, and a wincing exposure of human degradation, mark, for me, those middle-period plays. *Othello* continues the inquisition. If the triangular Sonnet-story *is* Shakespeare's, then *Othello* is the exposure and analysis of a complex of attitudes (all based on 'sentiment') which he had *rejected*. The comic of Iago marks one resemblance to tragi-comedy; and also the difference between this tragedy and *Hamlet*, *Macbeth* and *King Lear*.

What we say about *Othello* will necessarily depend greatly on our attitudes towards jealousy; and those will depend in turn on (1) what reflection we have given the subject—one it would be fantastic to describe as only of literary, critical importance; and on (2) whether we do or do not suppose that in the 1950s we are in a position to see deeper into the matter than people were in the psychological past. I do not mean Shakespeare; I mean those who have written on his play, or on the psychology or pathology of love. Popularly, conventionally, there is no love without jealousy; and jealousy is a measure of intense love. Its opposite is indifference, I suppose. A modern psychologist, however, ends his study with 'In short, jealousy is a sign of weakness in love, not of strength; it takes its source in fear, guilt and hate, rather than in love.' I say no more than that there is no possibility of compromise between those two positions (although *Sonnet 130* may suggest that Shakespeare found one). And outside Shakespearian criticism, your life may hang on which you take. I suggest that the whole meaning of *Othello* can be said to hang on how you interpret the half line 'of one not easily jealous'—or the one and a half lines that surround it: 'Of one that lov'd not wisely, but too well', and 'but, being wrought. . . '

Now only a concordance is required, and reflection, to show that *jealous* in Shakespearian usage *cannot* always mean 'sexually jealous'. Cassius, for example, 'And be not jealous on me, gentle Brutus' (I. ii. 71), and Brutus, 'That you do love me, I am nothing jealous' (I. ii. 162), both plainly mean 'suspicious': 'I have no suspicion of the genuineness of your apparent friendship: I think you sincere.' In *Hamlet* the Queen says,

> So full of artless jealousy is guilt
> It spills itself in fearing to be spilt (IV. v. 19–20):

'Guilty minds are so uncontrolled in their suspiciousness that they betray themselves by their very precautions.' Polonius 'beshrews his jealousy' in the same sense: he suspected that Hamlet was only trifling with Ophelia; whereas it was serious, he now thinks. Lear speaks of the neglect he has received in his daughter's castle: 'I have perceived a most faint neglect of late, which I have rather blamed as mine own jealous curiosity than as a very pretence and purpose of unkindness.' (I. iv. 67–9): i.e., he has dismissed it from his mind, telling himself that it is *finicking suspicion* on his part; but now he sees that it is more than that.

The word in Elizabethan usage has two clear meanings; and for the most part today we neglect the non-sexual one (although 'jealous' *is* used to mean 'envious', especially by girls). There is a good example of both senses together, yet distinct, in *King Lear*:

> *Edmund:* To both these sisters have I sworn my love;
> Each jealous of the other, as the stung
> Are of the adder. (V. i. 55–7)

We can assume (although the action has not yet shown it) that Goneril and Regan *know* of the rival attachment: hence *jealous* must mean 'sexually jealous'. But the comparison, trope, can only apply to a 'suspicious' situation, where *jealous* also means 'anxiously watchful, seeing dangers in every appearance': for, in a sane world, there is no competition for adders' favours; and, alternatively, if the adder is the rival, the fear lest it bite *me* does not fit the sexual situation. The double-meaninged word enables Shakespeare to say two distinct things at once: but the sense 'suspicious' is still the predominant one. *Henry V* (IV. i. 281–2)—

> My lord, your nobles, jealous of your absence,
> Seek through your camp to find you—

shows a sense one further removed from 'sexual' than this. They are 'anxiously apprehensive', not 'suspicious'. It should be noted how the dates of these citations are closely contiguous: 1599 (two), 1601, 1603, 1605. Confirmatory evidence is given by usages in *As You Like It, Twelfth Night, 2 Henry IV*.

If it be agreed that Othello's lines (v. ii. 350 ff.) contain an ambiguous term, 'jealous', then we can estimate what is being said, and, with that, its bearing on the whole Othello and on the whole play. If 'jealous' means *suspicious*, the lines can be taken at face value. Othello is 'not *given* to suspicion': he is trusting (Iago agrees there), and all his dealings with Iago demonstrate it. But a man who denies an ambiguous term may be denying either of its distinct senses. If he is simultaneously aware that he can truthfully deny the one, but not the other, then he is an equivocator. If he could, perhaps should, be aware of what he is falsely denying even in making a true denial of its equivoke, he is a self-deceiver, or is self-deceived. 'The fiend', we can say, if we like, 'equivocates with him (or within him).' The fault in him is not hypocrisy, but lack of insight, self-knowledge: i.e., of sincerity in its deepest sense of integrity. If 'jealous' means capable of or subject to extreme *sexual jealousy*, then Othello is, to say the least, deceived; for III. iii. has been a long revelation of just that: proneness to sexual jealousy. While Iago's game has been made the easier by Othello's *not* being jealous in the sense he still prefers to insist on (in v. ii).

The integrity of the '*noble Othello*' depends enormously on taking without adulteration:

> Of one not easily jealous, but, being wrought,
> Perplex'd in the extreme. . . .

His defence as not sexually jealous will hinge on when he can be said to have been 'wrought'. For that, there is nothing to do but to go back to III. iii. 34, and from there follow the character-deployment in detail. But I will anticipate by suggesting that in 'not easily jealous' Othello is right and wrong at once; and add that with his own continual behaviour behind him—and its consequence beside him—he has no good *reason* to be wrong ('excuse' is another matter).

I shall examine the stages in III. iii. and formulate conclusions as I go along. At III. iii. 34 Cassio exits:

Iago: Ha! I like not that.
Othello: What dost thou say?
Iago: Nothing, my lord; or if—I know not what.
Othello: Was not that Cassio parted from my wife?
Iago: Cassio, my lord! No, sure, I cannot think it,
That he would sneak away so guilty-like,
Seeing your coming.

We observe again Iago's trick of silence: a breaking off in his speech, leading to a different turn—or a sudden return to the same turn. It is only when the talk with Desdemona about Cassio is over, that these lines look like an insinuation. For, prima facie, Othello has the best of reasons for knowing why Cassio, demoted and degraded, should be shy of his presence. At l. 90 Desdemona and Emilia leave the stage; and there is a strange exaggeration, a baseless quasi-apprehension, in Othello's extravagance of doting admiration:

> Excellent wretch! Perdition catch my soul

But I do love thee; and when I love thee not
Chaos is come again.
Iago: My noble lord!
Othello: What dost thou say, Iago?
Iago: Did Michael Cassio, when you woo'd my lady,
Know of your love?

After a dozen lines, in which Iago says nothing but 'Indeed!', 'Honest?' and 'Think?', we have:

Othello: What dost thou think?
Iago: Think, my lord?
Othello: Think, my lord! By heaven, he echoes me,
As if there were some monster in his thought
Too hideous to be shown. Thou didst mean something:
I heard thee say but now thou lik'st not that,
When Cassio left my wife. What didst not like?

No need of more. We can speak justly of 'excitability by the most inadequate causes', whether that marks suspicion in general or jealousy.

About fifty lines further, and the words 'jealous' and 'jealousy' are being bandied to and fro. Iago (having defended his own 'good name'—his reason why he will not utter baseless thoughts) turns straight to his warning against jealousy; and the whole context of those lines (169–96) shows that he has good cause to: Othello *is* unambiguously jealous, in one of the obsession's earlier phases. There follows Iago's speech on the sexual life of Venetian women (l. 205 f.); the reminder 'She did deceive her father, marrying you.' (l. 210); Othello's denials that his spirits are dashed and that he is 'much mov'd'; then Iago's innuendo: 'Was there something strange in her tastes, in choosing *you* . . . in being so unnaturally obstinate?', where the ambiguous word 'will' (at ll. 236 and 240) means *lustful* underneath and only *wilful* on the surface; and immediately upon that the ego-wounding suggestion that she may come 'to match you with her country forms,/ And happily repent' (l. 241). Othello's reaction is 'Set on thy wife to observe'; and as soon as he is alone he is confirming those who have said that jealousy is marked by 'an eagerness to snatch at proofs'.

His speech beginning 'This fellow's of exceeding honesty' opens another field. A sense of inferiority, coupled with self-pity, leaps at a bound to near-certainty:

Haply, for I am black
And have not those soft parts of conversation
That chamberers have, or for I am declin'd
Into the vale of years—yet that's not much—
She's gone; I am abus'd; and my relief
Must be to loathe her. O curse of marriage,
That we can call these delicate creatures ours,
And not their appetites! (ll. 267–74)

The last two lines are ambiguous. 'We cannot call these delicate creatures' appetites ours': i.e., my wife is mine, but her desires and tastes are not always exactly the same as mine (a fairly egoistical complaint?). They can also mean: 'we can *say* that the delicate creatures are ours, and not recognize that they are creatures of their appetites—which they are—and that is the curse of marriage' (*appetite's* or *appetites'* is now a genitive, singular or plural; if singular, it means sexual appetite). What follows is gross in feeling, the idea of possession ('ours') being coarsened by the specific image:

I had rather be a toad,
And live upon the vapour of a dungeon,
Than keep a corner in the thing I love
For others' uses (ll. 274–7)

It is unnecessary to underline it by going ahead to l. 343 f.: 'What sense had I in her stol'n hours of lust? . . .' We can say that if jealousy is marked by 'a grossness of conception, and a disposition to degrade the object of passion by sensual fancies and images', Shakespeare's text gives authority to say, 'It is here.'

All this takes place in three hundred lines (or twenty minutes' playing-time), in a highly realistic, if blank-verse medium. The conclusion that Othello is markedly *unsuspicious* in listening, while being as markedly apt by nature to *jealousy*, is the only one that the text can support. To save time, glance ahead for the rest of the alleged characteristics of jealousy. In IV. ii. (the 'brothel-scene') are the concomitants and effects of the hints III. iii. has already given. The magnificent self-pity of 'Farewell the tranquil mind! farewell content!' (III. iii. 352 f.: magnificent, but still self-pitying: the contemplation of the fallen poetic glories of an admired ego) points straight to the passage at the end of which the *toad* image returns:

> Had it pleas'd heaven
> To try me with affliction; had they rain'd
> All kind of sores and shames on my bare head,
> Steep'd me in poverty to the very lips,
> Given to captivity me and my utmost hopes,
> I should have found in some place of my soul
> A drop of patience; but, alas, to make me
> The fixed figure for the time of scorn
> To point his slow unmoving finger at!—
> O, O!
> Yet could I bear that too; well, very well. (IV. ii. 48–57)

There is here not only some of that 'dread of vulgar ridicule, as distinct from a high sense of honour', which has been called typical of the jealous; but also (what is missed in quoting it by itself) the setting of this passage in Desdemona's utter incomprehension. 'Alas, what ignorant sin have I committed?': that is all *she* knows. Jealousy has been described as marked by 'a sense of shame at [the jealous man's] own feelings, exhibited in a solitary moodiness of humour, and yet from the violence of the passion forced to utter itself, and therefore catching occasions to ease the mind by ambiguities, equivokes, *by talking to those who cannot*, and *are known to be unable to understand what is said to them*—in short, by *soliloquy in the form of dialogue*.' It hits the 'brothel-scene' precisely.

And last, jealousy is characterized by 'a spirit of selfish vindictiveness'. Read what follows the too hackneyed 'O, Iago, the pity of it, Iago!' (IV. i. 192):

Othello: But yet the pity of it, Iago! O, Iago, the pity of it, Iago[1].
Iago: If you be so fond over her iniquity, give her patent to offend; for, if it touch not you, it comes near nobody.
Othello: I will chop her into messes. Cuckold me!

Next moment, it is 'With mine officer!'; and the next step follows immediately, the irrational leap to the idea of '*justice*' ('the justice of it pleases'; i.e., if he 'strangle her in her bed', as Iago suggests, and as Othello *does*—again with 'justice' on his lips: 'O balmy breath, that dost almost persuade/ Justice to break her sword!'). These ten lines epitomize the transition from self-pity (mingled with a sense of the pitifulness of his plight), through wounded self-esteem, turning the knife of insult in the wound, to insane self-love taking vengeance and calling it justice. However we read here, we shall carry our reading forward to the interpretation of 'It is the cause, it is the cause. . . .'

And I must, in passing, remark how Bradley[2] reads. He finds only the 'beginning of this passion' at III. iii. 262 ff. ('This fellow's of exceeding honesty . . . If I do prove her haggard . . . O curse of marriage . . . I had rather be a toad') and comments: 'Even there . . . indeed to the very end, he is quite unlike the essentially jealous man, quite unlike Leontes.' Then, having admitted that he has *some* of 'the feelings of jealousy proper' (his wife's being possessed by another is *intolerable to him*: he has a *sense of insult* and *impulse of revenge*), he goes on: 'But these are not the chief or the deepest source of Othello's suffering. It is the wreck of his faith and his love. It is the feeling, "If she be false, oh then Heaven mocks itself"; the feeling, "O Iago, the pity of it, Iago!"; the feeling,

> But there, where I have garner'd up my heart,
> Where either I must live or bear no life,
> The fountain from the which my current runs,
> Or else dries up—to be discarded thence! . . .'

And then, tactfully omitting the toad, etc., he says 'You will find nothing like this in Leontes' (which I quote for its relevant

[1] The Folio reading. [2] *Shakespearean Tragedy*, p. 194.

irrelevance), and ends 'Up to this point, it appears to me, there is not a syllable to be said against Othello.'[1] The ignobility of jealousy is fully admitted, but Othello disinfected from it. Bradley's reading of v. ii. follows directly from this: 'The deed he is bound to do is no murder, but a sacrifice. He is to save Desdemona from herself, not in hate but in honour; in honour, and also in love.' Thus: 'terribly painful as this scene is, there is almost nothing here to diminish the admiration and love which heighten pity. And pity itself vanishes, and love and admiration alone remain, in the majestic dignity and sovereign ascendancy of the close'. He ends by claiming that this 'most painful of all tragedies leaves us for the moment free from pain, and exulting in the power of "love and man's unconquerable mind".'[2]

If *that* falls, the whole of Bradley falls with it. I only say I find it utterly unacceptable; and instead of arguing with what he says, undermine by asking *why* he says it. There is no need to discuss the psyche of Andrew Bradley. Read Coleridge—*Table Talk* on 29 December 1822, and more on 24 June 1827 (both developments of what he said in his Lecture on *Othello* of 13 January 1812)—and the formula is unmistakable: 'Jealousy does not strike me as a point in his passion; I take it to be rather an agony that the creature, whom he had believed angelic, with whom he had garnered up his heart, and whom he could not help still loving, should be proved impure and worthless. It was the struggle *not* to love her. It was a moral indignation and regret that virtue should so fall: "But yet the pity of it, ... etc." ' (1822); and in 1827: 'I have often told you that I do not think there is any jealousy, properly so called, in the character of Othello . . . no predisposition to suspicion . . . If Desdemona had . . . been guilty, no one would have thought of calling Othello's conduct that of a jealous man. He could not act otherwise than he did, with the lights he had; whereas jealousy can never be strictly right . . .' (and with that he is back to Leontes).

It is time to go a little further and to show you what I have been doing in examining III. iii. and some of its consequences in

[1] ibid. [2] ibid., p. 198.

detail. After each 'move', or character-development, I gave you a generalization on jealousy—from a writer who considered himself a psychologist (and is generally regarded as a subtle one). There were six diagnoses. I shall now read the complete passage, from Coleridge's *Lectures on Shakespeare*, on *The Winter's Tale*:

> The idea of this delightful drama is a genuine jealousy of disposition, and it should be immediately followed by the perusal of *Othello*, which is the direct contrast of it in every particular. For jealousy is a vice of the mind, a culpable tendency of the temper, having certain well known and well defined effects and concomitants, all of which are visible in Leontes, and, I boldly say, not one of which marks its presence in Othello—such as, first, an excitability by the most inadequate causes, and an eagerness to snatch at proofs; secondly, a grossness of conception, and a disposition to degrade the object of the passion by sensual fancies and images; thirdly, a sense of shame of his own feelings exhibited in a solitary moodiness of humour, and yet from the violence of the passion forced to utter itself, and therefore catching occasions to ease the mind by ambiguities, equivokes, by talking to those who cannot, and who are known not to be able to understand what is said to them—in short, by soliloquy in the form of dialogue, and hence a confused, broken, and fragmentary manner; fourthly, a dread of vulgar ridicule, as distinct from a high sense of honour, or a mistaken sense of duty; and lastly, and immediately consequent on this, a spirit of selfish vindictiveness.[1]

It is a commonplace that Coleridge had 'a smack of Hamlet' in him and that *Hamlet* was distorted by that self-identification. It remains unrecognized that he had spices of Othello *and* Leontes also, and that Othello has been distorted too; only, now, by making the Moor a less questionably noble shape than Shakespeare drew. It is needless to explore the psyche of Coleridge, although it would have been morally and psychologically profitable to do so, had editors been honest and bold enough to print the evidence from his Notebooks. From the time of his return from Malta, 27 December 1806, to 1810–11, when

[1] Bohn edn., pp. 380–1.

his love for Sara Hutchinson fell to pieces, Coleridge suffered from morbid jealousy, and chiefly of Wordsworth; and in 1806–7 it touches the 'insane' or 'delusional' kind, as again in March 1810 (Sara's journey to Wales—for a marriage rigged by the Wordsworths, so he thinks). Side by side with this, there is lofty idealization, and a total dependence of his self-esteem on being loved. Coleridge's sense of inferiority to Wordsworth is everywhere; and with it, the trend towards making Wordsworth, or the Wordsworths, villains of the piece.

I give you all this to suggest a sound reason why Coleridge, criticizing *The Winter's Tale* in 1818, should see Othello as he does, and went on doing. Othello is *noble*: his love is the essential, not his jealousy; and Bradley follows quite directly from that. But let that suffice: I need not explore Coleridge's psyche any further, because the question can be taken out into a larger, less personal field.

The ambivalence of feeling in envy, and even more in sex-jealousy, is too obvious to need demonstration. It is a feeling with an ambiguity like that of the Elizabethan word 'jealous': i.e., it combines desire of owning (called 'love') with aversion, or hatred, or loathing, all antitheses of love or attraction. But the ambivalence can be resolved, as jealous people *do* resolve it, by making a virtue of the hatred. Iago does this with *envy*: presenting himself as an honest-spoken undeluded mind, in a self-deceiving hypocritical world. In this he exactly parallels Othello as agent of justice.

But 'jealousy' is itself ambivalent[1]: it is evil, a thing we feel shame about, and so a cause of guilt; it is also regarded as the index of love. The jealous-minded (like Coleridge) weight this second valuation until the first is at vanishing-point. What then happens with *Othello* is a distortion of the entire play, because the psychic mechanism of *projection* turns all the evil outwards and finds a villain in whom it is all centred (just as the jealous mind projects upon the suspected woman all the evil

[1] Contrast our normal attitudes to love, which is *not* ambivalent, but presumed *good*.

intent and conduct which would make the hatred justifiable; and therefore leaps at every 'proof', every 'trifle light as air'). Coleridge projects his own guilt-feelings on to Iago, who becomes the motive-hunter 'of motiveless malignity' (a comment quite inapposite to the soliloquy Coleridge's 1818 lecture shows it stems from: I. iii. 380 f.[1]). The Bradleyan Iago develops from those foundations: not only from Coleridge, but from this wider field of ambivalence, projection, distortion and falsification of Othello and *Othello*. All such critics project on to Iago the evil they know jealousy to be, making him the incarnation of their own unconscious *guilt*. Their guilt is his evil; and thus Othello and his jealousy are vindicated.

Critics who do not have this make-up, such as Dr. Leavis, reject the Coleridge-Iago and the Bradley-Othello utterly. Nor can I think that it is merely a matter of personal preference, and that one view is as valid as the other. For in this particular instance, although Dr. Leavis appeals to me neither, his judgement of the *shortcomings* in Othello and his self-proclaimed centre, his love, could be supported equally by the moralists (especially the French moralists[2]) before Freud; and by the psychologists, after.

It is the self-idealizing illusions of Othello on which Dr. Leavis fixes attention. He accepts him as 'truly impressive, a noble product of the life of action—of "the big wars/ That make ambition virtue" '; but insists: 'Othello, in his magnanimous way, is egotistic. He really is, beyond any question, the noble massive man of action, the captain of men, he sees himself as being, but he does very much see himself: "Keep up your bright swords, for the dew will rust them." In short, a habit of self-approving self-dramatization is an essential element in Othello's make-up, and remains so at the very end. It is, at the best, the impressive manifestation of a noble egotism. But, in the new marital situation, this egotism isn't going to be the less

[1] See Coleridge, *Lectures on Shakespeare*, Bohn edn., p. 388.

[2] e.g., Rochefoucauld: '*Il y a dans la jalousie plus d'amour-propre que d'amour*' (*Maximes*, 324).

dangerous for its nobility. This self-centredness doesn't mean self-knowledge.'[1] And Leavis sticks to it that it never *does.* Othello dies in a histrionic part, self-ignorant. On the love Leavis is unambiguous: 'his love is composed very largely of ignorance of self.... It may be love, but it can be only in an oddly qualified sense love of her: it must be much more a matter of self-centred and self-regarding satisfactions—pride, sensual possessiveness, appetite, love of loving—than he suspects.'[2] Finally, 'Othello's noble lack of self-knowledge is shown as humiliating and disastrous.'[3] By then, 'nobility' has acquired quotation-marks: 'The habitual "nobility" is seen to make self-deception invincible.'

I quote at this length because I believe a psychoanalyst would reach all those conclusions, travelling by a totally different road. In some respects he would be clearer than Dr. Leavis: e.g., over the 'oddly qualified sense' in which Othello's love 'can be love of her'. The psychiatrists would argue along these lines. First, there is no need to do more than remark the child-parents relationship; beyond stressing that to the child, love is not fulfilment, but answers *needs.* Secondly, love, passion, etc., can have functions other than their own. We can distinguish secondary from primary love, just as we can distinguish genuine *politesse du coeur*, arising from feeling for others, from formal politeness, artificial, mannered and assumed, which commonly masks fear, distrust, hostility. One kind of 'secondary love' similarly masks hate—used here as an extreme term to cover oppositions, frictions, disagreements—or sex-antagonism, if you believe it inevitable. Disagreement is inseparable from close human contact, unless you live in a universe of echoes or in delusion. Moreover, these dissatisfactions arise from disappointment, which can be the resentment of having to recognize that the loved one is not one's *ideal.* What the resentment is, whether it is 'hate' or not, depends on the kind of ideal: its remoteness from reality, etc.—and, of course, on the resenter's capacity, or lack of it, to

[1] 'Diabolic Intellect and the Noble Hero': *Scrutiny*, Dec. 1937, p. 265 (reprinted in *The Common Pursuit*, p. 136).

[2] ibid., pp. 268–9.

[3] ibid., p. 270.

adjust his egocentric ideal-demands if and when he has to face the realization that his 'seems' is *not* her 'is'.

The second accessory function of love ('secondary love') lies in its 'affording reassurance and security about one's self-value'[1] (particularly in the erotic sphere). It cancels '*un sentiment d'incomplétude*' (Janet). As with the man who drinks not because he likes it, but because he cannot do without it, it is a need. The needer of this kind of secondary love finds in it 'the inner security he otherwise lacks', becomes spiritually dependent on his love-object:

> The fountain from the which my current runs,
> Or else dries up;

'strictly speaking, this is not love at all, but a craving to be loved. He is not interested in the object of his affection as such, only in her relationship to himself.' It is this type which is most subject to jealousy. To say that the woman is an opportunity for the lover to demonstrate to himself his erotic capacity, his 'being a man', and that all hangs on that prestige-value, is too simple.[2] Rather, the 'sense of deficiency is connected with some inner self-dissatisfaction, a self-criticism that betrays some conflict within the self', i.e., *moral* inferiority underlies the self-dissatisfaction (and the psychoanalysts refer this to guilt, the child-situation, etc.). With such deficiency-feeling goes a compensatory self-love. It is 'self-love, self-esteem, self-respect which is wounded by the unconscious guilt': hence such persons' sensitiveness to criticism and constant demand for approval or recognition in various forms. Grant that black Othello, erring barbarian or no, feels himself inferior to sophisticated white Venice: his histrionic, self-admiring magnificence falls immediately into this pattern.

What such 'secondary lovers' seek can be variously described: security (from fears), certainty (from doubt), peace of mind

[1] Ernest Jones: 'Jealousy' (*Psyche*, July 1930, p. 41). The other quotations on this and the next page, for which no reference is given, are from the same source.

[2] Coleridge is a case in point: he was far superior to normal sexuality, so he protested.

(from troublings of unconscious guilt); but all are tied up with the assurance of absolute love and fidelity, because of the demand to be loved, the *need*. Take those away, and chaos comes again. The threat of this, meaning loss of confidence, causes regression to the infant phase: 'desire to *be* loved (in place of the desire *to* love)' and 'insistence on the lowly instinct of possessiveness'. To lose the woman's fidelity is 'not simply to lose the most desired thing that the world outside can give, it is also to lose the confidence in his own personality. This is the fear that underlies jealousy.' It exposes nakedly the moral inferiority and the guilt; and this guilt is projected on to either the woman or the lover (according to inner make-up): i.e., inner self-dislike, etc., is displaced on to others. Hence the deranged demand to be assured of the unfaithfulness: it justifies the hate, restores the inner sélf-esteem, provides an ego-compensation. This explains the pitilessness of morbid jealousy, '*le plus grand de tous les maux, et celui qui fait le moins de pitié aux personnes qui la causent*'.[1]

But this secondary love, which provides prestige for the ego, is intrinsically ambivalent. The need to be loved is positive; but the ego fears to be 'possessed'. Hence a positive craving and a negative dread, often shown in delaying marriage—from a fear of its dangers to the self. 'But that I love . . . ,/ I would not my unhoused free condition/ Put into circumscription and confine/ For the seas' worth . . .' (I. ii. 25–8). And this kind of inner insecurity predisposes to jealousy. So the psychiatrist: omitting as much Oedipus as I can, and saying *nothing* of homosexual patterns or pseudo-patterns.

In passing, I remark an uncertainty about Iago in Dr. Leavis's essay. He denies the 'diabolic intellect': 'Iago's power . . . in the temptation-scene is that he represents something that is in Othello—in Othello the husband of Desdemona: the essential traitor is within the gates.'[2] I agree—and feel more should have been made of that. Othello and Iago are not only antithetical types, noble and base: they have correspondences. On Othello's

[1] La Rochefoucauld, *Maximes*, 1503.
[2] F. R. Leavis, op. cit., p. 264.

love Leavis quotes Bradley, 'there is no love, not that of Romeo in his youth, more steeped in imagination than Othello's'; but only remarks that Othello was *not* young. I want him to say: 'If that is true, then imagination means *illusion*; and illusion-imagination in turn means . . . ?'[1] It seems to me to mean the rigid *exclusion* of the common realities of the world and of love from attention; a kind of romantic inhibition of awareness; and the antithesis of Iago's quality—what Leavis[2] calls 'his deflating, unbeglamouring, brutally realistic mode of speech'. Putting it my way, the ambivalences of human experience are made 'monovalent': the ideal exists by the inhibition of the real; and in the collapse of the ideal (unreal love), Othello is left with many views of Iago-like crudity and brutality. 'Goats and monkeys' in IV. i., to greet Lodovico's arrival in Cyprus, echoes Iago at III, iii. 407, 'as prime as goats, as hot as monkeys'; and reaches the level of Iago's opening jibes at Brabantio. 'I am bound to thee for ever'—irony, where it comes (III. iii. 217)—ends as a kind of analogy to 'Nelly, I *am* Heathcliff'. The underworld of 'Iago-nature' has 'steeped (him) in poverty to the very lips'.

Taking Iago thus, I am not troubled by what troubles Dr. Leavis: 'if Othello is to retain our sympathy sufficiently, Iago must, as devil, claim for himself an implicit weight of emotional regard that critical reflection finds him unfit to carry'.[3] This is obscure; and the subject is dropped immediately afterwards. It seems to me that, reading Elizabethanly or otherwise, Iago *has* some 'weight of emotional regard'; and if he does indeed 'represent something that is in Othello—in Othello the husband of Desdemona', then Leavis surely need not boggle? Moreover, Elizabethanly speaking, the power-hunting aggrieved machinator, especially one who is also a malcontent and professional cynic-critic, quite plainly *did* claim 'emotional regard'—even if the audience withdrew their sympathies at the first firm hint of

[1]With Othello's attitude contrast *Sonnet 138* ('When my love swears that she is made of truth'): the mature, ironic attitude.

[2] ibid., p. 267.

[3] ibid., p. 278.

'*und die Hälse schnüren zu* . . .'[1] It would be absurd to make Iago co-hero or villain-hero; but his wit, his cynical insights, his daring, his gusto in plotting, his gambler's sang-froid, all those *were* 'emotionally regarded' sides of these essentially ambivalent stage-figures (from Marston, through Vendice, to Bosola), emblems of the Jacobean moral confusion which I find in Shakespeare's Problem plays. While Othello talks of what happens if 'chaos is come again', Iago reiterates in *his* way the tough-cheerful aspects of the '*Blick ins Chaos*' of the seamier sides of *Measure for Measure*. And that is where, both by date and theme, despite Dr. Leavis on *Measure for Measure*, I place *The Tragedy of Othello*: next to that play, *Troilus and Cressida* and *All's Well*; in a sense, the last Problem Play.

Its themes are sex, seeming and being (especially seen as *reputation*) and the ambivalence of 'love' (an ambivalence of a particular kind). Sex enters by I. i. 89, in a pretty ugly guise: 'an old black ram/ Is tupping your white ewe' . . . 'You'll have your daughter cover'd with a Barbary horse' (I. i. 112); mitigated only to 'the gross clasps of a lascivious Moor' (l. 127). The rank sexual nastiness of much of the play surely needs no comment. But the antithesis to this fundamentally sex-loathing attitude (which seethes up in *Othello's* mind, note) is nowhere a normal acceptance of sexuality in human love. It is either a glorifying idealization or a glorified sensuality, as hyperbolic as the idealism and as little in touch with the real love of a real woman. We are shown extremes, with a kind of blank between.

> If the balance of our lives had not one scale of reason to poise another of sensuality, the blood and baseness of our natures would conduct us to most preposterous conclusions. But we have reason to cool our raging motions, our carnal stings, our unbitted lusts; whereof I take this that you call love to be a sect or scion. (I. iii. 325–31)

Could one forget who says this, would it be impossible to apply it to the un-reasoned Othello, and to his being conducted to 'preposterous conclusions' by the blood and by a baseness in his

[1] 'any throttling taking place' (Osmin in *Il Seraglio*).

nature (or in his love)?[1] 'Baseness' may sound a very wrong name for it. But I was thinking of baseness in metals—an alloy. If you call it 'idolatry', is it of Desdemona? ' 'Tis mad idolatry/ To make the service greater than the god,' says Hector, and he goes on to describe the self-deluding mechanism of the 'will' that dotes, in the ascription of false excellences. In his charge, to a Helen; but if so, why not to this pathetic, girlish, nearly-blank sheet, Desdemona?

I find that the peculiarly distressing effect of *Othello*—what Bradley calls its 'painful' quality—turns on this feeling of a hollowness at the centre, by the time the end is reached. There is a mixedness of feelings, an instability of apparently accepted values, an absence of stable ground underfoot in all the valuations of sex and so of those of 'love', which make me dislike the play's *Stimmung* as much as I admire its artistic contrivance. I think it is because, on love (its ostensible theme), it leaves me as much just nowhere as *Measure for Measure* does.

> Love is not love
> Which alters when it alteration finds,
> Or bends with the remover to remove. . .

The play is a beautifully contrived arrangement of *patterns*; and, with all possible suspicion of diagrams, I am put out by my own unlucky discovery that the vulgar view of *Othello* as 'the eternal triangle' is infernally true. I happened on this only by the mischance of reading Dr. Ernest Jones on 'Jealousy'[2], smiling loftily at his Oedipus-problems (every little boy finds himself in a triangle, etc.), and then starting to play with the idea of triangular arrangements of people in *Othello*—unable *not* to know about Mr. Shakespeare, Mr. W. H. and the Lady, but, I assure you, quite resolute on keeping the Sonnets, and homosexuality, right out of it.

I find the play works out to an infernal trigonometry: a perfect, highly complex pattern of incongruent triangles. Bear with me.

[1] We *should* see Othello more as we see *Angelo*. [2] op. cit.

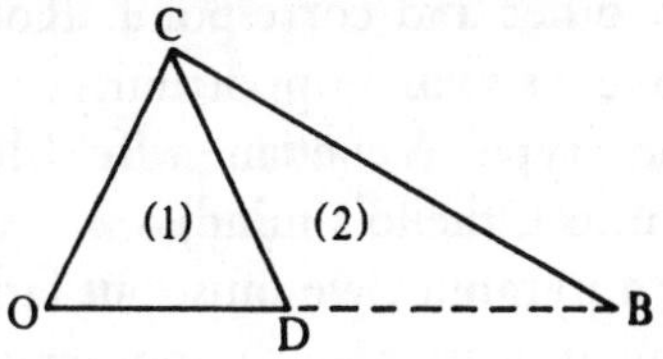

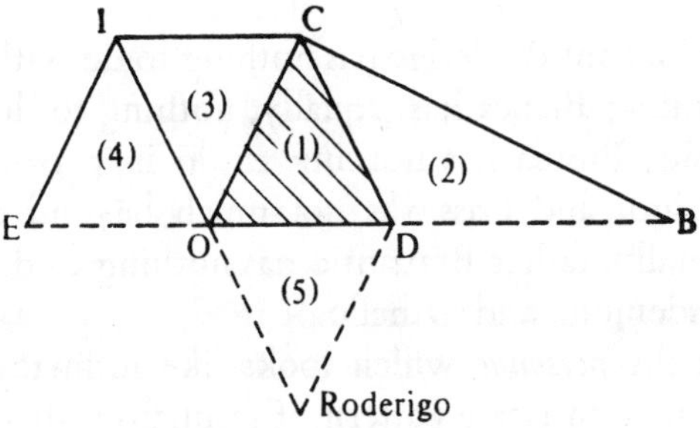

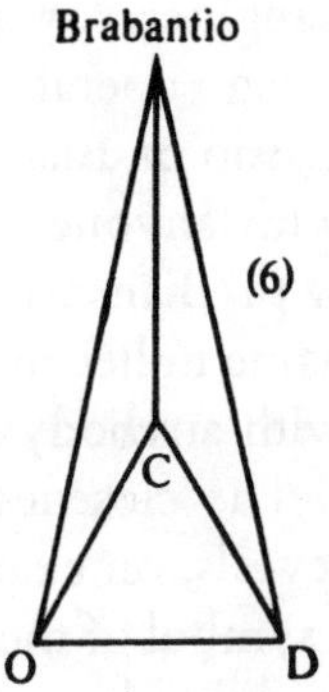

Centrally, there is (1) the Othello-Cassio-Desdemona triangle, in which Cassio does not love Desdemona; nor does Othello—except, as Dr. Leavis puts it, 'in an oddly qualified sense'. Attached to the right side there is (2) a false Cassio-Bianca-Desdemona triangle, where Bianca is the name 'my lord did say I was'.

That exactly pictures Bianca's place in the plot. Looking at the de-idealized Desdemona, Othello sees 'a Bianca'. On the left hand, there is attached (3) the '*envy-triangle*' of Cassio-Iago-Othello. This represents the same competition for 'favours' (Othello's favours of office) as Othello believes to be happening in the centre; and Bianca in *her* side-show. Attached again to that —we must get another straight line—is (4) the other *marital* triangle, Iago-Emilia-Othello (suspected of adultery by Iago: so that Othello is *his* pseudo-Cassio). In this Emilia is 'unfaithful', through her fidelity to her *mistress* being greater than her love to her *spouse*. Attached below to the line Othello-Desdemona and forming triangle (5), is the aspiring, befooled Roderigo, who *would* be (if he could) what Othello thinks Cassio *is*. The two triangles face each other and correspond. Roderigo represents the delusion of 'love' as sexual opportunity; and his imaginary Desdemona is the 'type' Venetian wife (the type Iago, at III. iii. 205–8, put into Othello's mind).

Finally, making a pyramid, we must put father Brabantio up aloft, as third point in a triangle in another plane, (6): father, daughter, lover.

Iago operates in all these: but Roderigo has nothing to do with Cassio or Bianca or Emilia; Bianca has, equally, nothing to do with anyone but Cassio; Emilia has nothing to do in person with Bianca or Roderigo; and Cassio is not much beyond a name in her mouth. Finally, father Brabantio has nothing to do with anybody but Desdemona and Othello.

The closeness of all the *personae* which looks like intimacy reveals, on examination, an intricate pattern of insulations. It is a symbol of the deranged self-absorption of all the 'triangulants' Each holds a monomania; and each calls it '*love*'.

11

Macbeth

MACBETH, like Richard III, is best interpreted through its themes and imagery, not through 'character' (contrast *Othello*); and after a consideration of order, kingship and 'the state of man' in the Histories. Its unusual shortness (it is the shortest of the tragedies: 2,086 lines, only 70 longer than *The Tempest* and 16 than *A Midsummer Night's Dream*) supports the theory that the Folio (the only text) is a cut version for court-performance. This is consistent with its complimentary allusions to James, his ancestors, his interests. Of the references which establish its date as 1606, that of the Porter to *equivocation* is the most important, because so much of the play turns upon the equivocal: saying both 'Ay' and 'No' to the 'same' thing. This perpetual antithesis is far more than could be inset as a compliment to James for a court-performance. Fr. Henry Garnet was tried on 28 March 1606 for complicity in the Gunpowder Plot, and relied on equivocation to justify his shifty and lying answers. 'Tres Sibyllae' greeted James at Oxford, August 1605. There *was* a corn-slump 1605–7; but the farmer 'that hang'd himself on th' expectation of plenty' was already a chestnut.

There are really three sources, and of two different sorts:

(*a*) The head and mind of State had been threatened by the powers of evil, who regarded equivocation as justifiable. England and her Scottish King had escaped the chaos of 'dire combustion', etc., which would result from blowing up Parliament, from insurrection, from civil war.

(*b*) Holinshed, in his *Chronicles of Scotlande*, has two different stories (of Duff at ii. 149 ff. and of Macbeth at ii. 168–76).

The Gunpowder Plot situation combined in Shakespeare's imagination with the ancient history of James's line; and that with quite another story. Thus Holinshed (p. 171) says that Duncan was a mild and incapable king, murdered by Macbeth with Banquo's connivance; and that Macbeth's wife was 'verie ambitious, burning in unquenchable desire to beare the name of a queene'. Macbeth reigned well seven years, then murdered Banquo, when 'every man began to doubt his own life'. Moreover (a detail), 'The pricke of conscience . . . caused him ever to feare, lest he should be served to the same cup, as he had ministred to his predecessor' (p. 172). The other Holinshed story is the murder of King Duff by Donwald for revenge (in a blood-feud), egged on by his wife, 'tho' he abhorred the act greatlie in heart' and did not do it himself. Duff is entertained as a guest; gives presents; the Chamberlains are made drunk and killed later by Donwald. Unnatural portents followed for six months (pp. 150–2). Further, Duff had been troubled by witchcraft at Forres. Holinshed's margin-notes would recall both stories to any reader who had been over the twenty-seven pages attentively (though the Siward episode is from his first volume, *The Chronicles of England*, i. 192.)

Shakespeare removed the *external* motive from both murders, i.e. the *coup d'état* from Duncan's, the blood-feud from Duff's; and correspondingly increases Duncan's trustfulness, piety, sanctity. The *wilfulness* of the murder is thus isolated; and Banquo set contrastingly apart from it.[1]

The outcome is a play about the disintegration of the state of man, and the state he makes his. It is commonly taken to be 'about ambition'; but ambition is only one of the names Macbeth finds for the impulsion in himself when looking into his own mind:

> I have no spur
> To prick the sides of my intent, but only
> Vaulting ambition, which o'erleaps itself. . . . (I. vii. 25–7);

[1] Over other alleged sources I am sceptical. Professor Kenneth Muir deals well with them (Introduction to Arden edn., 1951, pp. xl–xli), dismissing, for instance, the pleas of Mrs. C. C. Stopes and Dr. Dover Wilson that Shakespeare researched in the vast and deservedly obscure *Buik of the Croniclis of Scotland* by William Stewart.

and when he names it that, he rejects it: 'We will proceed no further. . . .' Better, I think, to call it 'particular will': a Shakespearian phrase for a force as much of the 'blood' as the intellect: Macbeth's *impulsion* (rather than his decision, as an ambitious man would feel it) to assert *his* pattern on the world: to make Macbeth Scotland. Instead, he finds he has made Scotland Macbeth: his damned soul has infected a whole country, even the whole universe. The forces *released* by the hope held in the Witches' prophecy; by the spurring of his wife, playing on his soldier's identification of honour (self-hood) with ruthless self-assertion through force: these give him the crown and sceptre. Both are hollow: the 'swelling prologue to the imperial theme' leads on to a *shrinking*, till 'there's nothing serious in mortality', and he becomes a tortured demon in a hell of his own begetting; glad of his own callousness; and (having half-conquered all), lord of nothing but chaos and the pitifully limited self-assertion of the will to fight until he drops.

A phrase of Coleridge's on the Weird Sisters states very well *what* it is that is released by Duncan's murder: 'they are the shadowy obscure and fearfully anomalous of physical nature, the lawless of human nature.' For Shakespeare, there is no compromise between order and chaos: the breakdown of ordered nature (in the mind, the state, the world) is absolute.

> Civilization is hooped together, brought
> Under a rule, under the semblance of peace
> By manifold illusion;[1]

or, rather, by one supreme illusion: a faith. But if that faith is once broken, then 'confusion' can 'make his masterpiece'. The very contemplation of the possibility of murdering the King brings the image and rhythm of confusion into Macbeth's mind:

> My thought, whose murder yet is but fantastical,
> Shakes so my single state of man
> That function is smother'd in surmise,
> And nothing is but what is not. (I. iii. 138–41)

This speech is exactly paralleled by Brutus's reflections before

[1] W. B. Yeats: *Supernatural Songs*, XII.

the murder of Caesar (*Julius Caesar*, II. i. 60 ff.): he too refers to the state of man, like to a little kingdom, undergoing 'the nature of an insurrection'; and though he can provide himself with motives far more rational than Macbeth's, he also faintly recognizes the shadowy presence of the 'anomalous', the fearful, the lawless and disordered, which his act ultimately releases. This parallelism of situation is emphasized by what are called 'the supernatural elements' in both plays. It would be more discriminating to call these elements 'sub-natural' or 'hypo-natural'; for they represent the irruption of forces *beneath* the normal order of integrated nature. In fact, they symbolize 'the horrifying old distrust of nature', the dread of the unintelligible, the threat of the uncontrollable world with which 'humanity . . . is helplessly and irrevocably involved'.[1] In Shakespeare's ethical symbolism, the macrocosmic universe, controlled by the unifying spirit of God, is imaged (I should prefer to say 'emblemed') in the State, controlled by the King seen as divine; and in the microcosm Man, whose ruling power holds in difficult subjection its lawless and passional undercurrents. It follows that the release of these mysterious and horrifying forces which strike at the illusion or faith that holds the State together as an organic whole, disturbs the complete order of all nature. The ultimate effect of Macbeth's 'horrible imaginings' at the very thought of breaking open 'the Lord's anointed temple', is felt in Ross's lines to Lady Macduff:

I dare not speak much further;
But cruel are the times, when we are traitors
And do not know ourselves; when we hold rumour
From what we fear, yet know not what we fear,
But float upon a wild and violent sea
Each way and none.[2] (IV. ii. 17-22)

They echo Macbeth's soliloquy-aside both in theme and in rhythm, ending with the same slip-away movement into sickening uncertainty. It is not merely that Macbeth's fears of

[1] P. H. Frye, *The Idea of Greek Tragedy*, in *Nebraska University Studies*, 1913.
[2] 'Each way, and move' (Ff).

the treachery he himself has taught have converted him into a cruel tyrant, so that no man knows where his safety ends, and fear reigns in all hearts—even of those who can tell themselves (vainly) that they should have nothing to fear.[1] But that, with the release of the sub-human (or sub-natural), it is impossible for men even to know themselves, for good and evil (or virtue and vice) have lost their outlines.[2] Men fear and do not know why, like brutes: but worse than brutes, in that they *know they do not know*, and experience the horror of the incomprehensible, the absolutely arbitrary: the thing that by all normal standards cannot be—yet is. It is this which gives what critics call the 'nightmare' quality to the play. It opens to the mind a vision of a world of men acting under hideous compulsions, in the unnatural wakefulness of 'murdered sleep'. This is easy to see in the case of Lady Macbeth; but Macbeth too speaks of 'the affliction of these terrible dreams/ That shake us nightly', and envies Duncan his death:

> Better be with the dead,
> Whom we, to gain our peace, have sent to peace.
> (III. ii. 19 f.)

As King of Scotland, Macbeth could appropriately cite those terrible words of Seneca, but turned to a still more terrible point:

> In regna mea,
> Mors impetratur.

This notion of the simultaneous and complete disintegration of the concentric orders of the mind, the State, the universe (or Nature in all three), puts difficulties in the way of the modern reader: for we normally think of all human order as comparative, and are (so long as we remain sane) assured of the law-bound nature of Nature. Even if we fear that war may bring about 'a return to barbarism' or 'the destruction of civilization

[1] cf. Lady Macduff at IV. ii. 73–8: 'I have done no harm. . . .'

[2] cf. 'Force should be right; or, rather, right and wrong—
Between whose endless jar justice resides—
Should lose their names, and so should justice too.'
(Ulysses in *Troilus and Cressida*, I. iii. 116–18.)

as we know it', the 'barbarism' we dread is comparative: we fear an increased ascendancy of the 'animal nature' in man—of violence, lustfulness, greed, instability—but not their absolute and universal dominion. I at least can imagine no crime so great as to destroy *all* order; and am therefore forced to consider Macbeth as a mind at the very verge of the abyss of insanity. When Bradley says that he regards the murder as 'done, one may almost say, as if it were an appalling duty',[1] I know what he is pointing to, but cannot accommodate the word 'duty' either to my own philosophy or to what I take to be Shakespeare's. Hence my use of the term 'compulsion'. It does prevent one's delving back into Macbeth's past biography after this fashion:

> But when Macbeth heard them [the witches' prophecies] he was not an innocent man. Precisely how far his mind was guilty may be a question; but no innocent man would have started, as he did, with a start of *fear* at the mere prophecy of a crown, or have conceived thereupon *immediately* the thought of murder. Either this thought was not new to him, or he had cherished at least some vaguer dishonourable dream. . . .[2]

Such speculative biography is beside the point. Macbeth is not a murderer in the dock, to have his spiritual history invented for him by a Q.C. bent on conviction: he is a symbol in a poem, and his only life outside it is in his effect on our minds. Later on (as he so often does), Bradley says the right thing: 'the temptation was already within him'. No man is, or ever can be, 'innocent' where his advantage is concerned. He can be blind; or he can see it, and then use his will to reject it, to follow it in moderation, or to follow it relentlessly. Macbeth does the last; and since he is the image of a normal mind, he recognizes at once that this means following those forces in himself whose domination can accept no competitor, no mitigation, and ultimately no restraint. For the desires of the subterranean forces of the mind are illimitable. They all prompt to the pursuit of happiness through their release from the bonds of order:

[1] *Shakespearean Tragedy*, p. 358.
[2] Bradley, op. cit., p. 344.

all lead to the tyranny of one anarch, or the anarchy of a host of tyrants. Macbeth, his intellect being quite the most normal—even commonplace—among Shakespeare's gallery of minds, recognizes at once the impulsion ('temptation' in Bradley's phrase) and the fearful surrender it demands. The extent and full consequence of that surrender are unknown: Macbeth is presented as a *man*, not as a prophetic or moral genius. But to substitute the memory of a specific guilty thought or plan for the experience of the upthrust of the essentially guilty undertow of the human mind, is to diminish what Shakespeare is offering. It substitutes a 'criminal' for whom we have 'a certain sympathy' for the contemplation of the potential evil of every human will. Shakespeare is not Dostoevsky; but if we cannot take Macbeth's guilt upon ourselves—*and* not forgive it—then the play descends from its high moral seriousness to the rank of a brilliant melodrama.

In referring to *Macbeth's* 'high moral seriousness', I have in mind the frequent comparisons made between this play and the greatest of Greek tragedies, in which we also feel a certain compulsive force driving on the hero or heroine to deeds either wrong in themselves or of direst consequence. But there is a difference. The Greek hero does not, as a rule, pursue *his own good*, but simply a mistaken good (the murder of their mother by Orestes and Electra is a perfect example of 'an appalling duty'). They do not wholly 'decide' their way; and whatever they may have done for Greeks, they compel us to consider what meaning—apart from the doers having to accept the consequences—is to be attached to 'responsibility'.

Shakespeare makes Macbeth simultaneously aware of three considerations, each of them normal enough, but abnormal in their co-existence: (*a*) the moral hideousness of the deed before him; (*b*) the inadequacy of the spur of 'vaulting ambition'; (*c*) the certainty of 'judgment here', and the utter impossibility of any act's being final enough to trammel up all consequence. The famous soliloquy begins with a strong movement *away* from the deed Macbeth is considering: the hesitation and hurry of the words imply the conclusion that 'it will *not* be done *with* when it *is* done', long before he comes to speak of justice:

> If it were done when 'tis done, then 'twere well
> It were done quickly. If th' assassination
> Could trammel up the consequence, and catch,
> With his surcease, success; that but this blow
> Might be the be-all and the end-all here—
> But here upon this bank and shoal of time—
> We'd jump the life to come. But in these cases
> We still have judgment here, that we but teach
> Bloody instructions, which being taught return
> To plague th' inventor. This even-handed justice
> Commends th' ingredience of our poison'd chalice
> To our own lips. (I. vii. 1–12)

Unlike the Greek heroes, Macbeth acts with a full sense of the evil he is submitting himself to; *and* a full realization that no good can come of it. Hence my speaking of 'a mind on the verge of insanity', of a 'compulsion'.

Surely we must find it incomprehensible that a man should be aware of all this, yet commit deadly evil simply because he cannot endure to be called a coward? Lady Macbeth has only three arguments to persuade Macbeth: (1) 'you thought of it first'; (2) 'you swore to it'; and (3) 'you swore to it in such terms that, had I used them, I would have murdered my own child sooner than belie myself'. The first is no argument at all; and, if keeping oaths is honourable, then Macbeth has a greater debt to his King. He cannot be 'afraid of being afraid', for he knows himself a dauntless soldier, and even now shines in the brightest gloss of 'golden opinions'. Why, then, does he kill Duncan? A man with a weak moral sense may do wrong because immediate emotional impulse (or 'temptation') is stronger than its check. But this is untrue of Macbeth. A stronger moral sense can be diverted by self-deception; but Macbeth is not in the least hypocritical or self-blinded. If he acts because his wife has poured her spirits in his ear and chastised him with the valour of her tongue, and for that only; if her persuasions are convincing to him (and since he does act, we must accept them as convincing): then Macbeth has no nobility of mind, and no independent strength of will. Such a man cannot be admirable, nor his fate of tragic importance. He becomes like those compulsive neurotics who must steal, or burn, or commit crimes of sexual violence:

> For aye entempesting anew
> The unfathomable hell within,
> The horror of their deeds to view,
> To know and loathe, yet wish and do![1]

This is what happens if we try to extract Macbeth as a 'character'—as a real person. *Qui facit per alium, facit per se.* If *this* is 'Macbeth', then the man is his wife's nearly-passive instrument; the murder of Duncan is hers, not his; and the eccentric (not to say incompetent) Shakespeare focuses his play on the tool, not the agent.

I submit that this is all wrong. We cannot take out Macbeth, Lady Macbeth and Banquo, and treat them thus. They are parts of a pattern, a design; are images, or symbols; and while a human being cannot simultaneously be full of the moral awareness of evil *and* fully engaged in doing it, wholly aware that the only motive he can offer himself is inadequate, those symbols we call *dramatis personae* not only *can* be, but must be, if the full weight and pressure of their acts are to be felt by the reader's or audience's minds. As Johnson put it, 'He has not only shewn human nature as it acts in real exigencies, but as it would be found in trials, to which it cannot be exposed'. In *Macbeth*, Shakespeare symbolizes the forces that operate in every moral conflict: and every deep conflict brings us to the contemplation of something powerful, anomalous and apparently ungraspable. I call that an impulsion, and use the name *will* for it for lack of a better: meaning thereby something less intellectual and consciously scheming, less argumentative, belonging more to the blood and the elementary passions, than we commonly think of

[1] Coleridge, *The Pains of Sleep*.

when we use the term. It is the passionate will-to-self-assertion, to unlimited self-hood, and especially the impulsion to force the world (and everything in it) to *my* pattern, in *my* time, and with my own hand. Hence the reflection, 'If chance will have me King, why, chance may crown me,/ Without my stir,' is powerless to restrain Macbeth. A similar force is in *Richard III*; but there it is more intellectual, more conscious: in *Macbeth* the springs of action are deeper, more mysterious and more alarming, because they seem so utterly beyond intelligent control, and so involved in the whole human scheme of things.

Shakespeare presents this self-assertive force as a force promoting disorder, in man, in nature, in everything. The two 'protagonists' symbolize complementary aspects of its existence and operation. Neither is complete without the other. Before Duncan's murder, Lady Macbeth is the embodiment of this will, but it is not her 'woman's will' only: it is also a force of nature—nature which is equivocal or ambiguous in essence. There is an aspect of everything natural which tends towards concord, peace, trust and reliability (love): a natural order. There is also an aspect tending towards chaos, or complete and meaningless disorder (hate). 'Evil' is rather too definite a term for the second, though it is evil: the word tends to suggest a conscious Devil, bent on a definite plan of damnation, with 'ambition' as his bait. But Shakespeare's vision goes beyond this Christian simplification. On the human plane, he shows how the results of hard-willed self-assertion develop. First, to success; then to the ingrown insensibility of Macbeth as King, with his human sensitiveness either nulled or a hindrance; simultaneously, to the terrifying separateness of the damned, which both criminals endure; then to the remorseful harassment of the night-wandering Queen; and finally to the state where Macbeth is merely monstrous, and outside him all are either enemies or tools or obstacles, in a world where 'everything includes itself in power,/ Power into will, will into appetite', and humanity preys on itself 'like monsters of the deep'.

At this level, *Macbeth* is the tragedy of success. Macbeth becomes the embodiment of everything antagonistic and self-directed; and yet he is made the symbol of the utter emptiness of mere antagonism and self-assertion. The two contrary experiences—determination to force one's way on everything, *coute que coute*, and despair at the impossibility *and* the futility of doing so—are brought to co-existence in the mind. It is *in us* that Macbeth, his Lady and Banquo happen. They are not three persons, but one event in a poem. Murderers and Porter apart, all the rest of the *human* cast are antitheses to the two protagonists: often they have different names, but one essence or being.

It is a great poem because the powers of the mind that it invokes are in all human beings; because those inchoate all-or-nothing forces I call *will* are universal, and universally tend towards that isolation, oppugnancy, negativeness[1] and chaos both in the individual and the world, which is shown in Shakespeare's stage-mirror of a past age, and through the difficult Jacobean machinery of a Scottish history of witches and royal murder, of magical kings and supernatural portents. Its 'theme' is not ambition, or sin, or guilt merely; but rather the equivocal nature of Nature: Nature in which all things exist, whether we call them good or evil; which builds and destroys; which has a natural order, to which man feels he belongs and is blessed in that hope; and which seems also to be moved by forces as potent and chaotic as the Witches:

> Themselves obedient,
> Knowing not evil and good;
> Obedient to some hidden magical breath.

[1] That is, humanly (or humanely) negative. Whatever has *any* power of effect is to that extent a positive: a mechanical positive. But this will makes human positives worthless: it inverts values. To put it at its contemporarily crudest, the determination to get on at all costs can only make affection, sympathy, co-operation, understanding, natural needs—such as meat and drink—and even procreation, into things either of no value, or into hindrances to the bustling spirit; or twist them into means of exploitation of others. The last is the Machiavellianism more particularly explored by Jonson; and especially in relation to natural appetites turned to greeds, as in *Volpone*. Our contemporary Macbeths make a desolation and call it 'Man's conquest of Nature': *solitudinem faciunt*, potestatem *appellant*.

They do not even feel, so abstract are they,
So dead beyond our death,
Triumph that we obey.[1]

This brings me to the Weird Sisters. They offer very great difficulties to the modern reader, and still worse ones to producer and audience. Coleridge remarked how utterly different they are from other stage-witches, and noted that they 'yet presented a sufficient external resemblance to the creatures of vulgar prejudice to act immediately on the audience'. That precisely hits the point. They *did* act immediately on the Jacobean audience: on us, they cannot. We are compelled to think up something for them to signify; for the threatening presence of a faceless and evil Unknown is as utterly absent from our séances as from our laboratories.

They are not the Fates; for they have 'masters', and the Fates do not need the chemistry of corruption to call forth their powers. They are not the real or supposed human witches that James tortured to the greater glory of God; for they predict the future and predict it truly.* They are not the Devil (and therefore not in control of Macbeth), because they cannot move Banquo to evil, though they do stir up ill within him.† It is not they who possess Lady Macbeth after her terrible invocation:

Come, you spirits
That tend on mortal thoughts, unsex me here;
And fill me, from the crown to the toe, top-full
Of direst cruelty. Make thick my blood,
Stop up th' access and passage to remorse,
That no compunctious visitings of nature
Shake my fell purpose nor keep peace between
Th' effect and it. Come to my woman's breasts,
And take my milk for gall, you murd'ring ministers,
Wherever in your sightless substances
You wait on nature's mischief. (I. v. 37–47)

They are, however, most closely associated with whatever

[1] W. B. Yeats: 'The Double Vision of Michael Robartes' (1919).
* See Note (*a*) at end. † See Note (*b*) at end.

ministers wait on the incomprehensible 'mischiefs' of Nature: i.e. they 'attend on the mischief wrought by any natural phenomenon, such as storm, tempest, earthquake, etc'.[1] That is to say, they too evoke the horror of that 'under-Nature' which is the compulsion in Macbeth, which is released in the portents (that display normal nature as running wild, turning unnatural), and which Lady Macbeth needs to be possessed of before remorse (i.e. compassion, or natural pity and sympathy) can be choked, and the 'compunctious visitings' of natural feeling denied their human way. They symbolize not our *idea* of, but our *feelings about* everything in the world that justice, humanity, morals, law exist to control; and that philosophy, science and religion strive to explain, i.e. to bring into the light of an intellectual and intelligible order. That is what Coleridge meant when he called them 'the shadowy obscure and fearfully anomalous of physical nature'; and therefore they are essentially equivocal. Like the impulsion of the will in Macbeth and the thickening of the blood Lady Macbeth prays for, they evoke the realization of a world in which 'nothing is, but what is not': where all human values are denied, and nothing is firm or faithful. The quality they have in common with the forces released in Macbeth by unnatural murder, is shown most clearly in the images of confusion he employs in consulting them at their second appearance:

> I conjure you by that which you profess—
> Howe'er you come to know it—answer me.
> Though you untie the winds and let them fight
> Against the churches; though the yesty waves
> Confound and swallow navigation up;
> Though bladed corn be lodg'd and trees blown down;
> Though castles topple on their warders' heads;
> Though palaces and pyramids do slope
> Their heads to their foundations; though the treasure
> Of nature's germens tumble all together,
> Even till destruction sicken—answer me
> To what I ask you. (IV. i. 50–61)

[1] Henry Cunningham in Arden edn. of 1912.

All destructive and disordered phenomena are associated with them; and most often those phenomena that devastate human society. The winds are to fight the churches; navigation is to be wrecked; corn and useful trees made useless; the castles which stand for security flung down; all is to end in such chaos that even destruction sickens. A similar, but subtly different, quality of suggestion is in the ingredients of the cauldron: poison; parts of repulsive, dangerous, cold-blooded, night-flying beasts; the sweat of a murderer's gibbet; the strangled bastard's finger: everything is obscene, grotesque and out-of-place in a nature men normally associate with kindliness, peace and bounty. Though I have little doubt that James I was filled with pious horror, I have always found these rhymed speeches grisly-comical, and have reached the conclusion that Shakespeare here intended the Witches to be hideous and undignified. There is nothing satanic about them; and they are meant, I think, to have become debased and vile in keeping with Scotland and Macbeth himself.[1]

In the stage-presentation of the play the Witches offer almost insuperable difficulties, because their *immediate* Jacobean effect is now utterly past recall, and no pious pretence can revive a hundredth of it. This necessarily alters the original balance of the play: instead of horror and what Bradley calls 'the incalculability of evil' being conjured up at once by their gestures and appearance and thence reflected upon Macbeth's troubled mind, these must now be moved by Macbeth's own internal vision of horror, and thence reflected upon the Witches. This plainly cannot be, at their first appearance; for, however we may come primed with ready emotions from our reading, those are not the same as the immediate emotions produced in the playhouse. The only way I can think of to make the Weird Sisters *immediately* effective would be to provide them with really abominable masks. The primitiveness of the visual sense makes it possible to compel through its means the emotive experience of a nameless

[1] Critics and editors who will have it that they are not 'witches', but Weird Sisters, 'ministers of fate and supernatural aid', etc., might with advantage study Reginald Scot's *The Discoverie of Witchcraft* (1584), or the pictures of Hexenküche. See Ploss and Bartels: *Das Weib*, Vol. iii.

horror of indefinable extent, even to a sophisticated observer.[1]

The Witch-scenes miss their original effect, and the same is true of what Coleridge lamentably called 'the disgusting passage of the Porter': a slip which has provoked too much attention. The Porter is now nothing but a skilful break in the dramatic tension, full of tedious Elizabethan jargon we know we ought to try to find at once comic and significant. On this there is nothing for it but the sad observation of Johnson in his Preface:

> It is to be lamented, that such a writer should want a commentary; that his language should become obsolete, or his sentiments obscure. But it is vain to carry wishes beyond the condition of human things; that which must happen to all, has happened to Shakespeare, by accident and time.

There is, however, no reason for not seeing what Shakespeare seeks to call out in our minds by his figures; and perhaps the best approach is by examining those passages which show images of the diametric opposite to all that the Witches stand for. In this way we can realize the elements of that order that is the antithesis to the chaos to which the Weird Sisters are native, and into which Macbeth plunges his mind and state.

The first of these passages is the descriptive commentary on Macbeth's castle given by Duncan and Banquo (I. vi. 1–9). It is one of the few moments of daylight and sunshine in a play sodden with gloom and midnight. The air of the castle is sweet and healthy; the martlet builds his loved mansionry under its eaves and mouldings; and the bird itself is 'temple-haunting', and builds only where heaven's breath is near. The irony has always been observed: like nearly everything in this play, the castle is equivocal. But these images of tender sympathy with the bird, its natural affection and its humbly skilful architecture,[2] unite with much more in the play. The murder of young

[1] As in negro masks, for example. See C. K. Ogden, I. A. Richards, and James Wood: *The Foundations of Aesthetics*, 1922.

[2] 'Her pendent bed and procreant cradle' catches perfectly the round 'wombiness' of the nest. Cf. Keats's famous remark about never seeing a sparrow without, as it were, becoming one and picking about in the gravel. Shakespeare gives the tactile image of the round nest in the eye's hand.

Macduff brings back these images of birds, mansionry and domestic affection, in his mother's reproachful reference to her husband:

> He loves us not;
> He wants the natural touch; for the poor wren,
> The most diminutive of birds, will fight,
> Her young ones in her nest, against the owl. (IV. ii. 8–11)

Then the child himself, told his father is dead, pertly remarks that he will live 'As birds do, mother'; and when Macduff is told of their murder, the same figure is repeated: Macbeth is a 'hell-kite' who has killed all his 'pretty chickens . . . at one fell swoop'. The artistic purpose of that slaughter of harmless and loved people is not merely, as Bradley puts it, 'to touch the heart with a sense of beauty and pathos, to open the springs of love and tears',[1] but far more to present impressions of the natural order which the spirit of Macbeth violates.*

A comparable use of what might be called 'images of construction and peace' is to be noticed in the apparently but half-relevant scene in England. This is introduced by the conversation of Lennox and a nameless 'Lord' (III. vi.), placed immediately after the banquet-scene in which the Ghost appears. It serves the functions of a Chorus-commentary, especially when the Lord says that Macduff has gone to England to beg help of the holy King,

> That by the help of these—with Him above
> To ratify the work—we may again
> Give to our tables meat, sleep to our nights,
> Free from our feasts and banquets bloody knives,
> Do faithful homage and receive free honours—
> All which we pine for now. (III. vi. 32–7)

The allusion to 'sleep' requires no comment: Macbeth has murdered sleep—for all who fear him as well as for himself; and with it he has murdered all those things that represent normality of life, security and human comfort. With this comment may

[1] *Shakespearean Tragedy*, p. 391.
* See Note (*c*) at end.

be compared his own, near the end of the play, where the opposites of what he now stands for are presented as his own failed hopes:

> I have liv'd long enough. My way of life
> Is fall'n into the sear, the yellow leaf;
> And that which should accompany old age,
> As honour, love, obedience, troops of friends,
> I must not look to have; but, in their stead,
> Curses not loud but deep, mouth-honour, breath,
> Which the poor heart would fain deny, and dare not.
> (v. iii. 22–8)

This is the Aristotelian *anagnorisis* carried to a more serious (and even a philosophical) plane. Not merely does the character, Macbeth, 'recognise' the falseness of his way: the passage also presents those constructive and positive things which are the opposites of the nightmare state of Scotland, and Macbeth's opponents.[1] It may be contrasted with the Queen's speech in III. ii., where only the negative emptiness of success is being considered:

> Nought's had, all's spent,
> Where our desire is got without content.
> 'Tis safer to be that which we destroy,
> Than by destruction dwell in doubtful joy. (III. ii. 4–7)

(A passage echoed in Macbeth's 'Better be with the dead . . .' twelve lines later.)

This building up of symbols of 'construction, concord, security and peace' gives the otherwise puzzling scene in England its place in the structure of the play. It follows the murder of Lady Macduff and her children, and is followed by the sleep-walking scene; and it links them by beginning with Macduff's lament on the horrible oppression of Scotland, and ending with the revelation by Ross of this last slaughter. The spirit of Macbeth is

[1] 'Troops of friends', for instance, is not our vague collective, but a sharp figure antithetical to the troops of enemies now mustered against the usurpers of darkness.

strongly present, first in the tainted air of suspicion that (for Malcolm) surrounds everything that comes from Scotland, and then again in Malcolm's deliberate vilification of his own character. At the superficial 'story' level, this is a device to test Macduff: if he still urges Malcolm on to invasion, after being told that he has 'no relish of the king-becoming graces', but 'abounds in . . . every several crime', then Malcolm will know he is a treacherous emissary sent by Macbeth to entrap him.* But at the deeper level of the play's poetic meaning, the positive things for which Malcolm (the rightful successor to Duncan) and England and the armies of invasion stand are being presented. Simulating an evil like Macbeth's, Malcolm says:

> Nay, had I pow'r, I should
> Pour the sweet milk of concord into hell,
> Uproar the universal peace, confound
> All unity on earth. (IV. iii. 97–100)

This is no mere Elizabethan bombast. The 'milk of concord' associates itself with 'th' milk of human kindness' that Macbeth was 'too full of, to catch the nearest way'; with Lady Macbeth's invocation to the spirits to 'take my milk for gall'; and with the lines where she speaks of knowing 'how tender 'tis to love the babe that milks me', before she dashes down that image with horrid violence.[1] The 'peace' which the spirit within Macbeth destroys is 'universal': the strong infection of Scotland's disease reaches England too:

> unnatural deeds
> Do breed unnatural troubles . . .

It is not only the Queen's sleep-walking that is 'a great perturbation in nature' (V. i. 9); those subliminal powers, released in Scotland and in her King and Queen, by their own nature 'confound all unity on earth'. To put it in the familiar abstract terms of our own day, the ruthless impulse of self-assertion, the blind urge to dominate through power, make a desolation in which

* See Note (*d*) at end.
[1] I. v. 14 and 44–5; I. vii. 54–9.

all men are enemies; and enemies not only to one another, but to all nature; enemies even to themselves. The final fruits of the assault on omnipotence are, first, to reflect that it is for Banquo's issue that Macbeth has defiled his mind and 'put rancours in the vessel of my peace' (III. i. 64, 66); then, to find that even to the most powerful of human wills there is always some further power lacking:

> Then comes my fit again. I had else been perfect,
> Whole as the marble, founded as the rock,
> As broad and general as the casing air,
> But now I am cabin'd, cribb'd, confin'd, bound in
> To saucy doubts and fears.[1] (III. iv. 21–5)

Beyond this again, there lies the desperate determination that verges on madness: 'For mine own good/ All causes shall give way' (III. iv. 135–6); and, finally, the abject collapse, where the would-be dominator of the world can see that world only as a procession of fools by candle-light; and life, even his own Titanic struggle for domination, as a ranting actor in an idiot-melodrama, 'signifying nothing'. Life, all human effort, appears as much of an equivocator as the Thane of Cawdor's appearance or the words of 'the instruments of darkness'. In that famous dismissal of life I look in vain for grounds for Bradley's belief that Macbeth's ruin is never complete: that 'in the very depths a gleam of his native love of goodness, and with it a tinge of tragic grandeur, rests upon him'.[2] There can be no gleam of goodness where the very meaning of good and evil is denied.

No. The positive forces whose currents sweep up in the second half of the play, after the murder of Banquo, are elsewhere: it is their extent and diversity, their very presence in every normal human heart, which is impressive, not their isolated intensity. What the holy King of England cures is simply 'the evil': the invasion of the English is the purging of a foul disease by the tides of unity, peace and concord; or, as the Prayer Book puts it,

[1] Few passages in the play show better how Shakespeare's imagery and rhythm exactly follow the changing passion of the thought.

[2] *Shakespearean Tragedy*, p. 365.

of 'unity and godly love'.* It is ironically symbolic that, to Macbeth, this appears as a plague: he wants the Doctor—the Doctor who has told him that a 'mind diseas'd' can only minister to itself—to cast the water of his land, find her disease and scour these English hence. Even 'good' has become equivocal as the result of Macbeth's inversion of all normal human values.

The last state of Macbeth is not great, nor fine; it lacks all touch of grandeur. Though Caroline Spurgeon[1] has made over-much of the recurrent image of the 'dwarfish thief' who has stolen a 'giant's robe', and appears almost ridiculous in his attempts to

> buckle his distemper'd cause
> Within the belt of rule,

the fact that this figure presented itself to Shakespeare is enough to demonstrate that the final stages of the hero represented to their creator a terrible *shrinking* in what had once been so potentially great. Shakespeare is no romantic with a peace-time attraction to the glories of violence. The poetic expressiveness of the 'Tomorrow and tomorrow' speech should not cloud over Malcolm's cold dismissal of 'this dead butcher, and his fiend-like queen'. Antony's speech over the dead Brutus, and Othello's 'Soft you; a word or two before you go', suffice to show that Shakespeare does not leave his last-moment gleams of grandeur in doubt. It is 'the State', and all that that implies for Shakespeare, by which Macbeth is measured: unlike Othello, who also was a madman and a murderer who murdered sleep, he cannot claim 'I have done the state some service . . .'.

The final Macbeth is a human mind dwindled down to one faculty: faith in force, against all sense and conscience. Bradley (thinking of Prometheus, perhaps) finds 'something sublime in the defiance with which . . . he faces earth and hell and heaven'. 'To the end,' he writes, 'he never totally loses our sympathy.' This is (to my mind) the inevitable distortion produced by

* See Note (*e*) at end.

[1] *Leading Motives in the Imagery of Shakespeare's Tragedies* (Shak. Assoc. Lecture, 1930).

Bradley's method of character-extraction. We certainly continue to feel that there is something illimitably pitiable in this frustration of human powers; but the desperate Macbeth has lost that touch of the demi-god he first possessed. He has hardened and dwindled till (as Bradley admits) 'he has no time to feel'; till he is too shrunk to fear, and therefore without any of the finer quality of courage. He dies less as a demi-god than as a gangster, playing an empty game to a finish by his own crude code. The man who spoke those penetrating lines on wilful opportunism and justice has been dead long since:

> . . . that but this blow
> Might be the be-all and the end-all here—
> But here upon this bank and shoal of time—
> We'd jump the life to come. But in these cases
> We still have judgment here, that we but teach
> Bloody instructions, which being taught return
> To plague th' inventor. This even-handed justice
> Commends th' ingredience of our poison'd chalice
> To our own lips.

I have tried to reveal a little of the inner structure of *Macbeth*, and to bring out the main emotional forces in the play: the principles (as they might be called) on which Shakespeare's intuitions of the powers at work in human minds and human society are ordered. The dramatic force of the events and of the passionate collisions of human energies, the faithful evocation of intense feelings, I have taken for granted. Instead of taking the play as a penetrating study of individuals, or a book of condensed psychology, illustrated with tense and vivid scenes, I have attempted to get down to that 'meaning which reveals itself gradually', and to which plot (in the widest sense) is a main essential. All the peculiarities of *Macbeth*—its brevity, its reduction to bare essentials, its terrific speed, the impression it gives of having been written in one continuous eruption of the mind —all those qualities (which every critic has noted) encourage one to believe that there is nothing otiose, nothing irrelevant to what Shakespeare felt to 'belong' to his dramatic vision of the soul at war. In other words, the play has an imaginative unity which makes every part essential *in its proper order*, like a knee or thigh-joint (which are only 'inevitable' or 'necessary' when we understand the organic body they belong to). The 'characters' we extract and analyse are only major *parts* of such a living body. When we understand all that that implies, we pass on naturally to the relevance of the seemingly irrelevant: the purpose of the images and scenes that the story could apparently do without.

If I have given overmuch attention to these considerations—to the images of concord and the 'unity of Nature'—it is to redress the balance of the play; and to substantiate a claim that Shakespeare is here writing with a mind full of considerations of the most immediate present importance. Without grasping a little of what was in that manifold mind—where, in the act of writing, as Coleridge said, 'he always by metaphors and figures involves in the thing considered a universe of past and possible experiences'—we cannot discern what human forces are embattled beyond (as well as within) the intensely gripping story he shows us 'in action'. Anyone can feel the excitement of his events; but that is insufficient.[1] We need to know how this supremely penetrating reader of human life saw its obscure and terrifyingly powerful forces lining up. For that reason I have talked about the will-to-power; about order and chaos; about concord and disintegration: instead of treating the emotional experience in terms of ambition and crime, remorse and conscience. I find these terms useful in their right place, but inadequate for my purpose: they cannot, for example, place in the unity of the play Macbeth's expatiation on the different degrees and valuations of dogs (when he tempts the Murderers against Banquo).* But once you can get past the difficulties of the setting of the fable in an imaginary world of witchcraft and demonic

[1] At this level, a contemporary thriller, such as Cain's *The Postman Always Rings Twice,* which almost exactly follows the *Macbeth* story, may easily prove more 'exciting'.

* See Note (*f*) at end.

states at once human and divine, then all these metaphors bring in 'a world of past and possible experiences'. The disintegrations brought about by the urge to power, which makes all mankind worse than the brutes, are near enough to our minds to make the experience of order and disorder worth our most painful exploration.

Notes

(*a*) If it be asked *how* the Witches can predict the future, if they are only forces of the abyss, and not agents of the Devil (which indeed Banquo suggests they might be), one can only reply that it seems likely that Shakespeare did not know. He was not a theologian. The fact of prophecy seems to prove nothing: for Edward the Confessor is also credited with it (IV. iii. 156–7). This, I think, proves that Shakespeare really did believe that true forecasts of the future could be made; but they are only another of Nature's inexplicable (and equivocal) phenomena.

(*b*) Banquo's 'Merciful powers/ Restrain in me the cursed thoughts that nature/ Gives way to in repose!' (II. i. 7–9) represents the touch of evil upon him, if we like to put it that way. But I rather take it as the Good Man's (*any* good man's) prayer, by which 'under-Nature' is held in check. In III. i. 48 ff., it is his 'royalty of nature' wherein something 'reigns', and a 'wisdom that doth guide his valour/ To act in safety', that make Macbeth determine his death. 'Royalty', 'reigns' and 'his valour' are not used loosely here. Bradley's analysis of his speech at the opening of Act III. is very pretty invention (*Shakespearean Tragedy*, pp. 384 ff.), but not more than that. Bradley is obsessed with Christian notions of sin, and so says that Banquo 'has yielded to evil . . . his punishment comes swiftly', etc., where Shakespeare is re-introducing the 'prediction-theme' in the most natural way available. It is not easy to see what Banquo would be expected to do about knowing that he has heard a prophecy, part of which has been fulfilled, and the rest of which applies to his own posterity. He cannot obliterate it from his mind; and if he is to be 'punished' for hoping, what are we to make of Dr. Bradley's idea of God?

Really, no such question arises. The speech is the Good Man's *chorus*, not a subtle piece of individual psychology. Where Shakespeare wants to show a character realizing a crafty advantage, he makes it plain enough: and more often than not, a trifle too unrealistically plain (as with Iago). The purpose of these ten lines is (*a*) to recall the predictions, (*b*) to show the utter impotence of Macbeth's disguises to elude suspicion, and (*c*) to mark the hollowness of the murder next to be plotted, *and* the importance of Fleance's escape. III. i. 15–18 is bottomlessly ironical: the 'tie' that binds his 'duties' (of attendance) to Macbeth is most damnably 'indissoluble'!

(*c*) Birds are creatures of the air, and air in *Macbeth* is a symbol of health and freedom. Macbeth *would* be 'as broad and general as the casing air'; the air the Witches ride on is 'infected'. In this scene, fear has made Macduff less 'natural' than the birds; and yet that fear was wise, as the murder shows: for presumably only Macduff *could* kill Macbeth. What is meant here, is not only the unnatural separateness that fear and treachery force on everyone, but also the transvaluation of values which occurs everywhere Macbeth's force is felt.

(*d*) Bradley is worth taking up sharply here:

> 'I grant him bloody,
> Luxurious, avaricious, false, deceitful,
> Sudden, malicious,
>
> says Malcolm; and two of these epithets surprise us. Who would have expected avarice or lechery in Macbeth? His ruin seems complete.' (*Shakespearean Tragedy*, p. 363)

A footnote reminds us that these lines are spoken by Malcolm, 'but it seems likely that they are meant to be taken as true throughout'. This law-court method of examining 'what the soldier said' is simply 'not evidence': not in poetry. 'Luxurious', which does, as Bradley tells us, mean 'lascivious' or 'lecherous', denotes nothing but another symbol of disorder in the microcosm, Man. Malcolm later accuses himself of an exactly similar catalogue of the opposites of the King-like graces. Immoderate lust is a way to, and a symptom of, the chaos, here as in *Lear*; and in neither case is there any question of biographical detail. On this point, the association of bestial lust and general licentiousness with rebellion was general to the Elizabethan mind (see the Homilies of the Church of England). As a usurper, Macbeth is rebellion itself, and all its vices are naturally associated with him.

(*e*) The prayer for the Church Militant, in the Communion Service. We should not forget that our official religion derives from the same scheme of beliefs as underlie Shakespeare's plays. An Irish priest recently observed that what was wrong with the world today was simply Pelagianism (reported in *Horizon*, Irish number, 1942).

(*f*) Macbeth on dogs. I made this deliberately puzzling in the original lecture, because it is a test-case. Either it is most irrelevant decoration (and not too good even as decoration), or it means something, and was worth including in a very short and compressed play (whether abridged or not). On my lines of examination of the play, it has a definite relevance, as indeed has all the conversation with the Murderers. Macbeth asks them if *patience* so predominates in their *natures* that they can *pray* for this *good man*; are they so *gospelled*? The Christian symbols are obvious enough, and with them the implication of Macbeth's sneering tone. (On being 'patient', *Lear* is worth comparison.) They reply, 'We are men', and we should recollect 'who dares do more, is none' from the earlier Macbeth himself. It is made plain that to mere *men*, only spite, recklessness and desperation are adequate motives for murder (III. i. 108 ff.). But Macbeth replies to the general term 'men' with an argument which cuts quite the wrong way; it is really ironical and condemns him from his own mouth: though we can only see this now by study of other plays. He says, 'Yes, you are men—but when we talk even of *dogs* we classify them according to their (social) purposes: the "valued file distinguishes" each by the particular service that "bounteous nature" has "enclosed" in it; and so each receives its particular respect (or even "honour"—for the word "addition" is used thus repeatedly in Shakespeare: cf. I. iii. 106). But for this, they would all be just "dogs". And the same is true of the "men" you claim to belong to. Now if you *have* any particular "proper place" in the general order of mankind, and that not the worst, let us hear what it is. You were recommended to me as brave and determined fellows, not just "men".'

Macbeth is really appealing to the principle of order, and particularly to the 'ordered' order of human society Shakespeare calls 'degree' in Ulysses' speech in *Troilus and Cressida*. But this principle of proper subordination, and 'knowing one's right place' (as ordained by God, or Nature), is the very thing he has struck against in making himself King. As in his twisting the Gospel phrase with his tone, he is here twisting what Tudor Christianity quite as religiously believed in, only now with his intellect. Shakespeare kept this passage in—or felt it as essential—because it marks the degradation of human society beneath the serviceable community of the dogs they breed.

12

Coriolanus

SHAKESPEARE may have felt some disappointment with *Coriolanus*. He would not be the last; for I think that few see or read it without feeling that they 'don't get as much out of it as they hoped to' or that it 'somehow doesn't seem to *pay*' or is 'less profitable than others I could think of'; or something like that. But whatever he thought he meant by the play is likely to be very different from what *we* make of it, unless we keep our attention fixed on what was going on inside Shakespeare's head in 1607—and what was going on in the year 1607 too. I do not mean that unless we know the barley-markets for 1606–8 and the state of malt-investments, we cannot understand *Coriolanus*. I suggest only this: that there are many ways of interpreting this play, and the one that begins nearest to Jacobean times is one that is necessarily a long way from our own. Moreover, so far as I can judge, the interpretations that arise spontaneously in our own times are so violently opposed to one another, and lead so inevitably into passionate political side-tracks, that almost any line of thinking that gets us away from them gives the play a better chance: a chance as a tragic play.

'Political': there I said it. *Coriolanus* is about power: about State, or *the* State; about order in society and the forces of disorder which threaten 'that integrity which should become 't' (III. i. 159); about conflict, not in personal but political life; and —the aspect which catches our minds first?—about the conflict of classes. I put that last deliberately, for two related but separable reasons. First, if we begin at that end, the play's tragic qualities are endangered at once: it tends to be seen as political, i.e. to be filled with imported feelings which are too partisan for the kind of contemplation which is tragedy. It also readily becomes polemical and seems to be giving *answers*, solutions to human conflicts, which tragedy does *not*. Secondly, it suffices here to summarize a few conclusions, merely as examples of 'passionate political side-tracks'.

1. Hazlitt: 'The whole dramatic moral . . . is that those who have little shall have less, and that those who have much shall take all that others have left. The people are poor; therefore they ought to be starved. They are slaves; therefore they ought to be beaten. They work hard; therefore they ought to be treated like beasts of burden.'[1] And so on. It is only necessary to read the text, to say that Hazlitt's Jacobinical comments are false and nonsensical. No question of politics arises: it is simply one of reading.

2. In December 1933, *Coriolanus* was played at the *Comédie française*. Every performance turned into a demonstration by Right-wing groups (it was the time of the Stavisky affair, and Parliamentary government itself seemed to be quite likely to come to an end); and the Royalists cheered every outburst against the 'common cry of curs', the populace, and the bald tribunes whose power should be thrown in the dust. The play was withdrawn; M. Daladier dismissed the director, put the chief of the Sûreté in his place; and events went forward to the great riots of 6 February 1934.[2] While one can admire the French enthusiasm for making Shakespeare really about something that matters here and now, this is still something other than Shakespeare-criticism. For the view that Caius Marcius should be—or ever could be—the good and great dictator, the integrator of a shaking state, is one that the play cannot support for a moment. Shakespeare's source, Plutarch, had indeed said precisely the opposite; and Shakespeare has put enough into the mouth of Aufidius alone (IV. vii. 35 f.) to make further reference superfluous.

[1] *Characters of Shakespeare's Plays*, 1817.

[2] See the *Manchester Guardian*, 21 March 1952, 'Class War by the Avon'.

3. I have been told that the Russian view is (or was) that this is an entirely acceptable play, on the class-war; but showing how the Revolution is betrayed by self-seeking demagogues who mislead the workers for their own private ends. So that Brutus and Sicinius are wicked persons (with their modern counterparts in the Labour Party, I suppose), since the deviationist is worse than the despot. This is only what I have been told.

4. But Mr. Donald Douglas, in the *Daily Worker* (March 1952), saluted the Stratford production with the interpretation that *Coriolanus* is a revolutionary play, but one gone wrong, and patched up at the end to appease the censorship. The crack can be seen in IV. vi., when the First Citizen leads the rest astray by saying

For mine own part,
When I said banish him, I said 'twas pity.
Second Cit.: And so did I.
Third Cit.: And so did I; and, to say the truth, so did very many of us;

—and it is not the Party Line at all. For the rest, let Mr. Douglas speak for himself: 'In the citizens' revolt against the Roman profiteers who are hoarding corn against a rise in prices . . . we have the fact of the people's power. In the banished Coriolanus, vowing destruction on his native city . . . we have the counterpart of the modern capitalist determined to ruin his country if only he can destroy the people.'

Those four views will do. I shall not argue with any of them, beyond saying that, given similar latitudes of interpretation (not to say perversion) of Shakespeare's words, I will demonstrate that Coriolanus is an allegory of more than one political idealist of our time, who followed his own inner counsels, despised common humanity, betrayed his trust, to become a lonely dragon in a fen; and then felt some new promptings of human nature, and threw away the game he had given away—to end in ruin and the mystery of the darkness of a mind that has set itself to stand

> As if a man were author of himself
> And knew no other kin.

Is that so far-fetched? In a sense, the three tragedies which belong to this stage of Shakespeare's writing are all about traitors and treachery. But treacheries of a particular kind. I remember Donne in *Twicknam garden*:

> But O, selfe traytor, I do bring
> That spider love, which transubstantiates all,
> And can convert Manna to gall.

Coriolanus, Antony, Timon of Athens: all could be called self-traitors, and their spider loves examined as Bradleyan 'tragic flaws'. But that is no line of mine; it will only lead round to moral advice, moral answers: and though moral are worth more than political answers, they cannot be the tragic heart of a tragedy. The 'tragic flaw' analysis is far too simple. It will never do to say that Coriolanus's calamity is 'caused' by his being too proud and unyielding and just that; for one of the play's central paradoxes is that though Caius Marcius appears as a 'character' almost unvaryingly the same, yet, for all his rigidity, he is pliant, unstable, trustless: traitor to Rome, false to the Volsces, then true to Rome and to home again, and twice traitor to himself. It is this 'self-traitor' element which makes one feel reservations over applying those words of Charlotte Brontë's in *Shirley*. Caroline Helstone recommends the play to Robert Moore, the factory-owner, whom Caroline wants to see that he cannot haughtily pass over the feelings of common men. He asks: 'Is it to operate like a sermon?' She replies: 'It is to stir you; to give you new sensations. It is to make you feel life strongly.' Taken by themselves, those words suggest a stirring experience, the romance of power, the stimulating contact with great characters or great events, a glory in history. It is assumed that to 'feel life strongly' has the opposite of a depressant effect. Yet the conclusion of *Coriolanus* is not one bit like that. It is flat, hurried, twisted off and depressing. One traitor steps off the other traitor's dead body: 'My rage is gone'; and turns sentimental traitor to his own successful treachery: 'And I am struck with sorrow.'

Look at it one way and you can say, 'That is exactly the way in which the unstable and trustless emotions of politics always *do* switch and swivel.' And sardonically wait for Aufidius to turn on the stock-rhetoric, as he does: capitalizing the occasion as glibly as Antony over the dead Brutus. How well we look, assuring our dead foes of 'a noble memory', a grand funeral! And it is only a Gilbertian candour that adds 'and fireworks in the evening. You won't be there to see them, but they'll be there all the same.' Look at it a little more deeply, and that is how *History* goes. Is it perhaps only Shakespeare's sense of fitness that makes his end so inconclusive, so unsatisfying? Because history does not end conclusively? Look at it like that, and the play not only takes on more meaning, but ends in utter blackness. To say that that was the outcome of 'feeling life strongly' would stamp me as a pessimist. Yet is it not the outcome of feeling history strongly? of a strong feeling for *political* life, epitomized in a Roman example? That is the approach I make to the play. It is a History, and about the historic process. It is political. And, being both these things, it makes intellectual demands which cause people to find it (in T. S. Eliot's phrase) 'not as "interesting" as *Hamlet*'.[1]

By 'political' I do not mean the class-war, nor even narrowly the Tudor system of God-ordained order. I mean *Coriolanus* plays on political feeling: the capacity to be not only intellectually, but emotionally and purposively, engaged by the management of public affairs; the businesses of groups of men in (ordered) communities; the contrivance or maintenance of agreement; the establishment of a will-in-common; and all the exercises of suasion, pressure, concession and compromise which achieve that *will* (a mind to *do*) in place of a chaos of confused appetencies. I have the impression that many who believe they

[1] He says this in the context of the comment that *Coriolanus* is, 'with *Antony and Cleopatra,* Shakespeare's most assured artistic success'. (*Hamlet*: *Selected Essays,* p. 144.)

feel strongly about politics (in the sense of this party or that) have but little of this 'political feeling' I am trying to suggest to you. They find it easy to back a 'side' (as if at a Cup Final), but not to feel about what makes a 'side' an entity—as the result or resultant of the forces of many separate wills. In the extreme case, such people are 'partisans' with no sense of State whatever. No, more than that: they lack all sense of party as an organic thing; for they desire the 'victory' of their party, and desire it so childishly, that, if they had the power, they would destroy the very principle by which party exists: the recognition of conflict and uncertainty in human minds, confronted with the complexities and uncertainties of human events. The partisan would destroy all opposed groups. That is, he would see complex human situations and eventualities only in his own terms.[1] That is, see them only simplified to his one-eyed creed. And that is, not see them at all. His assumption is that, given the power, right action is *easy*. All history refutes that. As W. Macneile Dixon said (on tragedy), 'In this incalculable world, to act and to blunder are not two, but one.'[2]

The political feeling of *Coriolanus* is different: utterly so. It concerns you (if at all) with the workings of men's wills in the practical management of affairs; with the making (by some), the manipulation (by others) of 'scenes', emotional eruptions of individual or group will; with all that unstable, shifting, trustless, feckless, foolish-shrewd, canny, short-sighted, self-seeking, high-minded, confused, confusing *matter* which makes up a State's state of mind; with all that can be made—but only through feeling—its determined will. Lack of feeling about such things means that much of the play seems frozen. For there lies its excitement. If you cannot be excited about what happens to the Roman State (a branch or *exemplum* of what happens in *States*), then you cannot feel the play. For it is a kind of excitement very different from that generated by 'What happens to George?'

[1] Like Brutus and Sicinius with the slave who brings the bad news from Antium: they want him whipped until he shares their desire to deny the inconvenient facts.

[2] *Tragedy*, 1924, p. 136.

The advantage of such an approach—'political' in the sense of the word in Aristotle's *Politics*—is that it leads you out of any academic or antiquarian restrictions, without landing you in the troubles which arise from prejudices about democracy imported from the nineteenth century or later. The terms in which the mob is described need not worry you. 'The mutable rank-scented many', 'the beast with many heads': those are Elizabethan commonplaces. The root phrase was Horace's (*belua multorum capitum*), and that was not original; a Stoic, Ariston of Chios, called the People *πολυκέφαλον θηρίον*; and versions and variants can be found in Bacon, Chapman, Dekker, Marston, Massinger, Middleton, Ford and (as we should expect) Beaumont and Fletcher. To get indignant with Shakespeare for such expressions is quixotic absurdity. He did not insult his audience, for the simple reasons that they knew nothing of voters' vanity, and *did* know, quite certainly, that they were *not* a mob. Yet, when I say that, do not imagine that a man does not *mean* a 'commonplace', merely because it is a commonplace. The many-headedness of those expressions is, surely, a measure of Shakespeare's fear: his fear of disorder, civil commotion, the disintegrated State. I shall return to that point.

The other advantage of responding to political feeling in the play is that we need not freeze it to a rigid Tudor-myth pattern of order. That is, we need not narrow it to what it doubtless showed to many *c.* 1607–8: an exposition of the evils which arise in the God-ordained microcosmic State when degree is neglected; when pride and Luciferian ambition make a great soldier into a 'limb diseased' of the body-politic; and when subjects attempt to judge what rulers are good for them—which is (as the 33rd Homily said, in a very convenient phrase too) 'as though the foot must judge of the head: an enterprise very heinous, and must needs breed rebellion'. That is by far the easiest way to systematize or pattern the play. Make the Fable of the Belly the key; turn all to Tudor-political moral allegory; throw in all the images of the body, disease, physic; and it all comes out pat. But you will have lodged the play back in Tudor distances, stopped all live political feeling, and set yourself the task of imaginatively thinking about the State solely in terms which can mean nothing whatever to your political self—unless you are highly eccentric and an anachronism in the twentieth century.

None the less, some imaginative attempt of that kind must be made; for the explicit political principles in the play are mainly put into the mouth of Coriolanus; and particularly in III. i., where he makes what is in effect a single political utterance, though in several parts. He says that the power of the people has increased, and must be diminished; the Senators have nourished the cockle of rebellion by the corn-dole: made themselves no better than plebeians to let these Tribunes play the Senator with their 'absolute "shall" '; the people think that concessions have been made through fear; no stable or ordered policy can come from direction by ignorant numbers through 'voices' (votes); and the State is ruined and disintegrated unless this power of disordering policy and vetoing wise decisions is taken away from them. No statement of policy could be more sincere: none less well-timed. It is Marcius's 'tragic blunder' (the Aristotelian *ἁμαρτία*) to state these convictions when he does. Yet so far as Shakespeare tells us what is right for the State in the play, there we have it. We may dislike it: we can say it belongs to a past age (and that Charles Stuart lost his head because he did not see that that age was past); we can say that we dislike the man who speaks (and there is no reason that I can see to *like* Coriolanus at any stage of the play). But the personality of Caius Marcius is one thing, and the convictions of Coriolanus are quite another. The rightness of a man's ideas or convictions is not affected by his unpleasantness; *or* by his popularity, his 'popular "shall" '. Indeed, being right is rarely too conducive to popularity. What is amiss with demagogy, but that it confuses popularity (what people like hearing) with rightness (expediency)? What do Brutus and Sicinius display, but just that?

In considering what Shakespeare gave Coriolanus to think right, we cannot overlook the fact that in May 1607 there was an insurrection which began in Northamptonshire and soon spread to other counties. It was a peasant insurrection; and partly about corn—anyway, about food. It was mainly against enclosures; but the engrossing of corn was a simultaneous grievance: an endemic economic evil of the day. The insurrection of the *Romans*, as told by Plutarch, was about *usurers* (they get a line at I. i. 79; but nobody would see it unless told to look for it). I wish no emphasis on Shakespeare's role as investor in malt. I only say: There were these risings, they kept happening in Elizabethan times; and if you ask what is his fear of the mob and disorder, it is answered at once in Marcius's mouth:

> my soul aches
> To know, when two authorities are up,
> Neither supreme, how soon confusion
> May enter 'twixt the gap of both and take
> The one by th'other. (III. i. 108 f.)

Taking that with what we find elsewhere, in this and other plays, I cannot doubt that those lines are heart-felt. They are (for once) what William Shakespeare also thought—in 1607. It follows that we must swallow our democracy, and, if we would grasp the play, accept it that the political convictions of Marcius are *right*.

The personality of Caius Marcius, his attempts to manage men everywhere but on the battlefield, are, you may say, wrong throughout. But his convictions about the State are good and right, however impolitically he may phrase or time them. There you have a tragic clash: the basis of a political tragedy, not a Tudor morality. And to achieve that, Shakespeare had to twist his source, for he and Plutarch are entirely at odds.

Plutarch has a real sense of democracy, and his Coriolanus is an ill-educated man, suffering from being brought up by a widow (and 'spoilt'), till by natural arrogance and wilfulness he is made quite incapable of any right ideas in communal life. He suffers from what Plato called 'solitariness'—whereby, from self-opinion and an obstinate mind, men 'remaine without companie, and forsaken of all men' (North's *Plutarch*, ii. 160). The charge that Marcius planned 'to take the soveraine authoritie out of the peoples handes' means nothing in the Shakespearian scheme of things. Shakespeare cannot conceive of sovereign power in the hands of the people. Thus the fact that they go on strike, so that the Senate cannot raise armies; and that the Roman way of life gives them a right to the exercise of their own wills through their elected representatives: all that is suppressed or missed by Shakespeare. In simplifying and Elizabethanizing his source, Plutarch's *Life*, he misses the point. But he gives it another, and quite different one, of his own: about history, and the valuations of men in the ceaseless Heraclitean flux of the drama of power.

Let me take but a single example of the peculiar clashes we can feel in the person of Caius Marcius. Mainly, Shakespeare views him with detachment. And yet he has achieved an amazing imaginative triumph in the affair of the Consulship: in his penetration to the very feel and surge of patrician hauteur, in all its passionate wilfulness, its physical loathing of the rubs and smarms of the 'democratic' bowling-green, where every Jack is there to be kissed by his would-be master. Do not jump to wild conclusions about my politics. Surely any man of any dignity must feel something base in the pranks that men (apparently) must employ to get the good opinion—and the vote—of other men? If so, there is a comical rightness in old Volumnia's image for the way he is to behave:

> Now humble as the ripest mulberry
> That will not hold the handling.[1] (III. ii. 79)

It is a derogatory image, worthy of Ben Jonson; and in its context, a satiric comment on all political candidates. Is there not ethical rightness, too, in Marcius's sudden revulsion against playing the male harlot to catch votes, piping like a eunuch, smiling like a knave, and whining for a hand-out like a beggar?

[1] Stratford, 1952, cut these lines. Is even Shakespeare's mulberry-tree forgotten there?

I will not do't,
Lest I surcease to honour mine own truth,
And by my body's action teach my mind
A most inherent baseness. (III. ii. 120)

He is excessive, no doubt. But if there is some truth and honourable rightness there, then so much the greater the conflict: the conflict proper to a political tragedy.

I shall not analyse his character; but these few comments seem worth offering. Marcius's pride and arrogance need no examples. But the comic touch that that kind of self-greatness invites is by no means absent from the play. It is nonsense to call it a satire—as O. J. Campbell [1] did—yet throughout there are deft touches of ironical suggestion that strike the iron demi-god between the joints of the harness. The sadistic ways of Marcius junior with unamenable butterflies are neatly pointed home by his mother's 'One on's father's moods.' (I. iii. 66.) Shakespeare is keenly interested in this terrifying man, and certainly not standing aloof to condemn his sinful pride; yet he is aware of a potential absurdity. Or, put another way, he is aware of the *precariousness* of this self-greatness. Marcius's rages totter on the edge of a line which Jonson would have pushed them over—into ridicule. And when Menenius is putting the fear of the demi-god into the Tribune Sicinius for the last time, this Jonsonian topple does occur, revealing a grotesquely comic aspect of the bogey-man which had been kept under till then:

> The tartness of his face sours ripe grapes; when he walks, he moves like an engine and the ground shrinks before his treading. He is able to pierce a corslet with his eye, talks like a knell, and his hum is a battery. (V. iv. 17 f.)

We laugh—at the scared Tribunes, or at Menenius's *Schadenfreude*; but the comment still rebounds on Marcius. It is a queer preparation for the death of the tragic hero.

This comic irony is paralleled by the ironies of the major political scenes, where we watch great events being determined;

[1] *Shakespeare's Satire*, 1943.

yet watch them with some infiltration of an awareness that there is a preposterous unreasonableness about the ways in which the destinies of peoples are settled: much rather by the shortcomings and littlenesses of men than by anything great about them. It is an awareness of potential absurdity (as in the Galley-scene in *Antony and Cleopatra*). Our reaction may be only *discomfort*: it depends on one's ironic capacity. Pursue that irony—present all through Act III.—and another aspect of Marcius is found: one near the heart of his tragedy. It is an irony of frustration; and when I hit on that phrase, I almost find it all prefigured in the little incident in I. ix. 79 f. when, after the battle, he asks for the life of the poor man who was his host at Corioli. Cominius, as General, gives him it at once; but what happens?

> *Lartius:* Marcius, his name?
> *Cor:* By Jupiter, forgot!

No such forgetting in Plutarch. It is Shakespeare's invention. 'New-made honour doth forget men's names', he wrote in *King John*. The man's self-greatness frustrates himself, his own good aims, endangering not merely life but honour. As here.[1]

Now look at Marcius as a political force. He has had, from Volumnia's upbringing and from active life, the profoundest concern for the Roman State: not merely as conqueror, but from his feelings for law and order ('*Tu regere imperio populos Romane memento*'). But his very nature, passionate and wilful, makes it impossible for him to contrive or carry out those things which will maintain the unity of the State, that very unity he values so highly, 'that integrity which should become't': the source of any man's (or any group's) power to make the State do good.

All this gives Menenius his place in the pattern: Menenius whom Shakespeare *made* from two lines in North's *Plutarch*: 'certain of the pleasantest old men, and the most acceptable to the people. Of those Menenius Agrippa was he, who was sent for chief man.' And that, with the fable of the Belly, is all.

[1] Stratford, 1952, cut this incident!

Shakespeare did the rest: to give his play a humorous, ironical, experienced, sensible, critical commentator; and, simultaneously, in the Roman political world, an 'anti-type' and counterpoise to everything that is Marcius.

Menenius is much more than a comedian. He is 'humorous' (both in the Elizabethan and our senses), but a 'humorous *patrician*': a mocker, but one who can 'spend my malice in my breath'; and he spends or vents it largely in irony, covering it with an air of sorely-tried moderation and good nature; so that even in rebuke, he implies that it is all really the other man's fault, for being so unreasonable. (e.g. at IV. vi. 115 f.) He is a conciliator, aims at political compromise, but is not a weak old man. He handles the rebellious mob skilfully, and is apt with hecklers:

> *1st Cit.:* What could the belly answer?
> *Menenius:* I will tell you;
> If you'll bestow a small—of what you have little—
> Patience awhile, you'st hear the belly's answer.
> (I. i. 122–4)

The rhythm that Shakespeare gives those lines *is* Menenius (or one side of him). So is it earlier, when at I. i. 106 Shakespeare gives him the only belch in English blank verse: the

> kind of smile,
> Which ne'er came from the lungs, but even thus—

These touches show the politician as well as the 'humorous' man. As politician Menenius is able to move with the dialectic of events. He is pliable, but like the reed in the fable; Caius Marcius is the oak. All through the central Act III. he is saying things like 'Be calm, be calm'; 'Well, well, no more of that' (III. i. 115, on Coriolanus's corn-speech); 'Come, enough.' But his 'mildly . . . calmly . . . temperately' is not the positive side of him. That comes out in his bulletin-phrase after the riot in III. i.: 'This must be patch'd/ With cloth of any colour.' There speaks a mind which is able to keep before itself the 'political feeling', or emotion of political life, which I tried to outline to you: a mind which does not lose the great aim of integrity in the State, whatever immediate personal provocation it may encounter. Menenius is, therefore, a direct contrast to Caius Marcius, the hyper-sensitive battleship, so strangely constructed that though no weapon can harm it seriously, there is an open way to the magazine for the word '*traitor*', which blows the whole fighting-machine to ruins. Say that to Coriolanus (and the Tribunes know this), and his private honour makes him lose every thought of the integrity of the State. He becomes like Achilles in *Troilus and Cressida*:

> Imagin'd worth
> Holds in his blood such swol'n and hot discourse
> That 'twixt his mental and his active parts
> Kingdom'd Achilles in commotion rages,
> And batters down himself. (II. iii. 167–71)

Indeed, the Marcius-Menenius pattern repeats—in a very different tone—much of the Achilles-Ulysses pattern in that earlier play; as it also repeats the themes of power, honour and war. But Menenius is not lacking in feeling (as Ulysses is, perhaps). He is quite sincere in saying that he too would put his armour on, before Coriolanus should thus stoop to the herd. But in between comes the all-important proviso:

> but that
> The violent fit o' th' time craves it as physic
> For the whole state. (III. 2. 32)

That is: he would *not* put his armour on to fight the plebs. He accepts the necessity of 'stooping', for an aim beyond self: beyond himself or Marcius's self.

With those few passages I have examined, you have the central significance of Menenius. His love of Marcius; his breathless tumble of words in welcoming his warrior back from victory; his pathos; his comically cruel treatment by the sentries: all those have their importance. But they do not give his main significance in the tragic pattern. To develop that further I should have to examine the other counterpart-*cum*-contrast to Menenius: Volumnia. Throughout, Caius Marcius hangs between the influence of the two. They are opposites; and the irony is that they both desire the same victory for him. Only it never could be the same: for in political life, means determine ends, and the 'identical' end, won by opposite means, is quite another end.

Menenius's significance is one thread to take hold of the tragic pattern by: he is (what Marcius is not) a political mind which moves with the dialectic of events. As he can *think* (and will) *dialectically*, he remains true to the major loyalties: Rome and himself. Marcius, the man of 'principle', does not. In this play, Bradley's generalization is entirely true: 'To meet these circumstances something is required which a smaller man might have given, but which the hero cannot give.'[1] Thus Marcius's 'greatness' is fatal to him. But *is* it great? I do not propose to answer that: only to insist that the comic ironies of the action (and phrasing) push the question at us; and that reflection offers the paradox that Menenius is 'greater' in mind than Marcius.

The valuation of Marcius is, however, offered by Shakespeare himself: in Aufidius's speech at the end of Act IV. (IV. vii. 35 f.), a speech which perplexed Coleridge utterly.[2] It is, as he rightly says, 'out of character'; but in it Shakespeare sums up Marcius. He was first 'a noble servant' to Rome; but whether from pride, or defect of judgement, or unadaptable rigidity of nature (which made him attempt to manage peace as he did war)—and he had 'spices' of all these—he came to be feared, hated and banished. That he epitomizes any of these faults is explicitly denied. But two of them particularly concern what I used Menenius to focus: the qualities of a political mind, able to remain effective in a changing world of events. Whatever pride may be, rigidity (however high-principled) and 'defect of judge-

[1] *Shakespearean Tragedy*, p. 21.

[2] *Lectures on Shakespeare*, 1818. Coleridge cherished the hope that he would become wiser, and discover some profound excellence in what he could only see as an imperfection; but I think he could never see it except as 'out of character'.

ment' are the opposites of those qualities. But Aufidius (and Shakespeare) adds:

> So our virtues
> Lie in th' interpretation of the time.

Now that, in one and a half lines, gives the essence of the play. Run over the whole action, act by act, and each is seen as an 'estimate' or valuation of Marcius: enemy of the people—demigod of war—popular hero home in triumph—Consul-elect—and then (through his assertion of what he always *had* asserted) public enemy and banished man, 'a lonely dragon' (IV. i. 30). Throughout all this, he himself is almost an absolute *constant*. Then, on his way to Aufidius at Antium, we have his one soliloquy:

> O world, thy slippery turns! Friends now fast sworn,
> Whose double bosoms seems to wear one heart,
> Whose hours, whose bed, whose meal and exercise
> Are still together, who twin, as 'twere, in love
> Unseparable, shall within this hour,
> On a dissension of a doit, break out
> To bitterest enmity. (IV. iv. 12 f.)

It is strangely reminiscent of the sad midnight reflections of Henry IV, looking back over Richard's time; yes, and thinking about history. But what is Marcius's speech about, if not that same world of history, where all is change, nothing absolute; where all 'virtues' lie in the interpretation of the time, and all times lie about the virtues they have lost the use for?

This is very near to what Ulysses tells Achilles about Time's wallet and the 'one touch of nature' that 'makes the whole world kin'. The 'touch' is an incessant writing-off of past values, an interminable revaluation-series. This is what happens in the historical process: history always *goes on*; goes on, if you like, to the sad and cynical tune of *Frankie and Johnnie*:

> This story has no moral,
> This story has no end,

> This story only goes to show
> That there ain't no good in men . . .

Or shall we say, 'There is not enough good of an effective kind, in men as they appear in the historical process'? Be that as it may, this is what happens in that process. History always goes on; and in this play even Bradley could not say that re-established order and rightness are left to console us. There is no Albany; not even a Fortinbras or a Malcolm; the survivor is Tullus Aufidius.

Coriolanus is the last and greatest of the Histories. It is Shakespeare's only great political play; and it is slightly depressing, and hard to come to terms with, because it is *political tragedy*. The idea of the State runs through it:

> the Roman state; whose course will on
> The way it takes, cracking ten thousand curbs . . .
> (I. i. 67)

And ten thousand men. Yet it is *not* the ideal or cosmic state of the other plays: rather, an abstraction from an organism, or a real state. Real states are dynamic: hence the constant irony in the play, especially of Marcius and Aufidius saying what they *will* do, and then not doing it or doing it in a way that neither had foreseen.[1] Hence too the changing valuations of the same Marcius by Aufidius, or by the comic servants in Antium, who snub him muffled and then say they knew all along he was Somebody. This re-estimation of Marcius goes on to the bitter

[1] Examples are Marcius's statements about what he will do to Aufidius:

> Were half to half the world by th'ears, and he
> Upon my party, I'd revolt, to make
> Only my wars with him (I. i. 231–3);

and

> At Antium lives he? . . .
> I wish I had a cause to seek him there,
> To oppose his hatred fully (III. i. 18–20).

Others are: Aufidius's early threat to murder Marcius 'were it/At home . . . even there/Against the hospitable canon' (I. x. 24–6); and Marcius's assurance to his mother, as he leaves Rome in exile, that he 'Will or exceed the common or be caught/With cautelous baits and practice' (IV. i. 32–3). Here the irony is double: both things happen, but in no foreseeable sense.

end: to Aufidius's stepping off his stabbed body—'My rage is gone'—and calling for a hero's funeral. 'O world, thy slippery turns!'

But, in a sense, Caius Marcius *Coriolanus* was dead already. That fine speech which Shakespeare made by transforming North—

> My name is Caius Marcius, who hath done
> To thee particularly, and to all the Volsces,
> Great hurt and mischief (IV. v. 65 f.):

what is it but the equivalent of a *dying*-speech, a summary of expiring greatness? 'Only that name remains' is no more than truth: he is no more *Coriolanus*—as Aufidius will tell him, before he stabs him.

The final depressing paradox is that Marcius's unyieldingness and would-be self-sufficiency make him so pliant to force of circumstance. All told, he is as unstable and trustless as those whom he abused with:

> you are no surer, no,
> Than is the coal of fire upon the ice
> Or hailstone in the sun . . .
> . . . . . . and your affections are
> A sick man's appetite . . . (I. i. 170 f.)

Shakespeare spares him that last twist of bitter reflection: the words were spoken to the mob. But the reflection is there, in the play. And on my view, it ends—as J. W. N. Sullivan says that Beethoven's *Coriolan* ends—'in utter darkness': the darkness of history, from which Shakespeare finally absconded—with *Cymbeline*. I cannot accept Bradley's hint to make this the bridge-head towards the Romances: but I rejoice to concur with Mr. Eliot: *one of* Shakespeare's most assured artistic successes—as perfect in control as *1 Henry IV*.

13

Shakespearian Tragedy

CAN WE arrive at a conception of Shakespearian Tragedy? The easy way is *a priori*: not to arrive *at*, but to arrive *with* one ready-made; to start with previous notions derived from the Greek, from Aristotle (or from Bradley, whom many still mistake for a pseudonym for Aristotle). If we take the Aristotelean previous notion, there is nothing to add to what Mr. Trotter says in Shaw's *Fanny's First Play*:

> If you had been classically educated . . .
>
> *Fanny:* But I have.
>
> *Trotter:* Pooh! Cambridge! If you had been educated at Oxford, you would know that the definition of a play has been settled exactly and scientifically for two thousand, two hundred and sixty years.

As I was not educated 'classically', I find that unacceptable.

The testing of Shakespearian drama by the *Poetics* is recognizably a consequence of the eighteenth century: part and parcel of their demonstrations of how much that is 'classical' was to be found in this apparent Goth. This is not to say that Shakespearian tragedy cannot be seen more clearly by contrasting Greek and English, on the basic assumption that tragedy is a rare literary product, cast up only in *some* cultures or cultural stages; and that there is (if no more) a 'tragic sense' in common between Sophocles, Racine, Ibsen, Pirandello and Shakespeare. But it cannot be assumed that Aristotle's generalizations are relevant to Elizabethan-Jacobean tragic writing. There is no evidence that Sidney knew the *Poetics*. There is apparent evidence that Shakespeare did not know much about Aristotle, who is mentioned twice: once as pre-Homeric (*Troilus and Cressida*, II. ii.); once by Tranio as the opposite to Ovid. And only once does any Elizabethan mention *catharsis*: and then only to mock at it.[1] All this (so far as Elizabethan popular stage-writing goes) can be dismissed with Dryden: 'It is not enough that Aristotle has said so, for Aristotle drew his models of tragedy from Sophocles and Euripides; and, if he had seen ours, might have changed his mind.'[2]

The other way—*a posteriori*—is to find out what the Elizabethans (including Shakespeare) had to say about tragedy; and to add to that by inference from their practice, whether with words or with the names of plays.

Shakespeare uses the word *tragedy* eleven times: once in mere jest (*A Midsummer-Night's Dream*); twice merely descriptively (*Hamlet*); of the eight occasions left, only one usage, in *Henry V*, is later than *Richard III*. *Tragic* (eight times) and *tragical* (five times) add another thirteen usages, of which eight are in early plays. Thus of twenty-four occurrences, fifteen are as early as *Richard III*, and three are in jest (*A Midsummer-Night's Dream*). We can say, then, that over 70 per cent are very early; the three usages in *Hamlet* only concern the Players' repertoire; and that leaves but three for plays anywhere near the Tragedies in time of composition. *Othello* is the only tragedy in which any of the three words is found; and 'the tragic loading of this bed' did not mean, to the Elizabethans, anything as weighty as we feel from it.[3]

Tragedy, in Shakespeare's own usage, seems to mean 'an alarming calamity, usually bloody, and often determined by the plotted designs of someone'. When not plotted, it means simply 'a calamitous fall'; and can be applied to defeat in battle (as used by, e.g., Warwick at Towton, or the Archbishop of Canterbury on the Black Prince in France). It is associated with 'dire induc-

[1] Robert Peterson in *Galateo of Manners and Behaviours*, 1576: see J. W. H. Atkins, *English Literary Criticism of the Renaissance*, 1947, pp. 223–4.

[2] *Heads of an answer to Rymer's Remarks on the Tragedies of the last Age.*

[3] cf. the 'stern and tragical' look of Winchester in *1 Henry VI*, where 'tragical' means 'murderous'.

tion' and 'prologue'; and 'this scene of rude impatience' is the same as 'an act of tragic violence' (Queen Elizabeth in *Richard III*, II, ii. 39). In short, it seems to refer exclusively to the kind of 'tragic' of Kyd: not to modern critical associations at all (although the newspaper-sense is represented: Salisbury [*1 Henry VI*] is shot by cannon—has his eye out and his cheek missing—and that is 'this woeful tragedy'). The only usage with any hint of wider, more philosophical implications is in *Titus Andronicus*: Titus asks why Nature made 'so foul a den' as the place where Lavinia was ravished, 'unless the gods delight in tragedies'.

The next place to try is the Stationers' Register, where the names of plays were entered before legitimate printing. It is arguable that the players would be reasonably careful to put down the right titles, and that (though Shakespeare may have had no hand in it) what we can read *was* what the plays were called.[1] The Stationers' Register has *Richard III* and *Richard II* both down as tragedies; *Hamlet* (1602: Robertes's entry) is 'the Revenge of Hamlett Prince Denmarke'; *King Lear* (1607), the 'history of Kinge Lear'; *Antony and Cleopatra* (1608), 'a book called Antony and Cleopatra'; *Othello* (in the Register of 1621), 'The Tragedie of Othello, the moore of Venice'.

If we consult the early Quartos, printed during Shakespeare's lifetime, we find the same uncertainty. *Romeo and Juliet* (Q2: 1599) is the 'most Excellent and lamentable Tragedie'; but *Hamlet* (1604) 'The Tragicall Historie' (as was Q1), and *King Lear* (1608) the 'true chronicle Historie'. In the Folio we have not only the presence of *Troilus and Cressida* between the Histories and Tragedies (which may be explainable), but also *Cymbeline* as a tragedy, fully entitled.[2]

Now we might *guess* from all this, that by *c.* 1599 Shakespeare was aware that he was writing something different from what had *been* 'tragedy' at the time when he most used the word in

[1] With the Folio we can be certain of no such thing. The date is 1623; and the editors are committed to their tripartite division of the canon.

[2] The very least I can infer from that, is that it was never called a comedy (conceivably it was a 'true chronicle Historie', and analogy with *King Lear* did the rest: both being stories of ancient Britain).

his plays, five to ten years earlier. Accordingly, he avoided the word in his Tragedies. This is only a guess; but better than supposing that he had no conception of tragedy, or only a crude one. He must at any rate have been perfectly aware that he was writing something totally unlike the most respected kind of tragedy; the highbrow kind that imitated Seneca directly (or at one remove), with a Chorus and at least a compromise with the neo-classical principles which required that the time represented should be as near as possible to a single day, that the scene should remain as far as possible one and the same throughout, and that scenes of violence should be described rather than presented (in keeping with the Horatian *Ne pueros coram populo Medea trucidet*). About this kind of tragedy there is no lack of first-hand Elizabethan information; in fact, most of the contemporary tragedy-criticism is about *form*. Sidney and Jonson give representative comments; and their main relevance to Shakespeare is that they show what he must have known he was *not* attempting to do.

Not that Jonson was the strict pedant he is often supposed to be. In 'To the Readers', before *Sejanus*, he admits the play's classical deficiencies (in the unity of time, and there being no Chorus), but continues that it is not 'needful' nor perhaps 'possible in these our times, and to such auditors as commonly things are presented, to observe the old state and splendour of dramatic poems, with preservation of any popular delight'. Webster says much the same, but ill-temperedly, in *The White Devil*. It would be no good his offering 'the most sententious tragedy . . . observing all the critical laws': the breath of the 'uncapable multitude' would poison it. And he quotes Horace's Epode about the horrid garlic—*O dura messorum ilia*—and rounds off the paragraph with a further civility about giving pigs what is meet for pigs.

I mention both these views (*a*) because Webster is a dramatist of the 'school of Shakespeare'; (*b*) because there is nothing to show that Shakespeare was dissatisfied with what he was making of the changing 'tragic-history' form; and (*c*) to emphasize that there were two forms of tragedy[1], and that Shakespeare's choice was consistently for the *lower*. Consistently: because there is no sign that he ever tried to tighten his form in tragedy; for his last tragedy (*Antony and Cleopatra*) and his greatest triumph (*King Lear*) are the loosest-woven of all. What 'lower' means is shown by a passage of 1604. Anthony Scoloker is writing an 'Epistle' as preface to his *Daiphantus*. He wants it to please all; and, to express this, he uses first an allusion to highbrow reading, and then turns to something more vulgar and popular: something which appealed to those who were not up to Sidney's *Arcadia*. This is how he puts it:

> It should be like the *Neuer-too-well read Arcadia*, where the *Prose and Verce* (*Matter* and *Words*) are like his *Mistresses* eyes, one still excelling another and without Corriuall: or to come home to the vulgars *Element*, like *Friendly Shakespeares Tragedies*, where the *Commedian* rides, when the *Tragedian* stands on Tip-toe: Faith it should please all, like Prince *Hamlet*.

But though Shakespeare worked in 'the vulgars Element', that does not mean he therefore abandoned what high-sententious tragedy had to offer. What that was, to the Elizabethans, Sidney and Jonson can tell us; and I see no reason to suppose that Shakespeare could have taken an entirely different view of what tragic writing included (the most important differences concern what orthodox tragedy would *exclude*).

Jonson includes among the 'offices of a tragic writer', 'truth of argument, dignity of persons, gravity and height of elocution, fulness and frequency of sentence' (*Sejanus*: 'To the Readers'). In modern terms we should say: a veracious *plot*;[2]

[1] i.e. excluding Latin performances and unstageworthy sedulous apings of them.

[2] I say 'a veracious plot' to avoid the difficult question of what was regarded as 'truth of argument' in a play. Jonson presumably means the same as 'my integrity in the story', which he 'shows' by footnote-quotations from Latin historians. It is obvious that Shakespeare attempted no such historical accuracy; and that he must often have been aware of how he altered alleged records of fact (e.g., in *Macbeth* and *Coriolanus*). It is arguable that he was conscious, in this, of his own efforts to reach at a higher, more general human truth, obscured by chroniclers and historians: what Sidney called the 'golden' world of poetry, as

great or distinguished *characters*; seriousness and elevation of *style*; and a richness of sound moral teaching, memorably expressed.

Sidney is relevant, for all that he does not write for 'the vulgars Element'. In his *Apologie for Poetrie* he has three main criteria of tragedy: (1) In his criticism of *Gorboduc*: it should keep the classical forms (i.e. the unities), and should teach morality 'most delightfully'—that being 'the very end of Poesie', i.e. 'the end of well dooing and not of well knowing onely'. (2) it 'maketh Kinges feare to be Tyrants, and Tyrants manifest their tirannicall humors'; (3) it 'teacheth the uncertainety of this world' by 'sturring the affects of admiration and commiseration': i.e. it makes *felt* the 'mutability-ethic' of the Middle Ages, and especially through *exempla* of men-of-power (cf. his quotation from Seneca's *Oedipus*: *Qui . . . duro imperio regit/ Timet timentes, metus in auctorem redit*).

The first of these principles adds nothing to what we have had from Jonson. Modern inquiries have shown that there is far more 'notable moralitie' in *Richard III*, *Julius Caesar*, *Macbeth*, *Coriolanus*, than used to be supposed. But the moral framework of the Histories (Order, degree, the magical King-figure, the order of the State as a branch of Natural Order) is less than the *moral pattern* of *Macbeth*; and in *Hamlet* and *King Lear* the extractable Elizabethan morality is trivial beside the total effect of the play: even if we do not feel that this total effect *runs contrary* to what we suppose an Elizabethan would take for its moral teaching.[1]

The second is slightly comical, if we think of a row of stalls

compared with the 'brazen' that Nature gives us. But it seems quite certain that the *audience* knew of no such refinements. The poets may have had their own 'philosophical' standard of 'truth'; but their hearers in the theatre assumed that the staged events really happened. As Hamlet told the Court, 'This play is the image of a murder done in Vienna . . . the story is extant, and written in very choice Italian.'

[1] One has to guess. But I cannot see that *King Lear*—seen from the Elizabethan moral point of view—says anything very different from what *Gorboduc* did. Both are about kings who split up the State, destroyed the magic bond of subordination, and let loose unnaturalness upon themselves, their children and their people.

full of kings being shown what happens to tyrants. It might apply to *Richard III*, but is too crude for *Richard II*. 'Tyrants' manifesting 'tirannicall humors' is more promising—if translated. 'Tyrant' is a Senecan word, and by it Sidney means the kind of character (Atreus, Oedipus, Lycus, Eteocles) who is, to Stoics, an *exemplum* of tyrannic '*passion*' (will-to-power; will to revenge; passionate will, as in Phaedra; madness).

> The overgrowth of some complexion
> Oft breaking down the pales and forts of reason

might well be applied to Othello (and to Iago too?), to Coriolanus, and perhaps to Romeo and to Antony: all are in some sense obsessed or infatuated men. So is Timon: victim of two consecutive and opposite obsessions. But the view (Masefield's) that the tragedies are tragedies of obsession is again too crude: though it does show how easily Sidney's Senecan-extracted fear of passion can be made Christian for those who are neither Senecan nor Stoical. If Shakespeare started with some such conception of tragedy, he not only went far beyond it by 1600: he was doing so even in *Richard III*, where that very sardonic humorist has (for all his naked villainy) an engaging gusto and a daring resoluteness which run counter to the moralists' requirements. Sidney's 'tirannicall humors' does not signify anything at all like the sarcastic, grimly ironical, often profane sense of humour which Richard displays. The Senecan 'tyrants' are, in fact, if not mad, as humourless as madmen.

Sidney's last principle is the widest and the best. 'The uncertainety of this world', the demonstration of what weak foundations gilded roofs may rest on: that touches the old primitive distrust of Nature. Both Stoic and Christian have capitalized it as 'world-contempt', yet it remains primitive still. There is a murmur behind calamity which tells us, in the words of Lafeu, that 'we have our philosophical persons to make modern [commonplace] and familiar things supernatural and causeless'. And what follows? 'Hence is it that we make trifles of terrors, ensconcing ourselves into seeming knowledge, when we should submit ourselves to an unknown fear.'[1] That 'unknown fear' visits us in our own catastrophes. 'Why this, to me?' 'Why should it happen as it did? Why just then?' And the *sense* of tragic poetry is there, though the words are lacking: 'I am a man/ More sinned against than sinning'.

It is a manifest quality of Shakespearian tragedy that it visits us with such unknown fears, and in almost as high a degree as if the fates of imaginary creatures were our own. All the tragedies deal with men and women caught in traps of circumstance: though the degree of mere 'accident' varies enormously (e.g., as between Romeo and Macbeth or Coriolanus). So too does the extent to which the hero has made the circumstances in the first place. Hamlet does not make his at all. Richard II has apparently made his. Antony, Macbeth, perhaps Lear, we watch making theirs, almost absolutely. Othello we watch having the circumstances made about him: he stands somewhere between Hamlet and Macbeth. The heroes' characters are partially determinants of their sufferings and destructions; but their ends are either so *different* from their intentions as to *seem* unjust (Romeo, Brutus, Hamlet, Othello), or so entirely excessive in misery that there is no question of 'seeming' about it (Lear, Gloucester). The two most arguably 'just' ends are those of Macbeth and Coriolanus: Macbeth, only if we keep our eyes strictly on the hero (*not* on the ruins around him); in *Coriolanus*, the hero is the only real sufferer.

I take occasion to quote Bradley here. He labours to believe that the gods *are* just: that a moral principle re-establishes itself at the end of *King Lear*; and yet he writes: 'to assert that he deserved to suffer what he did suffer is to do violence not merely to language but to any healthy moral sense'.[2] On the next page he says: 'Let us put aside the ideas of justice and merit . . .'; and I have used Sidney's tragic principles as an approach to Shakespeare, because it seems to me that what Shakespeare had to do was to put aside those ideas, in order to become a Shake-

[1] *All's Well*, II. iii. 1–6.
[2] *Shakespearean Tragedy*, p. 32.

spearian, not an Elizabethan, *tragedian*: a writer of genuine tragedy, not 'moral-tragicall' Histories.

Set beside Elizabethan tragical principles (as in Sidney), Shakespeare's tragedies have rejected the 'Tudor-Christian' conception of a moral and just world. I do not mean that their author has 'accepted' the opposite of that conception: only that it is distanced—like a hypothesis, not a faith. The *personae* themselves, in their suffering and uncertainty, try to jump to superstitious or pessimistic conclusions; and we may be tempted to accept them emotionally: 'There is a divinity that shapes our ends';[1] 'The time is out of joint'; 'It is the very error of the moon'; 'It is the stars'; 'The wheel is come full circle'; 'As flies to wanton boys'; 'O, I am fortune's fool!'; 'the false housewife Fortune.'

But these are not philosophic utterances. 'I see men's judgements are/ A parcel of their fortunes', Enobarbus says. The 'uncertainety of this world' is not only its hidden threats of terrible consequences following from human actions which seemed right (or, at least, quite safe); but the blind, explosive 'spread' of retribution. Witness the fates of Ophelia, Desdemona and Cordelia. Fools, knaves and innocents go the same way, though we feel less about them than about the heroes. County Paris, Polonius, Rosencrantz, Roderigo, Oswald (a servant rather maligned in the interests of sound morality), all die. Cassius, much more on terms with evil than Brutus, shares his fate (and suffers less). Hamlet is destroyed with Claudius, Othello with Iago; Cassio (of doubtful 'daily beauty') escapes; Emilia is killed. This alarmingness of circumstance is only evaded by the theory of 'tragic flaw' or 'tragic weakness'. The theory (extracted from Aristotle) says that the hero's nature is 'flawed' and his fate follows from this excess or deficiency. Its effect is to shift all blame from the universe (or to give that consoling im-

[1] Or 'There is a special providence in the fall of a sparrow', which comes in the very scene where Hamlet says: 'I am constant to my purposes [which he is *not*]; they follow the King's pleasure' (which is true. Claudius *is* being the divinity that shapes his end).

pression),[1] and it is popular enough: both because of the ease with which 'tragic weaknesses' can be diagnosed (or devised) —when we know how the story ends; and, again, because it re-establishes the comforting belief that the universe is moral, and the fates of tragic heroes somehow just.

Take *Othello*. Critics jump to conclude that Othello *was* 'one not easily jealous'; or that he 'loved not wisely, but too well'; or (with Bradley) that 'credulousness, excessive simplicity' must go in the list of 'marked imperfections or defects' which begins with 'irresolution, precipitancy, pride', and ends with 'excessive susceptibility to sexual emotions'.[2] 'Credulousness, excessive simplicity' look all right in the list, till I turn to my texts. I find:

> The Moor is of a free and open nature
> That thinks men honest that but seem to be so;
> And will as tenderly be led by th' nose
> As asses are (I. iii. 393–6);

and remember:

> He, being remiss,
> Most generous, and free from all contriving,
> Will not peruse the foils; (*Hamlet*, IV. iii. 134–6)

and:

> A credulous father! and a brother noble,
> Whose nature is so far from doing harms
> That he suspects none; on whose foolish honesty
> My practices ride easy! (*King Lear*, I. ii. 170–3)

Why are these qualities in Othello, Hamlet, Edgar, to be called 'evil'—even 'in the wide sense of the word'?[3] When Bradley adds, 'Evil exhibits itself everywhere as something negative, barren, weakening, destructive, a principle of death. It isolates, disunites, and tends to annihilate not only its opposite but itself,[4] I have to say that the noble frailties in his list are not 'evils' at

[1] It only gives an impression, because it does not even attempt to answer the question: 'Is there any cause in nature that makes these hard hearts?'
[2] *Shakespearean Tragedy*, pp. 34–5.
[3] Bradley, ibid., p. 35. [4] ibid.

all. He is right enough about the quality of evil in Macbeth or Iago or Goneril; but with the others he has turned a nobility (generosity of mind) into an 'evil', to evade the issue, and to avoid the embarrassing position of Auden's schoolmistress, 'giving the Universe nought for conduct'.

I do not think it an exaggeration to say that to press these patterns of 'tragic weakness' is to destroy tragedy.[1] They reintroduce the Elizabethan moral machinery under various disguises; and, so to speak, go back to *Richard III* and Sidney against the current which took Shakespeare from *Hamlet* to *Macbeth* and *Lear*. The play, in fact, to which the 'tragic weakness' pattern applies neatest, *Timon*, is the most ignored of the later tragedies; and the next nearest to it, *Coriolanus* (where Shakespeare does alter Plutarch to increase Coriolanus's recalcitrant pride), is not commonly bracketed with *Antony and Cleopatra* as 'Shakespeare's most assured artistic success'. None the less, there does seem to be a problem here. Shakespeare wrote these two plays, either before *Antony and Cleopatra* or between that and *Cymbeline* and the Romances. It is possible that they represent a going-back from the tragic conception of *Lear* towards something more moral, simpler and less terrifying: towards the Histories, in fact. Both Timon and Coriolanus are alienated from a *social* world: the universes of Macbeth and Lear shrink to a *πόλις*. Their passions are more like the 'ruling passions' of the eighteenth century.

Shakespeare's conception of tragedy plainly and constantly concerns the man who *is* 'passion's slave'—in the extended, Senecan sense of 'passion'. Hence the distinguishing mark of his emotional effects: that even among his violent contemporaries he is a past-master at scenes of pain. He gives us not only the pure pathos of Lear kneeling before Cordelia, utterly humbled

[1] There is an English complacency which evades the hurting contemplation of misfortune or misery by finding that the victim is to blame (as he may be): to blame for *all* of it. Coleridge knew this very well in Wordsworth, settled, married and a man of propriety and property. If he could have brought that knowledge alive into his criticism of tragedy, 'hamartia-hunting' might have been strangled at birth.

('If you have poison for me I will drink it'), or the rages of Othello, Lear, Antony, Coriolanus; but the immense variety of 'on the torment of the mind to lie/ In restless ecstasy' in Brutus, Hamlet, Othello, Macbeth. Suffering beyond solace, beyond any moral palliation, and suffering because of a human greatness which is great because great in passion: that, above everything else, is central to Shakespeare's tragic conception. 'The man who is not passion's slave' gets his passage in Hamlet's mouth, and the invitation to make Horatio a paragon of animals is duly accepted by your even-tempered Christian. But before we make too much of that, we should call in those others to whom the term applies: Bolingbroke, Octavius, for example; and perhaps we should ask whether, if cool self-management is a virtue, we can exclude Claudius and Iago?

If, then, 'distinction' is Shakespeare's tragic subject—*passional* distinction, and as much *through* suffering as despite it—a phrase of Bradley's casts an immediate light on one essence of that tragic quality. He says that the hero is so circumstanced that his greatness is fatal, adding: 'To meet these circumstances something is required which a smaller man might have given, but which the hero cannot give'.[1] And if you ask what quality that implies in the hero, the answer is *pride*: Renaissance pride, seen as self-greatness. Hence such heroes as Richard III and Macbeth, distinguished in flat defiance of their time's morality; hence too the approach *towards* being tragic figures of all the History kings. The Shakespearian tragic universe is such that mediocrity is pretty safe, for all that 'some innocents escape not the thunderbolt' (as Cleopatra said). I see no sign that Shakespeare has any conception of bourgeois tragedy: to him, I suppose, *Arden of Feversham* (or *Women Beware Women*) was not tragic; for his heroes go beyond something greater than the Common Law, the trap of retribution in domestic crimes.

Much rather, he offers adumbrations of a fundamental antimony. The universe produces human greatness, which is therefore *natural* to it; and yet it is antagonistic to distinction. If we

[1] *Shakespearean Tragedy*, p. 21

approach the tragedies through the Histories, then we must see that, in so far as cosmic order still appears, it has become the *antagonist*. In *Julius Caesar*, *Macbeth* and *Lear*, this is so explicitly. In the Roman plays, the world seems to be conceived as a polity, in which there is, at most, room for one great man—*and*, it would appear, for only certain sorts of greatness (not, for example, for that of Brutus or of Antony). By its destruction and the calm that ensues—if Bradley is right—greatness seems *unnatural* to this world. Virginia Woolf said the same of *The Mayor of Casterbridge*: 'Henchard is pitted, not against another man, but against something outside himself which is opposed to men of his ambition and power.' I had rather she said it of Captain Ahab and *Moby Dick*, but that makes no odds here. We cannot 'accept' this apparent 'unnaturalness' of the qualities we are moved by and admire; and that contradiction is at the root of the 'sense of mystery' which all critics agree to find in Shakespearian tragedy. The emotional experiencing of this universal antinomy is what Aristotle called *φόβος*: the tragic fear which is not self-regarding.

If this view is acceptable, then *Hamlet* ceases to be an awkward and perplexing aberration—as it is, if approached through the Histories. For though Prince Hamlet has had a King-father murdered and a throne usurped, he *never* refers to cosmic order, Divine Kingship or curses on State and posterity. Hamlet is a cosmic non-conformist. If seen as the good mind in an evil world, as alien to it—as *all* the heroes are alien—I see no problem. And indeed *Hamlet's* evil world-frame follows logically on the collapse of the ideal pattern of cosmic order in *Troilus and Cressida*.

I do, however, find the greatest difficulty over Bradley when he tells us (p. 23) that the central tragic feeling is the impression of waste; and then (p. 37) that, by the end of a tragedy, 'it [the moral order] has lost a part of its own substance—a part more dangerous and unquiet, but far more valuable and *nearer to its heart*[1] than that which remains,—a Fortinbras, a Malcolm, an

[1] Not Bradley's italics.

Octavius'. I feel the 'waste'; but my difficulties over that 'nearer to its heart' are insuperable, unless I conclude that the 'moral order' has a *double* heart: i.e. that the universe is quasi-Manichean, and that human greatness (which is *one* God's 'good') is the evil of the *other* God (i.e. the God of order and degree). I cannot think Bradley meant this. Yet such a view can result from seeing Renaissance *virtu* superimposed on Christian order: *Virtu contra Ordinem*. If I do make myself accept Bradley's Hegelian terms, I find myself irreverently remembering Peer Gynt, when he is marooned in Africa and suddenly sees the yacht that has dropped him blow up: 'Ah! God *is* a Father to me after all . . . but He's not what you'd call economical about it!'

But that is not the whole picture. Not only is the vulnerability to fortune of human distinction Shakespeare's theme, its special liability to intense suffering and destruction. He also emphasizes the precariousness of its very *quality* of greatness: of its right to regard, respect, admiration, awe. A regular concomitant of his tragedies is that the pettier and less dignified aspects of heroes and heroines are insisted on; and, more than that, that comic and even farcical scenes, persons and effects are thrust against the main figures and episodes.

I turn back to Jonson and Sidney, and take up my point about 'what orthodox tragedy would *exclude*'. It is what Sidney called 'mungrell Tragy-comedie': the thrusting in of 'Clownes by head and shoulders, to play a part in majesticall matters', clean contrary to the orthodox principle of 'strict separation'. It is, again, what Scoloker meant with his '*Friendly Shakespeares Tragedies*, where the *Commedian* rides, when the *Tragedian* stands on Tip-toe'.

This insistence on the *comic* is entirely absent in *Richard II*; nearly so in *Julius Caesar*; fumbled or uncertain in *Titus Andronicus* and *Romeo and Juliet*: but from *Hamlet* to *Antony and Cleopatra* it is always there, though never constant. It is by no means entirely dependent on conventional clowns. So, although the traditional clown explains its *evolution* as a factor in true-

English tragedy, it cannot be argued that Shakespeare included it simply because the clown had to have a part. Hamlet mad,[1] Ophelia mad and bawdy, Iago cynical, Cleopatra raging or mocking Antony till he looks ridiculous, Menenius, Enobarbus: none of those are clowns' parts.

Again, as can be shown from the Fool's part in *Lear*, the characteristically Shakespearian effects are far less ludicrous than *grotesque*. They *might* be laughable, if they could be noted with a heart devoid of sympathy, but by an intelligence keenly aware of their immense incongruity and of the mocking wit which seems to have devised them. They somewhat resemble tragic irony, of the kind where a man's words seem as if malevolently mis-designed for him, by a witty spirit which foreknows how true they are,[2] but in a sense quite other than he imagines in uttering them:

Macbeth: Is't far you ride? . . . Fail not our feast.
Banquo: My lord, I will not.

Or *Othello*:

If it were now to die,
'Twere now to be most happy; for I fear
My soul hath her content so absolute
That not another comfort like to this
Succeeds in unknown fate.

But in these comic ironies is more of a spirit of witty *rascality*: a sly derisiveness, which not only emphasizes men's blind ignorance of their ends, but seems (by mocking it) to question their intrinsic value—their very quality of distinction. This mockingly *critical* function, which criticizes by making game of what men respect, admire, feel sympathy towards or are drawn to, is expressed in Goethe by Mephistopheles. '*Der Geist der stets ver-*

[1] 'In his shirt' appears to have been the Elizabethan idea: too much for Olivier, that!

[2] Or, of course, how ridiculously *false*, when all the truth (of later events or latent natures) is known. *Coriolanus* has much of this irony: e.g., Aufidius at I. x. 19–27, or Coriolanus himself at I. i. 231. 'Tragic irony' is really verbal *peripeteia*.

neint' ('the spirit that ever denies') he calls himself. But before the Lord Almighty, in the Prologue, his comic-derisive quality of 'rascality' is at once stated, and by the Lord himself. To Mephistopheles' 'Dust shall he bite, ay, lick it up with zest', the Lord replies:

> Ich habe deinesgleichen nie gehasst:
> Von allen Arten Geisten, die verneinen,
> Ist mir der Schalk am wenigsten zur Last.
>
> (In that you also have a dispensation.
> Your kindred never had my hate or scorn:
> Of all the spirits of negation
> The scamp is least of burdens to be borne.)[1]

There the resemblance ends: for Goethe cannot write tragedy, and his spirit of negation must 'toil to serve creation, though a devil'.

As an example, take the element of bawdry in Ophelia mad, which tends to *negate* the suffering by rousing (Elizabethan) hilarity.[2] Or Hamlet at the grave-side, quibbling on mortality, ignorant that it is Ophelia's grave. The Clown's 'You lie out on't, sir,' is a sardonic jest with three edges to it. It is another, that Hamlet talks of *equivocation*: for all he says to the Gravedigger is equivocal, and death is creeping up behind him while he prattles. How comical a set-up for a Chaplin! Othello in the 'brothel-scene', treating Emilia like a professional bawd, has moved towards the pure grotesque. This has a quality of horrifying absurdity, because Othello is playing to a 'Desdemona' only of his diseased imagination; and yet playing the scene to caricature-like excess before Desdemona herself. This equivocal quality also appears in the coarse parallels of Bianca and Emilia, not to Desdemona herself, but to what Othello imagines as 'Desdemona'. Bianca *is* a whore; Emilia not over-scrupulous, given her price; and Iago's Desdemona, and Roderigo's too, are similar 'light' illusions.

[1] Philip Wayne's translation. Penguin, 1949.

[2] Experimental producers might attempt inserting contemporary smutty songs to try out a genuine Elizabethan effect?

It is a wide jump: but in *Twelfth Night* the grotesque delusion of Malvolio, in love with an illusion called Olivia, is a parallel instance of this kind of malevolent gulling. Few things undermine dignity more than a display of ridiculously misplaced confidence in a man's own misjudgement. There is a beautiful example of it in *Coriolanus*, in Menenius's mission to the Volscian army (v. ii.). The Sentinels bar his way, and then—when Coriolanus appears—the old man tells them what they have let themselves in for: 'Behold now presently, and swoon for what's to come upon thee'. But it is he who is left near swooning: utterly snubbed; allowed to say two words only ('How! away!'); and abandoned to the Sentinels' mockery. If funny, it is also moving—with that strange pathos of the Clown's tragedy, which only the greatest comedians understand.

'Ridiculously misplaced confidence in a man's own misjudgement': the phrase might also be applied to *some* of Shakespeare's tragic patterns. Richard III (setting aside his diabolic sense of comedy) does set to work on a programme summarized in Queen Margaret's curse. But though he hears the curse, it never crosses his mind that he is fully 'working to rule', and that *he* is last on the list. Othello sets out to prove his love false; and does. Coriolanus would stand as if a man were author of himself and knew no other kin; by the end, he has achieved the total separation this implies; and the intolerable word 'traitor' is true of him *vis-à-vis* both Rome and Corioli. Lear, having made his everything turn on the truth of his youngest daughter's love, having staked all his force of passion on it, has to play to that stake. He wins; and it costs him everything.

All these simplified patterns suggest a view in which 'Fate' has taken the hero, the magnificent egotist, at his word; only 'Fate' is a sardonic *farceur* who 'gives with subtle confusions', and deals out supple equivokes. The same outline-patterns could create comedies (a commonplace, I know, but not the flat truism people seem to think it). I mention those four plays, because critics have exaggerated the amount of inner conflict in them. Some would exclude *Othello*. But here too we should contrast *Hamlet*, *Macbeth*, *Antony and Cleopatra*—and the first wavering hero, Brutus. The point is that all these 'patterns' repeat the inverting effect of so-called comic relief.

It is impossible to do more than touch on the comic-ironic grotesque in *Lear*. Nothing elsewhere approaches the phantasmagoric quality of the 'Farmhouse-scene', the trial of Goneril and Regan. But let two points suffice. First, the Fool. His loyalty and his half-dazed sufferings are only *one* side to him; for the other, no Spirit Ironic from Hardy could more wittily strike Lear and us on the raw than the Fool, 'Lear's shadow', does with his pitilessly clear-sighted *comical* statement of what Lear's folly has done, and is. Bradley is uninterested in such comic effects. Then, for a more grotesque example of a heartless and comic aptness in words, take the scene where the blinded Gloucester meets Lear, mad and 'every inch a king', inveighing against sexual hypocrisy, simpering dames. Lear offers him money for civet.

> *Gloucester:* O, let me kiss that hand! . . . Dost thou know me?
> *Lear:* I remember thine eyes well enough. Dost thou squiny at me?
> No, do thy worst, blind Cupid; I'll not love. Read thou this challenge; mark but the penning of it.
> *Gloucester:* Were all thy letters suns, I could not see one.

That is the Shakespearian grotesque. Utterly unlaughable, it has all the wit of a malevolent commentator as pitiless and well-informed as the records of the Day of Judgement. 'Blind Cupid' for Gloucester: bastard Edmund's father, who tells us 'yet was his mother fair; there was good sport at his making'. The only possible comment is Edgar's:

> I would not take this from report. It is,
> And my heart breaks at it.

There remains the problem of *Macbeth*. Looking ahead, we find belittling and half-derisive commentaries, similar to those we have already examined, in Menenius and Enobarbus. The effect of much they both say is to call in question, with witty common-sense or cynicism, the heroic qualities of Coriolanus, Antony, Cleopatra. But in *Macbeth* there is only the Porter, finely equivocal in a play about nothing else *but* equivocation; otherwise an absence of these witty, malevolent sidelights which do more than catch the hero off his guard. There seem to be two possibilities to explain this. The first is that Macbeth is a hero too precariously heroic to stand this biting comic irony. This is true both of Richard II and of Brutus. It 'explains' why Mercutio dies when he does.[1] The mordant force which undermines the value of passionate sexual love is *bawdry*: light-hearted, witty derision of the whole undignified business which young men make such a fuss about. Mercutio is an expert at that form of masculine amusement. His commentary would wreck the delicate, sentimental catastrophe; and therefore, to keep the play together, either he must stop being Mercutio, or he must cease altogether. Shakespeare stopped him.

The second explanation is this. *Macbeth* is a heavily cut text. It may just be that the figure of the 'giant's robe upon a dwarfish thief' represents an element in the play as Shakespeare *wrote* it. That it represents an element in Shakespeare's true *conception* of Macbeth himself seems to me quite certain. In Dr. Caroline Spurgeon's words, the imaginative picture is of 'a small, ignoble man encumbered and degraded by garments unsuited to him'; and she calls attention to the use of this appearance by comedians. It may be that this devaluation and comic aspect was marked by other comic scenes in the uncut play, which have vanished as a result of abbreviating it for Court-production. It would be pure Shakespeare to give here too an *aspect* of the hero—especially the power-hero—which, by itself, would belittle him. We know, from the report of an eye-witness in April 1611, that in the Banquet-scene 'the ghoste of Banco came and sate down in his cheier be-hind him. And he turninge About to sit down Again sawe the goste of banco, which fronted him so, that he fell into a great passion of fear and fury.'[2] This is an

[1] As Dryden saw.
[2] Simon Forman: *The Bocke of Plaies.*

undeniable detail of Elizabethan production; and one that no modern producer dare attempt, because it would seem funny.

These examples sum up the last essential of the Shakespearian conception of tragedy: that the tragic includes its seeming opposite. The final alarmingness is not loss of life (with no promise of any after-life); nor the injustice of excessive or too widespread retribution: but the threat of indignity, of the loss of heroic *existence*, by the mocking devaluation of those very qualities by which the hero commands our admiration. Here it is that the commonplace about tragedy and comedy conjoining at their limits is demonstrable. In that generalization to which Coleridge was so excessively and profoundly attached, 'extremes meet'. We can see from the performance of half a dozen Elizabethan dramatists that tragi-comedy was the distinctive *English* practice; and it is a practice for which no Aristotelean or classical precedent can possibly be invoked. The other great tragic qualities of Shakespeare can be paralleled. This alone is uniquely his.

And why? Because of the immense value of human dignity to Renaissance man. That 'sense of vertiginous insecurity' which has been called the true 'tragic qualm'[1] was not, for Shakespeare's age and mind, evoked by the threat of suffering or death. Imaginatively at least, the Elizabethan owed it to himself to die in the grand manner: as Caesar and Antony and Cleopatra do, and Othello (to Mr. Eliot's annoyance). And many real Elizabethans did indeed die like that: like stage-heroes. But the full tragic qualm, the image of the terrifying uncertainty of human actions and human fate, could *only* be rendered through the illusions of the theatre by the hint that all the heroic gestures, all human distinction and greatness, might be played by strutting, fretting humans against a vast cosmic background which made them small, 'full of sound and fury,/ Signifying nothing'.

To sum up. Shakespeare's tragic conception of *order* is medieval and Christian; his conception of human *greatness* verges towards the antithesis of goodness in that order, and in-

[1] Prosser Hall Frye, *The Idea of Greek Tragedy*, op.cit.

cludes much of what his age called *virtu*: a complex ideal of self-sufficiency, pride and will, derived *via* Marlowe from Seneca read by English candle-light, but with much Italian illumination added. Just as those two principles are antithetical, so again is the clash between the pathetic or passional aspect of the heroic, and the comical or derisive. Here the whole hangs between two poles: 'We that are great, our own self-good still moves us'—and Isabella's

> But man, proud man,
> Dress'd in a little brief authority,
> Most ignorant of what he's most assur'd,
> His glassy essence, like an angry ape,
> Plays such fantastic tricks before high heaven
> As makes the angels weep.

And the angels (she continues) would 'laugh mortal', *if they could.*

Somewhere in his *Tragedy*, W. Macneile Dixon quotes Garibaldi: 'Let those who wish to continue the war against the stranger come with me. I offer neither pay, nor quarters, nor provisions. I offer hunger, thirst, forced marches, battles and death.' And he goes on to say, 'Explain to me the force of this appeal, why it warms and not chills the heart, and I will listen when you speak of tragedy'.[1] My own answer would be something like this: 'It appeals because it implies that those who *can* hear those words are men enough to meet and face the worst, and with open eyes; and also that (unlike those others whom these facts of war intimidate) they are "free men". Even if free will is a delusion and were scientifically exploded, they would still have more degrees of freedom than those others have.'

Garibaldi offered strength to overcome the world, if only in will. But only the tragically aware, the open-eyed, are aware how uncertain that greatness is—not only in its *fate*, but at its very centre in the mind of man: that centre which Shakespeare's tragedy touches, not only with the fear of the proud man's blindness, but with the other (and opposite) apprehension of his potential littleness, in the comic obverse of his pride.

[1] [p. 159.]

14

'Comic Relief'

At the end of Plato's *Symposium* is a strange little serio-comic episode. Socrates has drunk down everyone but Agathon and Aristophanes—but the doctor, Aristodemus, wakes at cock-crow: the three are still talking, drinking from a huge bowl (passed widdershins), and Socrates is still arguing. Aristodemus could not remember much of it; he had missed the beginning and was still half asleep: 'but the gist of it was that Socrates was forcing them to admit that the same man might be capable of writing both comedy and tragedy—that the tragic poet might be a comedian as well'. Socrates clinches his argument—to a now negligent audience—and goes off to give his first morning lecture. And thus Plato drops his notion teasingly, leaving posterity to guess whether the emphasis should fall on *In vino*—or on *veritas*.

The separateness of comedy and tragedy is taken for granted by those who never think of inspiration by separate and jealous Muses. Because of that assumption the term 'comic relief' exists and persists: to signify those parts of a 'serious' play which stand like a row of grinning dots in an interrupted (not broken) tragic sentence. The purpose of these dots, it is argued, is to give relaxation from what would otherwise be unbearable. The analogy is that of the bow, which loses its spring if kept too long bent. The whole theory is neatly summarized by Dryden:

> A continued gravity keeps the spirit too much bent; we must refresh it sometimes, as we bait in a journey, that we may go on with greater ease. A scene of mirth, mixed with tragedy, has the same effect upon us which our music has betwixt the acts; which

we find a relief to us from the best plots and language of the stage, if the discourses have been long.[1]

Those who write unreflectively of comic relief are equating Shakespeare's comic intermezzi with the Tweedledum and Tweedledee string and woodwind noises that lowered the immense tragic tensions of the Restoration audience at the heroic play. It is not eccentric to be dissatisfied with this.

The existence of *some* comic relief of this interruptive kind is admitted in Greek tragedy, though there is but little, and Aristotle is silent about it. There is the Nurse in *The Choephoroe*, the simple old King Aegeus in *Medea*, the Messenger in *The Bacchae*, Herakles in *Alcestis*. There was also the 'relief' of the burlesque satyr-play after the trilogy: a primitive survival, but 'functionally' explicable as making a deliberate return to the commonplace and undignified levels of the ordinary or the everyday. None of this amounts to much; nor is it helpful with Shakespeare, who is writing in quite another tradition. It is, moreover, easy to read *back* the *Romeo and Juliet* Nurse into Aeschylus, and to convert relaxed tension into the 'comic'.

Dryden's view is too simple. It does not even explore what *happens* in the convenient period of rest, much less explain the question 'why *comic*?' This alleged use of the so-called 'healing laughter' in tragedy—to let the mind readjust itself—is perhaps best studied by examining those plays which do *not* supply it. The strain turns to indifference as 'afflictions induce callosities'; or the audience finds its own relief by giggling in the wrong places.[2] In 1951, for instance, the B.B.C. broadcast Middleton's tragedy, *The Changeling*, cutting out all the sub-plot. For some, the thing became more and more absurd; others felt it go dead. Again, in *King Lear*, IV. ii., after the mad-scene in the farm-house

[1] Neander in *An Essay of Dramatic Poesy*.

[2] This can be studied by listening to the response to films which deal unaffectedly and unforcedly with hurting themes: not violent, but heart-twisting ones. In Cambridge, the callow giggle can often be read like a pressure-gauge. Elsewhere, you find that the less educated *whistle*. Both are, I presume, hysterical symptoms.

and the blinding of Gloucester, Goneril, giving her favour to Edmund as he leaves, turns away and exclaims:

> O, the difference of man and man!
> To thee a woman's services are due.
> My fool usurps my body.

Audiences often laugh at this, and before the line making a sexual innuendo possible is spoken. Presumably it implies that Shakespeare has unduly neglected 'relief' in this long and painful sequence.

Even a mildly 'tragic' situation in real life induces some degree of hysteria in a fair proportion of otherwise normal people. Since powerful imaginative situations can do the same, a practical dramatist must face this fact as a practical problem, whether he agrees or not with Johnson that 'the mingled drama may convey all the instruction of tragedy or comedy', and 'approaches nearer than either to the appearance of life, by shewing how . . . the high and the low co-operate in the general system by unavoidable concatenation'.[1] More than this—and whether 'life' is to be instructively presented or not—the *dramatic* not only lives by, but *is* tension and relief: screwing-up and relaxing, driving up and letting down. Things are rightly styled 'dramatic' when they tense us up sharply, by no more than springing a realized situation on us suddenly enough: as, for example, Donne does in that tremendous screwing up to an agony of trepidation and spiritual terror in

> What if this present were the world's last night?

or in his totally different, but no less dramatic

> For Godsake hold your tongue, and let me love.

Lowered tension is apt to verge towards the comic; and 'incongruity' is not always the most convincing explanation of *why* it does so. If it does explain it, then it is most often incongruity of *tone*. Donne, Heaven knows, has enough incongruities:

[1] *Preface to Shakespeare.*

yet only a few act like comic or sardonic switches—that, for example, which begins *The Relique*:

When my grave is broke up againe
Some second ghest to entertaine,
(For graves have learn'd that woman-head
To be to more than one a Bed).

The simplest instance is the 'pompous promise and lean performance'[1] which ends not only in bathos, but bathos which boomerangs a contemptuous comment back on to the performer: the Political Speaker, for example: 'I am going to ask myself a question.' Voice: 'An' a bloody silly answer you'll get.' J. C. Gregory (quoted above) thinks that in this kind of laughter 'the mind is eased from effortful understanding'; but he adds that, besides relief, 'perception of incongruity' plays the maximum part. Surely Hobbes put this theory better: '*Sudden glory*, is the passion which maketh those *grimaces* called laughter'; and the reason why people laugh is (*a*) 'some sudden act of their own, that pleaseth them', or (*b*) 'the apprehension of some deformed thing in another, whereof they suddenly applaud themselves'. (*Leviathan*, VI.)[2]

Now a 'sudden glory' at some debasing and unanticipated turn, of figure or of events, says a great deal about the discontinuities of Shakespearian tragedy—and of Shakespearian comedy too. If we disregard his editors, and admit that Shakespeare does *not* separate the 'tragic' and 'comic', then we see at once that his *comedy* is largely built out of contrasts of tone. In the early plays, this is often very simple: a 'loves of the parallels' pattern is used,

[1] J. C. Gregory: *The Nature of Laughter*, 1924.

[2] On this, consider Gregory's story (op. cit., pp. 24–5) of the workman engaged in blasting who dallied too long and was blown up. The foreman timed him, and at the end of the week his wages were docked for 'time off' in the air. Gregory explains, 'the beginning . . . makes a big call on sympathy, the end a small one. It is distressing to have even sixpence deducted from one's wages . . .' That makes the effect sound like *relief*. But what if a physicist says, 'even *sixpence*! If he gets £12 a week for an 8-hour day, the man works one minute for a penny. At this rate a *halfpenny's* worth would send him up a matter of 7,000 feet'. If this is a laughable comment, then 'sudden glory' seems nearer the mark than 'relief'. The butt is the 'deformed thing' to the expert psychologist.

and the affairs of serving-man and maid (or 'country copulatives') echo those of lady and gentleman. It is apparent in *The Taming of the Shrew*; in *Love's Labour's Lost*, where Costard and Jacquenetta are a comment on the high-falutin' notions of the gentry, on 'academes' and on three years' womenlessness; in *The Merchant of Venice*, where it is quite trivial; in *As You Like It*; and in *Twelfth Night*, which has a complicated pattern of sentimentalities, on the one subject of love, in very different tones. We can still talk of 'relief' here: farcical or satiric, with some vinegar in the sweetness (Touchstone, for example, in and on love). The dominant tone can be supported by an echo in a slightly different key, or stiffened by a discord: when the shifts from one to the other become *like* the changes of tension in tragic comic-relief. Shakespearian tragi-comedy hangs precisely between; and a play like *Much Ado* hangs as precisely between these comedies and tragi-comedy. It has three plots, three quite different tones; and each plot is 'about' seeming and being, pinned down to the un-tragic matter of verbal misunderstanding. The Hero-Claudio relationship is the rhetorical question: Dogberry the 'bloody silly answer'. Moreover, in the mature comedies (as in *Henry IV* too) tone-contrast means conflict of *values*. That conflict is the real *plot*, as distinct from mere story, in *As You Like It*, *Twelfth Night*, *Measure for Measure*, etc.

In *tragedy* a mere gap, as a space for possible mental adjustment, is rare. The followers of Dryden's theory can point to Cinna the Poet in *Julius Caesar*, the Clown in *Othello*, but will not get much support from them. They can claim the fig-bearing Clown in *Antony and Cleopatra*; but he is not without sinister reflections on the main theme; as (still more so) is *Macbeth's* Porter. Neither is really just a gap. Both Porter and Fig-bearer would have been accepted by Lope de Vega (1562–1635), who defended the comic in tragedy, but stipulated that it should have an integral part in the main plot and not take the form of inserted 'episodes'. The precept was followed exactly by Calderon, whose servants, etc., burlesque the serious action in deed or by comment. But they do not *add to* the tragic effect, as Shakespeare's do. For

Shakespeare the relaxation-theory is quite inadequate. There is too much 'relief': and not seldom where there has not been enough tension to need *any*. The Galley-scene in *Antony and Cleopatra* is of this sort. Worst of all, for the theorists, *Othello* and *Lear open* with bawdy laughter at Iago and Gloucester. This is a very interesting kind: 'relief' not *from* but *for* the serious to follow. The dramatist makes bawdy jokes and the audience is softened up, made suggestible, and its morale lowered. Public speakers know this—and some lecturers. To say that it is 'getting the listeners on your side' is too simple. Rather, it is making an audience of them. Laughter is public, suffering-of-soul private (unless weeping is in fashion): the one suggestibility leads on to the other. *Julius Caesar* begins this method of protasis.

What is it that *happens* when a harrowing or tense, strained passage is followed by a comical one, no matter of what sort? 'The mind readjusts itself.' Yes; but in the comic interim it cannot be that *nothing* is happening to it, unless the insertion is totally without meaning or relevance to the theme. The mind is having new experiences, perhaps emphasized by their very difference. Unless these are quite null, the final state cannot be the *status quo ante risum*. Is the laughter analogous to what happens when an iron bar is hammered, made to vibrate, in a magnetic field, permitting the molecular magnets to orientate themselves along the 'lines of force'—so that the bar becomes magnetic? If so, the field of force is double. The mind must then be quite discontinuous; *or* it must be afflicted with two worlds, both separate; *or* there must be a striving for interaction and a re-established, but complex, unity. I presume only that the comic episode somehow 'belongs'—that it is not a merely funny irrelevance, for which another comic turn would do as well. If the comic twist or episode has a relevance to the serious theme, then the same things may be seen in an altered light, which makes them very different 'things'.

In *Julius Caesar*, for example, I suggest that the mob-scene, where the poet Cinna is beaten up, with the cry 'Tear him for his bad verses!', is *comic*. It is comic when the angry person hits the wrong man. But the sadistic humour of tearing bad poets to pieces, or the comically presented horrors of rage, are aspects of the breakdown of order, following Caesar's murder; of the forces which Brutus and Cassius have let loose. The Plebeians are generous-minded in their gratitude towards Caesar. Antony has played on this; and their gratitude takes the form of vengeance—on an innocent man. Order in collapse is not only tragically terrible: it is grotesque, horrible and absurd, like a shocking practical joke. The same is true of the Cade scenes in 2 *Henry VI*, where the revolutionary terrors appear as grotesquely comic, as gargoyles let loose, with minds to match. The mob has become a kind of collective Caliban, like the Hydra that Bosch makes of it in his *Ecce Homo*.

As Coleridge observed: 'Indeed, paradoxical as it may appear, the terrible by a law of the human mind always touches on the verge of the ludicrous. Both arise from the perception of something out of the common order of things—something, in fact, out of its place; and if from this we can abstract danger, the uncommonness will alone remain, and the sense of the ridiculous be excited.' 'The close alliance of these opposites', he adds, '—they are not contraries—appears from the circumstance, that laughter is equally the expression of extreme anguish and horror as of joy. . . .'[1] These notions could be developed at length in analysing the Farm-house scene in *King Lear*.

Shakespearian tragedy takes the contrast and collision of opposites to extreme lengths. The true Shakespearian 'relief' trades in apparently wanton incongruity, where every risk is taken in using discord or clash; where the most heterogeneous *moods* are yoked by violence together, and no 'classical' principles can discern if it is with controlled purpose. *Comprehensiveness* is one term we can use to mark off the aim of this sort of play-making from the other sort (where comic relief does imply 'relief' in the pain-stopping sense). But where there is *true* relevance, then we can speak rather of '*interinanimation*'. The Gravedigger-scene interacts with Hamlet's own approaches to

[1] Notes on *Hamlet*, 1818.

death; the Galley-scene with Antony's self-defeat in the political game of world-strategy. Yet the word 'relief' is still usable, though the Galley-scene does *not* follow any great dramatic tension. We can use it as in *sculpture*: low-relief or high-relief, whereby the figures are 'brought out' by being laid against a something, or an absence of something, so that the two effects interact, to produce a unified but complex reaction of the mind. A bust or statue is here a limiting-case: a shape laid against a nothing.

But in this case there need be no 'relief' whatever in the 'toothache' sense: for the absence which makes the object in relief stand out may be a hurting *lack*. In humanist tragedy, and in tragi-comedy, the lack is lack of dignity, of greatness. It is the antithesis to humanist pride—and therefore *comic*. In *Measure for Measure*, for example, a transitional play, the utterly undignified figures of the underworld (Pompey, Mrs. Overdone and, in a different way, Lucio) are funny; yet they vigorously present incontinence, lust and the snares of the flesh, which are tragic matters in Angelo, Claudio, Isabella. At the comic base-string level, sex, lust and the dread of flesh are bawdry, smart smut, 'rather . . . a merriment than a vice' (as Angelo accuses Isabella of trying to make him think of her brother's 'sliding', at II. iv. 115–16). And that is the *lack*: the absence that negates the seriousness by transposing it all into terms of 'codpiece-rebellion' and the like. The constant joking on venereal disease, on the other hand, though conventionally laughed at, is not funny. In that setting it is vile and hateful, for all that we recognize in it a stock joke, sometimes a clever one.

The aim of all this trading in incongruity is a highly complex emotional effect, perhaps impossible to those who cannot face violently mixed feelings; and the relations of that to irony are obvious enough. Irony (of one sort) is the abstracted effect of such mingled emotional reactions: the irony which appeals to those who see almost all human ways and human situations with a constant and irremissive doubleness. It may result, too, in 'ironic detachment' being ascribed to the author. He appears to record the clashes and discords of life, its inextricable mixture of base and noble, fair and filthy, and to leave it without comment. Like Don John the Bastard in *Much Ado*, he seems to be saying: 'Sir, they are spoken, and these things are true.'

This doubleness was encouraged by the Elizabethan stage-environment and by the heredity of both history-plays and tragedy. On the environment, Landor was right in his second Imaginary Conversation with Southey: 'It may be questioned whether the people in the reign of Elizabeth, or indeed the Queen herself, would have been contented with a drama without a smack of the indecent or the ludicrous. They had alike been accustomed to scenes of ribaldry and of bloodshed; and the palace opened on one wing to the brothel, on the other to the shambles.'[1]

As for heredity, the habit of juxtaposing the religious and the farcical, the moving-pathetic and the brutal-comic, in the Miracle Plays, often gives a naïve variety of exactly the kind of 'relief' I distinguished just now. It at least *suggests* a background of diabolism, of the spirit which is the *denial* of all that the Cycle (as religious ritual) is about. The ambivalence of the most striking Miracle Play episodes entirely anticipates those uncomfortable, ironic or puzzling scenes in Shakespeare, when he seems to have wrenched and strained the frame of his stage, to cram into it as much as possible of the gamut of human experience. The grotesque of the Gothic drama could hardly be better illustrated than by the babbling sottish Porter, by Lear's half-wit Fool and by Edgar disguised as Tom o' Bedlam, with his patter about how he has been a bawdy serving-man. Behind each there lurks a shapeless horror.

Elsewhere the ambivalence is sharpened to irony. In *Antony and Cleopatra* the Galley-scene has been described by Mr. Eliot as 'a prodigious piece of political satire'.[2] The same might be said of the Fig-bearing Clown. But it seems more Shakespearian to

[1] cf. Robert Bridges: *The Influence of the Audience on Shakespeare's Drama*. See p. 287, *post*.

[2] In 1933. We have seen enough Conferences at sufficiently high levels since, to appreciate the comment.

see these as apt ambivalences. The Clown is only a yokel with a glimmering that the lady is in trouble and is choosing a way out which he does not intend to see too clearly. But, at another level, he is the essential mechanism in a movement of history: the ultimate agent to make great Caesar into 'ass unpolicied'. Cleopatra slips away to her Antony, through the fingers of Caesar, the man of destiny; just as the mastery of the world had slipped through Antony's fingers, after he picked up *his* serpent; or through Pompey's, when Menas the pirate offered him the throats of the three triumvirs, and all he could say was:

> Ah, this thou shouldst have done,
> And not have spoke on't. In me 'tis villainy:
> In thee't had been good service. Thou must know
> 'Tis not my profit that does lead mine honour:
> Mine honour, it.[1]

Examples of this comprehensiveness are endless. One interesting one, leading towards other considerations, is where one and the same man is at once tragedian and clown. Richard III, for instance, provides his own sardonic comic relief, often profane, always chuckling:

> Simple, plain Clarence, I do love thee so
> That I will shortly send thy soul to heaven,
> If heaven will take the present at our hands. (I. i. 118–20)

And Hamlet is at once the hero and the sarcastic, satirical commentator—*and* 'almost, at times, the fool'. Again, there is Cleopatra raging at the messenger, snapping at Charmian (who reminds her of Caesar), or mocking the almost *miles gloriosus*-like 'herculean Roman' with play-acting to match his.[2]

We cannot say that such things are *derived* from the two-sidedness of the Miracles—the direct dramatic connection is non-proven. The Miracle Plays survived till Shakespeare's time: that

[1] II. vii. 72–6.

[2] With all these we can contrast *Richard II*, and perhaps *Henry V*, where the attitudes presented cannot stand the test of ridicule; and *Macbeth*, where the derisive image (the dwarf in giant's robes) is there, but Shakespeare does not use it in open mockery. See p. 228.

is all we know, except that he does refer to them ('out-herods Herod', etc.). We can look back to the 'Wakefield Master' and to the queer releasing of indecent sexual curiosity about Christ's birth in the 'N. towne Plays' (or *Ludus Coventriae*) and say, non-committally: 'There is the same spirit; and it can be labelled "Gothic". Pity and admiration stand side by side with derision: as in Bosch's *Crowning with Thorns* in the National Gallery.' But when we turn to the Morality Play line of descent, the connections are close and clear. The seriously treated vices became 'the Old Vice', a clown. The morals faded and the Fool remained: often a tricksy, malicious villain in the making. Hence the depiction of the Machiavel as a cynical jester: for *Il Principe* is not what any unassisted reader could take for a jest-book. The Moralities turned from religion to controversy, and so to politics; and from that diversion the so-called 'Chronicle Histories' developed. They did so exactly on the lines of the Moralities, with their 'interludes of vice', i.e. comic or buffoonish turns.

Cambyses represents an historical story maltreated in just this way; and since 'the Vice', Ambidexter, has a real part in the historical plot, the same tragic story is treated simultaneously as farce.[1] In *Dr. Faustus* there is the same clashing incongruity. Faustus raises the Devil seriously, terrifyingly, damnably. Immediately afterwards, the clown Wagner does the same, to be comically terrified—and only that. A travesty of the serious action is laid beside it, in juxtaposition. Faustus, in the middle reaches of his own tragedy, is turned over to the farcical, practical-joking imp of mischief or disguised Devil of the *Till Eulenspiegel* and Friar Rush traditions.[2]

Now *Dr. Faustus* is an Elizabethan play, and therefore establishes economically the connection between the Morality (and Interlude) and what I might call 'the Elizabethan play in two tones', the play of constant ambivalences. The tones are 'the

[1] We find the same *kind* of treatment in *The Troublesome Raigne of King John*, *The Famous Victories of Henry V*, and *Woodstock*.

[2] See F. P. Wilson, *Marlowe and the Early Shakespeare*, 1953, p. 69.

serious' and 'the farcical', high relief and low; and the total meaning of the play is only grasped when the effect of comprehensiveness is reached. But even if the effort is defeating, that is no reason for not seeing that *2 Henry VI* essays the undignified in history; that *1 Henry IV* achieves perfection in its difficult kind; and that *Measure for Measure* and *Troilus and Cressida* are shaped on exactly the same pattern, that of *Cambyses*. Only whereas neither the 'University wit', Thomas Preston, nor Marlowe, knew how to use it, Shakespeare did. Of plays of the time and type of *Cambyses*, Sidney could reasonably complain that they 'thrust in Clownes by head and shoulders, to play a part in majesticall matters', of 'their mungrell Tragy-comedie', and so on. Later, after Shakespeare, Middleton could reply:

> There's nothing in a play to a Clown, if he
> Have but the grace to hit on't, that's the thing indeed.
> The King shown well, but he sets off the King.

I claimed for *1 Henry IV* 'perfection': i.e. perfection, in the plotting, of the use of travesty. The Prince is double-faced throughout: he tells us so in his first soliloquy—and why should we disbelieve him? Nobody really knows him, and he deceives everyone. He might indeed say, with Richard III, 'I am myself alone'. His Eastcheap-self is too obvious a travesty of all he ought to be to need remark. Hotspur is at once a fine, energetic figure of impulsive knighthood *and* a figure of fun: the braggart swaggerer who 'kills me some six or seven dozen of Scots at a breakfast'. The comic episodes themselves parallel and criticize their serious counterparts. The entirely serious, pathetic and noble meeting of misunderstanding father and misunderstood and offending son is travestied *before* it happens, by the Prince's and Falstaff's interlude of play-acting in the tavern. Within the interlude, too, is a double character-portrait of Sir John: the one, by Sir John himself, a travesty of the truth; the other, by the Prince, a scurrilous travesty of the travesty. Even after the Prince's solemnly sworn repentance, his promise of reformation and a new life—which he bears out at Shrewsbury on Percy's head—there follows *immediately* Sir John with Bardolph, also about to reform:

> Well, I'll repent, and that suddenly, while I am in some liking; I shall be out of heart shortly, and then I shall have no strength to repent. An I have not forgotten what the inside of a church is made of, I am a peppercorn, a brewer's horse. The inside of a church! Company, villainous company, hath been the spoil of me. (III. iii. 5–10.)

The whole idea of abrupt, determined reformation in a man's life is made derisible. Shakespeare sets up a greatness in a gesture and then switches to a plane where all is mockery. And when he ends his play—to go no further in extracting his ambivalences for your admiration of Coleridge's 'myriad-minded man'—he does the trick again. The Prince meets Hotspur and heroically destroys him, nobly drops a tear on his mangled brow, and even has a good word for the dead Falstaff. It is all very sad and fine. And then comes the glorious resurrection. Sir John sits up, and after reassuring his pavid heart that Percy is not shamming too, re-kills the bear and goes off to sell the skin—and to buy honour.

From that one can pass to a detailed examination of the 'reliefs' in the tragedies, going the right way, through *Measure for Measure* and *Troilus and Cressida*. But I leave that, to run farther afield, and to ask *why* there should be this hold of the Gothic comic underworld on the Elizabethan mind? What total meaning can we extract from the general presence and principles of derisive, debunking, low or critical comedy or farce in the major tragedies? Here we are confronted with a plain choice. Either we say, 'These are mere juxtapositions, and there is *no* unity, no coherence, no singleness of vision, in the "myriad-minded man". All is chaotic, though Shakespeare only expresses his sense of this at intervals.' (Or, should we rather not say, 'Shakespeare descends to his audience's level, at which there *is* no coherence or unity, and never was.'? If so, we must accept Robert Bridges's opinion of that audience and its influence:

Shakespeare should not be put into the hands of the young without the warning that the foolish things in his plays were written to please the foolish, the filthy for the filthy, and the brutal for the brutal; and that if, out of veneration for his genius, we are led to admire or even tolerate such things, we may be thereby not conforming ourselves to him, but only degrading ourselves to the level of his audience, and learning contamination from those wretched beings who can never be forgiven their share in preventing the greatest poet and dramatist of the world from being the best artist.[1]).

Or, if we cannot accept this, then we take our cue from Coleridge on the Imagination, by means of which the poet 'diffuses a tone and spirit of unity, that blends, and (as it were) *fuses*, each into each, by that synthetic and magical power to which I would exclusively appropriate the name of Imagination: that power which reveals itself in the balance or reconcilement of opposite or discordant qualities: of sameness, with difference; of the general with the concrete . . .'.[2] Mr. Eliot can be called as a further witness here: 'When a poet's mind is perfectly equipped for its work, it is constantly amalgamating disparate experience; the ordinary man's experience is chaotic, irregular, fragmentary. The latter falls in love, or reads Spinoza, and these two experiences have nothing to do with each other, or with the noise of the typewriter or the smell of cooking; in the mind of the poet these experiences are always forming new wholes.'[3] He goes on to refer to drama: 'The poets of the seventeenth century, the successors of the dramatists of the sixteenth, possessed a mechanism of sensibility which could devour any kind of experience.'[4]

[1] *The Influence of the Audience on Shakespeare's Drama*, p. 29.

[2] *Biographia Literaria*, Ch. XIV.

[3] *The Metaphysical Poets* (*Selected Essays*, p. 287).

[4] This passage makes it surprise me that Mr. Eliot did not see more clearly into the parallelism of plot and sub-plot in Middleton's *The Changeling*, beyond speaking of the play (with all his admiration of it) as 'disfigured by ribaldry or clowning' (*Selected Essays*, p. 165) and adding the half-aside, 'nauseousness of the secondary plot' (*The Use of Poetry and The Use of Criticism*). The sub-plot—that of 'the changeling'—is on the identically same theme as the Beatrice-De Flores plot: only it is in a tone which marks what 'blasts a beauty to deformity' (as Beatrice

On either view a derisive or devaluating use of the comic or farcical can 'belong', in a complex artistic unity. It also 'belongs' in English Renaissance tragedy, because it is a *humanist* tragedy. For the effect of comic devaluation is to throw strong shadows of doubt on the dignity and worth of man; to switch Hamlet's 'What a piece of work is a man!' into the opposite tone of contemptuous mockery; to cast the hint that heroism is ridiculous, nobility a sham, all dignity the pomp and circumstance of a poor bare forked animal, or the pretensions of an 'angry ape' playing 'fantastic tricks before high heaven'. Or again (to touch on what stings us more than the lapse of human greatness) it can suggest that all love is a smutty joke wrapped round a brutal act, common to beasts ('Ay, madam, it is common').

This is not so much the contrast of 'good' and 'evil' in the traditional moral sense, as of 'values' and 'non-values'. The Devil is a nihilist: he has lost his Satanic dignity, and become like that dreadfully vulgar and greasy vision which Ivan had of him in *The Brothers Karamazov*.[1] In this devalued world, supposed absolute, Man has no dignity: not even that of being damned. His tragic conflict is about nothing but his own fantastic notions, which have no validity beyond 'the small circle of pain within the skull'—a pain resulting from delusions and self-importance. He is utterly subject to the spirit of denial; and all his glories and sufferings are empty, his fine speeches mouthings to cover his hollowness with sounding words.

That is a *comic* view. Man's vanity is the comedian's province. Yet it is not a glib phrase that 'extremes meet', and that comedy

says of the word 'whore' and its 'horrid sound' in v. iii). Its 'ribaldry' denies, by implication, the *nobility* of sex-motivated villainy; is counterpart to De Flores's ugliness. Middleton has amalgamated 'disparate experience' in a way that the creator of the Typist and the House-agent's clerk ('carbuncular')' might have been expected to appreciate. Every shift to the sub-plot in *The Changeling* has the same effect, in sexually emotive terms, as the movement of 'She entertains Sir Ferdinand/Klein . . .'

[1] We might remark here how the distressing spirit of negation is only the *extreme* or absolute of what we all expect 'a sense of humour' to do (especially for friends and others than ourselves) in reducing the emotional importance of things.

and tragedy can use almost identical patterns of situation. Consider tragic irony. One simple kind is where a man's words state his true situation, or fate, but in terms that conceal it from him. The changes of the action make it true, but in a sense opposite to any he intended. It happens with Buckingham's speech in *Richard III*, v. i. 20 f.:

> That high All-Seer which I dallied with
> Hath turn'd my feigned prayer on my head
> And given in earnest what I begg'd in jest,

where the feigned prayer was back at II. i. 32 f.: his inviting God to punish him (very specifically 'with hate in those where I expect most love' and with supreme treachery in friendship) when he turns against the Queen. He does; and he gets what he asks for. *Richard III* is largely built out of such practical-ironical jokes.

Dramatic irony can be on exactly the same *pattern* as the comic situation where X says, 'Just you see what I'll do——', and the event shows what he really *does* or does *not* do: Bobadil, for example, bragging about killing armies, and then beaten by George Downright; Menenius and the Volscian Sentinels; and (not comic at all) Aufidius saying what terrible things he will do to Martius, if he is given the chance—and then embracing him when they do meet. There is a complete gradation here, from farcical comedy through 'comic relief' to tragic irony (reversal of sworn intention). The technical terms seem to mark them off in classes: but the patterns are the same. One man is proved an unattended prophet by the fact; another a liar. It is the same pattern.

In *tragedy*, the devaluations of man's prescience, of his awareness or his magnitude—the revelations of his blindness—turn outwards, as it were. The clash with heroism, with the quality that we expect of the tragic hero, is so direct, so 'unacceptable', that we are urged to see in it the implication of some power in life, or of 'Fate' or 'Destiny', which, as in dramatic irony, is making a fool of him, though in a terrible way. The alternative is theologically intolerable, unless we can adumbrate a universe with a mocking and pitiless practical jester behind it. And it comes near to that when we see Macbeth turn into a trapped and snarling rat, and Othello into a gibbering, horn-mad black monkey. We feel it even when Menenius makes us see Coriolanus as a lunatic machine of pride, running madly to destruction, as confident and conceited as a tin god. It is present, though less forcefully, when Ophelia becomes a painted courtesan to Hamlet's eye; when Cleopatra flytes and scolds like a whore—and thinks like one (a side of her matched by the sexual badinage of her court).[1] Shakespeare does what the Greeks and Racine *never, never* do—what Corneille dare not do, even more than those others—he makes his hero lose his dignity. This is not 'comic': it only *could* be. I call it '*grotesque*'.

In all these instances one has—and shies away from it—the suggestion of a universe with a malevolent grin on its face: or, worse, one from which the grin has faded away, like the Cheshire Cat's. *King Lear* is informed throughout with that drastic and terrifying suspicion. For it is not the feeling that suffering is inevitable that shatters human pride and resolution: it is that man's whole endurance may be totally meaningless. As Joseph Conrad wrote to Cunninghame Graham (far more exactly hitting off himself): 'You have a fiendish gift of showing the futility, the ghastly jocular futility of life.' This is a thing neither Greek nor later classical drama can touch. It is in essence romantic. In *Lord Jim* (Ch. ix.) Conrad catches it for once triumphantly. It is the crucial moment of Jim's tragic life. He is a ship's officer, self-dedicated to the code of honour of the sea, and he deserts a sinking ship, which—because of the desertion of the superior officers—is *his* ship. The *Patna* is a rotten old crate carrying pilgrims; she collides with a water-logged wreck; only the bulging forward-bulkhead rests between the crew and passengers and immediate sinking. The officers know: the Moslems do not. The worthless captain and other officers launch a boat and try to slip away; Jim resolves to stay on board. But at

[1] Cf. pp. 268–70.

the tremor of a squall, long seen approaching, he finds that he has jumped. He did not jump—he only found he *had*, and was there in the boat: safe, dishonoured. The ship does *not* sink, and the whole tale comes out at an inquiry. Thereafter the story follows him—nobody minding it but himself—and he moves farther and farther East, a pilgrim bound for a Mecca he can never reach by moving: because it exists only in himself, in his romantic soul; and because the only way of finding it is 'to the Destructive Element submit yourself. In the Destructive Element immerse . . .'.

> The boat was heavy; they pushed at the bow with no breath to spare for an encouraging word: but the turmoil of terror that had scattered their self-control like chaff before the wind, converted their desperate exertions into a bit of fooling, upon my word fit for knockabout clowns in a farce. They pushed with their hands, with their heads, they pushed for dear life with all the weight of their bodies, they pushed with all the might of their souls—only no sooner had they succeeded in canting the stem clear of the davit than they would leave off like one man and start a wild scramble into her. As a natural consequence the boat would swing in abruptly, driving them back, helpless and jostling against each other. They would stand nonplussed for a while, exchanging in fierce whispers all the infamous names they could call to mind, and go at it again. Three times this occurred. He described it to me with morose thoughtfulness. He hadn't lost a single movement of that comic business. 'I loathed them. I hated them. I had to look at all that,' he said without emphasis, turning on me a sombrely watchful glance. 'Was ever there any one so shamefully tried?'
>
> He took his head in his hands for a moment, like a man driven to distraction by some unspeakable outrage. These were things he could not explain to the court—and not even to me; but I would have been little fitted for the reception of his confidences had I not been able at times to understand the pauses between the words. In this assault upon his fortitude there was the jeering intention of a spiteful and vile vengeance; there was an element of burlesque in his ordeal—a degradation of funny grimaces in the approach of death or dishonour.[1]

[1] *Lord Jim*, ch. IX.

It is that element of burlesque which is the true 'Destructive Element' in Shakespeare. From its derivation, or evolution, it can be called diabolical: the interstitial farce of Elizabethan plays being the Gothic 'comic-devilish' in origin. But in its ultimate and deepest purpose, where it is 'something more serious and philosophical than history', it adumbrates a profound intuition of the human mind, which is not in the least limited to Shakespeare's plays. Attempts on it are particularly noticeable in E. M. Forster's novels. There is the unsuccessful essay on the Devil himself in *The Longest Journey*; there are the goblins of Beethoven's Fifth Symphony in *Howard's End*; the *oom-boom* echoes of the Marabar caves in *A Passage to India*.

You can take all that, and much more besides, from post-Renaissance literature back to Shakespeare, and end perhaps with going beyond Tennyson's 'That is the greatness of Shakespeare: he shows you the incongruities of things.' One wonders how deeply Tennyson had felt and pondered that remark. The incongruities of things can be very terrible. They can be like Rubek the sculptor's faces in *When We Dead Awaken*, which have always a bestial sub-suggestion under their speaking likeness; or they can present us with that ironic twist of *John Gabriel Borkman*, when Foldal says 'It's a terrible tragedy' (meaning Borkman's life), and Borkman adds 'But looked at from another point of view, it's really a sort of comedy as well.' Shakespeare's view is the double-eyed, the ambivalent: it faces both ways.

15

Wordsworth and Shakespeare

I SUPPOSE we think of Shakespeare as the 'poet of humanity' (though not 'not of Nature') and of Wordsworth as 'a (perhaps *the*) poet of Nature'. Accepting those terms for convenience, I must begin by remarking that the terms 'poet' and 'poetry' are different items in the two cultures of *c.* 1570–1616 and 1770–1807. If we use a concordance, or book of 'Familiar Quotations', it is easy to set up an illusion of resemblance. Giving to 'airy nothing/ A local habitation and a name' seems to be exactly the poetry of what Wordsworth says in prose in the Preface to *Lyrical Ballads* ('delighting to contemplate . . .'); and Timon's tame poet's 'Our poesy is as a gum which oozes/ From whence 'tis nourished' seems near enough to the 'spontaneous overflow of powerful feelings'. In *The Prelude*, Bk. xii.,[1] with the matter and value of his *Lyrical Ballads* in mind, Wordsworth even gives us lines which seem to stand for the substance of Shakespearian tragedy:

> Sorrow that is not sorrow, but delight,
> And miserable love that is not pain
> To hear of, for the glory that redounds
> Therefrom to human kind and what we are (xii. 245–8)

If we bring ourselves face to face with the question, 'What is a poet?', Wordsworth gives his answer: 'He is a man speaking to men.' The paragraph which follows seems so applicable to Shakespeare that it may make it appear only my delusion to

[1] All references to *The Prelude* in this lecture are to the text of 1805.

talk of 'an illusion of resemblance':

> a man . . . endowed with more lively sensibility, more enthusiasm and tenderness, who has a greater knowledge of human nature, and a more comprehensive soul, than are supposed to be common among mankind; a man pleased with his own passions and volitions, and who rejoices more than other men in the spirit of life that is in him; delighting to contemplate similar volitions and passions as manifested in the goings-on of the Universe, and habitually impelled to create them where he does not find them.[1]

I would not accuse Wordsworth of 'writing in the air': although the passage does take on a different (and more revealing) sense if we re-read it with 'I', 'my' and 'me' in place of 'a man', 'his' and 'him'. Analysis is not required; for Wordsworth has himself pointed to important differences in various passages where he has his own poetic practice specifically and sharply in mind. There are three stanzas in the Prologue to *Peter Bell*, including the lines:

> The common growth of mother-earth
> Suffices me—her tears, her mirth,
> Her humblest mirth and tears.

There is also the too familiar stanza from *Hart-Leap Well*:

> The moving accident is not my trade;
> To freeze the blood I have no ready arts;
> 'Tis my delight, alone in summer shade,
> To pipe a simple song for thinking hearts.

That echoes *Othello*. It was Othello's cue to speak 'Of moving accidents by flood and field'. That echo is an almost explicit exclusion of some of the major Shakespearian themes.

Nor is that all. Mr. Eliot remarks (in *The Possibility of a Poetic Drama*) how 'The *framework* which was provided for the Elizabethan dramatist was not merely blank verse and the five-act play and the Elizabethan playhouse; it was not merely the plot. . . . It was also the half-formed ὑλή, the "temper of the age" (an unsatisfactory phrase), a preparedness, a habit on

[1] Preface to *Lyrical Ballads*.

the part of the public, to respond to particular stimuli.'[1] It is unnecessary to point to the Advertisement to the first edition of the *Lyrical Ballads*, or to the Preface of 1800, to remind you that Wordsworth met (and minded) an *un*-preparedness on the part of his public: the very opposite of a 'habit', where specifically Wordsworthian stimuli were concerned.

Hence one very important difference. Wordsworth's greatest poem, *The Prelude*, was addressed to Coleridge and to Dorothy Wordsworth. Shakespeare's greatest poetry was addressed to the Globe Playhouse. I intend no derogation, only definition. We are bound to remark a change in the place of poet and poetry in a culture. Shakespeare is beyond cavil 'a man speaking to men'. But in Wordsworth we can see the outline of another kind of poetry: where the poet is a crony talking to cronies. Paradoxically, it is the intimate poet, Wordsworth, who is emphatic on his public aims, the *purpose*, the 'worthy purpose' which will be found (he says) to distinguish his poems. The confessional of 'thinking hearts' aspires to elevate itself into a pulpit. There is the mark of it even in his portraits, even in the Nether Stowey one of 1798, with the Jacobin hair-style; a touch of clergyman. From the start he is more than a 'pastoral poet'; he is a would-be Pastor, with an attitude like that of Paul in Athens: 'Whom, then, ye ignorantly *do not* worship, *that* declare I unto you. . . .' Near the end of his life, he summed himself up in a sentence in a letter: 'What I should myself most value in my attempts [is] the spirituality with which I have endeavoured to invest the material universe, and the moral relations under which I have wished to exhibit its most ordinary appearances.'

Shakespeare gives no indication that he saw himself as a man with any important public aim. What *he* would himself most value in his attempts, we simply do not know. As for moral purpose: well, two of his plays have overt morals, *The Taming of the Shrew* and *Troilus and Cressida*. One is for rebellious wives, the other for panders. Neither need detain us here.

To do Wordsworth any justice whatever, the *comic* must be

[1] *The Sacred Wood*, 3rd edn., 1932, pp. 63–4.

set aside. It is not only that, as Johnson wrote, Shakespeare seems to luxuriate there, to be utterly at home; but that Wordsworth is simply *not* at home to the Shakespearian comic, be it sweet or tart, mild or bitter. Miss Helen Darbishire may do her best for *The Waggoner*, but it amounts to much ado about very little. It is less comic, human and alert than *All's Well*. The only funny lines in Wordsworth are lines which he meant seriously. 'Lord what fools these mortals be!' is almost the antithesis to any Wordsworthian approach. The author of *The Idiot Boy* and *Simon Lee* was not equipped to produce a Dogberry, an Elbow or a Shallow.

With the comic must go the tragi-comic. The sense that a person is ridiculous, yet suffering or pathetic; an episode or situation absurd, yet *navrant* (or 'quick-grating', like a broken nail on silk): all that is quite absent from Wordsworth. It is what makes some of the pathetic *Lyrical Ballads* what they are: appreciable only to the most willing suspension of—derision. Greatness, passion or dignity shot through with irony is foreign to Wordsworth's notion of man. It seems almost that there is nothing for him between glory and a nullity, as we can see, for example, from the revealing passage on Bartholomew Fair at the end of *The Prelude*, Bk. vii., where the teeming world of London on holiday is dismissed as a 'spectacle' that lays 'The whole creative powers of man asleep!' (l. 654) and as 'the press/ Of self-destroying, transitory things.' (l. 739). There at least he lays bare his lack of sympathy with man-as-he-is; and although his *credo* (Bk. iii. 191)—'there's not a man/That lives who hath not had his godlike hours'—sounds fine enough and generous enough, it implies a drastic limitation, no less. We have only to think of Pompey Bum in *Measure for Measure*. I would not dwell on Pompey's 'godlike hours'; nor on Froth's (if he had any).

It would be academic to cite *The Borderers* to demonstrate that Wordsworth has no *dramatic* talent. It is notorious that the Romantic Revival produced some great actors, but no playwrights: notorious, and logical. The inspired individual vision of the 'single I' is antithetical to Keats's conception of the chameleon poet, who is 'for all waters' (like Maria), and enters into a Iago and an Imogen, a Quickly, a Goneril and a Hermione with equal zest. The romantic 'I, I, I, always I' poets may long for 'negative capability': in so far as they remain poets of the inspired egocentric vision, it is *ipso facto* denied them.

Now Wordsworth does remain such a poet. His 'characters' are either projections of Wordsworth himself or of Wordsworthian ideas; or they are broken-off, 'semi-detachable' pieces of nature, like the Leech-Gatherer, who begins as a cloud or a rock, and ends by fading back into unitary Nature. He is constantly in difficulties over bringing mankind-as-met-*generally* into any vital relationship with Man, as encountered in moments of vision. The Old Soldier, the Old Cumberland Beggar, Michael, the Shepherd in *The Prelude*, Bk. viii., are all like figures in Russian films, photographed from ankle-high or lower: 'In size a giant, stalking through the fog' (*Prelude*, viii. 400). Wordsworth thanks 'the God/ Of Nature and of Man',

> That Men did at the first present themselves
> Before my untaught eyes thus purified,
> Remov'd, and at a distance that was fit (ibid., 436–8),

adding:

> And thus
> Was founded a sure safeguard and defence
> Against the weight of meanness, selfish cares,
> Coarse manners, vulgar passions, that beat in
> On all sides from the ordinary world
> In which we traffic. (ibid., 451–6)

The contrast with Shakespeare is sufficiently marked in the passage (Bk. iv.) where, as an undergraduate, he comments on what he calls (betrayingly) 'that vague heartless chace/ Of trivial pleasures'. He writes disparagingly of exactly what Shakespeare's mind was most alert to, most absorbent of:

> 'Tis true, some casual knowledge might be gain'd
> Of character or life. (iv. 307)

But

> Far better had it been to exalt the mind
> By solitary study; to uphold
> Intense desire by thought and quietness. (ibid., 311–13)

Without what he calls 'that religious dignity of mind', he believed that Man

> Seems but a pageant plaything with vile claws
> And this great frame of breathing elements
> A senseless Idol. (ibid., 302–4)

(Lines which, echoing 'this goodly frame, the earth, etc.,' seem to show that without this 'inflation' of the human currency, he would be in danger of falling into the melancholy of Hamlet.)

It is, of course, the dilemma of humanism, this ambiguity of man. But I am only concerned with the inevitable limitation which the Wordsworthian view imposes: the incapacity to enter imaginatively into other human beings; and the confusion between the valuation of man *in posse* and humanity *in esse*. One side of it is expressed in

> Society has parted man from man,
> Neglectful of the universal heart (xii. 218);

and that is, again, a measure of the different climates of poet and poetry in 1805 and 1605. But another aspect is *implicit* in

> The still sad music of humanity
> *Not harsh nor grating*,

where the siren dream of a mysterious calm lures us to forget the clash and conflict that is *man*. It is not merely the Shakespearian *plenum* that is lacking, that full involvement with life, with all its grating and harshness; nor that Wordsworth merely *mishears* the terrifying orchestration of the world. Rather, his attention is on the Solitary (not to say 'The Recluse': the poem of which *The Excursion* was to have been a part); and the Solitary (to commit an Irishism) 'sees humanity with his back turned'.

Set beside Shakespeare, this is his weakness; but it also defines his strength, the power which speaks out in

Our destiny, our nature, and our home
Is with infinitude and only there;
With hope it is, hope that can never die,
Effort, and expectation, and desire,
And something evermore about to be. (vi. 538–42)

The juxtaposition is outrageous, indeed laughable, if you imagine the two men together; but these lines show Wordsworth as more like Marlowe as a poet than like Shakespeare.

It is true that Wordsworth has a kind of interest in psychology: the *Lyrical Ballads* were intended to offer situations 'tracing . . . the primary laws of our nature' and especially 'the manner in which we associate ideas in a state of excitement'. Wishing to reveal 'the essential passions of the heart' is the ground he gives for choosing 'humble and rustic life'. And *Nutting*, *The Highland Reaper*, *Strange fits of passion* are about psychological *aperçus*; as too are the boat and skating episodes in *The Prelude*, Bk. i. and, in Bk. xi., the 'sequence' of the mouldered gallows, the 'naked pool that lay beneath the hills' and the girl with a pitcher (although all these reach something greater than the associationist formula). Wordsworth has this 'apperceptive' power by glimpses ('I see by glimpses now . . .'). But it would be a queer collection of 'essential passions of the heart' which a resolute researcher would extract from his works. Put it beside Shakespeare and you must call it 'domestic', perhaps 'provincial' (although is it really as much as 'the essential passions of the English Lake District, *c.* 1770–1810'?); and recognize (call it what you will) that with Wordsworth 'humanity' lacks range, lacks strength and is indeed highly selective and exclusive.

Man . . .
As of all visible natures crown; and first
In capability of feeling what
Was to be felt, (VIII. 631–5)

sounds utterly comprehensive. But where in Wordsworth's conspectus of 'primary laws', 'essential passions', is there a glimpse of the animus of Cassius against Caesar, the amiable conceit of Dogberry, Angelo's torment of the divided mind? It is no better if we look at 'humble life'. His world has no room for Pompey ('Truly, sir, I am a poor fellow that would live'), nor for Parolles ('Simply the thing I am . . .'). And we shall not improve the matter by trying out ladies instead, still less lady's-maids: for Wordsworth was not the man to listen to the often naughty tongues of Beatrice or Rosalind—or of poor Ophelia mad.

Far be it from me to defend 'the language really used by men'; but I do recollect one queer, engagingly yokelish touch in 'Residence in London' (*Prelude*, Bk. vii.), where Wordsworth remarks that it was three years since he had first travelled two hundred miles south,

> And for the first time in my life did hear
> The voice of Woman utter blasphemy (VII. 416–17).

Presumably he is tactfully indicating the *latitude* of Cambridge. I find it a strain on my credulity, none the less; and do sometimes wonder how well Wordsworth really *knew* the Cumberland people he turned into ideal 'anti-types' to those of Cambridge and London.

This seems the place for a note on Wordsworth's theory of language. Much of his stylistic polemic amounts to maintaining that there is no language of feeling, there is only the language of men; and metre is a mere notation that a man (the poet) is going to speak feelingly. For Wordsworth this was *true*: the simplicities of his diction allowed him to say, and with profound emotion, all that he felt (as near as we can judge). But he need only have looked into his accepted great poets (Shakespeare, Spenser and Milton) to see that for them, it was false. But why did he not also observe that even the vocabulary and syntax of quite ordinary people tends not only to change with stress of emotion, but to become, in some sense, *literary*? No doubt he did; and, if so, 'the language really used, etc.' becomes misleading; for the word 'used' suggests 'what men are accustomed to use in usual speech', rather than 'what is not normal usage, but could be employed in unusual circumstances'. This latter must be what he meant; and he *had* to go to naïfs, simpletons, etc., for it around 1800, because the well-bred, well-educated of Cambridge and London prided themselves on *not* falling into abnormal language when their feelings were moved (as, of course, the well-bred still do).

Yet my last remark is manifestly false: it is about what the well-bred *appear* to do—or did. Either Wordsworth was very ignorant of the real language of contemporaries (outside Cumberland) or he thought that when they did show feeling, it was unworthy (e.g., ill temper, spite, anger, jealousy, meanness). Or, again, he judged more from books than from men. It is not only that Wordsworth is not a man who has 'been here and there/ And made himself a motley to the view'; nor only that *wit*, even of the simplest, is no part of his language. That is certainly true as well. There is a sort of verbal play which Shakespeare almost *standardized* as an English habit: you can see it today in advertisements, which do occasionally reach the level of quibbling of Shakespearian serving-men. Wordsworth avoids it as sedulously as ever an Addison would. Yet it is not simply wit that he lacks: it is that capacity, behind wit, of being able to catch at things from abruptly contrasted points of view, and to snap them together in a pun or a paradox. None the less, this lack does have an effect on Wordsworth as a word-user. He most earnestly and always means what he says; and that is why he is so vulnerable to *irony*.

Now Shakespeare's viewing of humanity—even at humanity's greatest—holds its own ironies. It is time wasted to devise derisive lights on his people: he has supplied them (and usually outdistanced you) before you start. In *Hamlet*, *Lear*, *Antony and Cleopatra*, as in the major comedies, contrast, antithesis, paradox, deflationary or derisive parallelism are normal media to him. He is, you might say, his own parodist; and whenever deflationary parallelism or comic-to-farcical commentary is lacking, his plays are tricky and unstable. We find this in *Richard II*, *Julius*

Caesar[1] and (at a lower seriousness) *Henry V*: plays with something less than the full Shakespearian greatness in the central role.

With that I turn from humanity to Nature. But first (bear with the portentous platitude!), Wordsworth may be, in his own way, a poet of humanity: he is no poet of *satanity*. The self-amused malice of Richard III; the intense black-diamond-like cutting concentration of Iago and Edmund; the cursings of Lear and Timon; even the obsession of Leontes, the nagging sense of resentment in Don John or of envy in Thersites: none of those has any place in Wordsworth's range of 'capability of feeling what/ Is to be felt'. 'Pageant playthings . . .'? Or do we find a similar absence in the moods and modes of nature? At the end of *Landscape into Art* (1949), Sir Kenneth Clark observes how we of the twentieth century have utterly lost the entrée to the 'enclosed garden of Nature' of the fifteenth century: a Nature that was 'friendly and harmonious'. 'Science has taught us that Nature is the reverse.' It is against the implied background of that remark that I want to talk now.

Sir Kenneth thinks there may still be a future for landscape painting, as an expression of projected human emotions; and that 'it is possible that the . . . excitement and awe' of 'this terrible new universe' will find expression in some such way as 'the old forest fears' of the Germanic peoples did, in the art of Bosch and Grünewald. Theirs is an art of apocalyptic revelation, of grotesque and bedevilled nightmare-visions, of cruel agony, fantastic and absurd distortion, and above all of *terror*. Sir Kenneth is thinking predominantly of our mental foreground of nuclear physics; but that is not essential to the question I am asking: whether we are by now shut out of the national park of Wordsworthian Nature (which many naïvely associate with the Lake District; though I do not)?

I do not see how anyone who *thinks* about Nature can have any faith in the famous lines:

[1] It is not eccentricity, it is critical insight which makes Sir John Gielgud play Cassius. The playing of Brutus as a great Liberal—a Roman Mr. Gladstone in circumstances more trying than the Irish Question—is of the nineteenth century. We know 'liberation' as a highly equivocal term.

> Knowing that Nature never did betray
> The heart that loved her; 'tis her privilege
> Through all the years of this our life, to lead
> From joy to joy. (*Tintern Abbey*, 121–4)

Let me comment, with a thoroughly Shakespearian irony. In 1848 the Duke of Argyll visited the Wordsworths, and *Tintern Abbey* was read to him. He was struck with the fervent emphasis with which Wordsworth read 'My dear, *dear* friend . . . in thy wild eyes . . .'. He thought, it seems, that Mary was meant—Mrs. Wordsworth (our text reads, 'My dear, dear Sister!'). However, he found out. His letter continues: 'It was not till the reading was over that we found out that the old paralytic and *doited* woman we had seen in the morning was the sister to whom *Tintern Abbey* was addressed . . . it was melancholy to think that the vacant silly stare which we had seen in the morning was from the "wild eyes" of 1798.'[1] Dorothy became a paralytic imbecile: Nature only led from joy to joy if we accept Meredith's bitter lines in *Modern Love*:

> If any state is enviable on earth,
> 'Tis yon born idiot's, who, as days go by
> Still rubs his hands before him, like a fly
> In a queer sort of meditative mirth.

And although Wordsworth sedulously revised *The Prelude*, no line of his to Nature ever touched the notes of

> No, no, no life!
> Why should a dog, a horse, a rat have life,
> And thou no breath at all? Thou'lt come no more,
> Never, never, never, never, never.

That is a 'statement' about Nature, if we *think*; and by 'think' I mean no more than old Gloucester, answering Lear's 'yet you see how this world goes' with 'I see it feelingly'. Do I need to demonstrate that *Shakespeare's* Nature is unchanged in validity?

[1] The Duke of Argyll to the Revd. T. S. Howson: *The Poetical Works of Wordsworth*, ed. E. de Selincourt, 1944, II, 517.

Never mind atomic energy, neutrons, gamma-rays, derangements of chromosomes. It is no good saying that men have gone mad in the last fifty years, or since the Renaissance: Nature has not changed in the last four hundred years. As Jonson said, 'She is always the same, like herself. . . . Men are decayed, and studies: She is not.'[1] The Wordsworthian conception of Nature, *as generally received*, is not far from the *Tintern Abbey* lines to the effect that nothing in mankind can disturb

> Our cheerful faith, that all which we behold
> Is full of blessings.

Against that I only cite Lafeu, on what he calls 'our philosophical persons'.[2]

We are forced to recognize something germane to our 'sense of Nature' in the art of the sixteenth century, with its revelation of 'a terrible new universe': a world which has, as it were, split open to reveal its core, an *under-nature*, which invites artistic expression in terms of agony, distortion, clashing paradox, diabolism. We are also made to recognize the validity of feeling like that about both external nature (macrocosmic or ultra-microscopic) and *internal* (human) nature *equally*.

Think now not of Nature as something comfortably in our English pockets: but of the awesomeness of great storms, great floods, earthquakes, fires; of great mountains, not as cool marmoreal photographs labelled Kamet, North Devi, Chumolhari, Kanchenjunga, Anapurna, K.2, but as icy hells of murderous wind, shaking thunders of avalanche; and all 'so slippery that/ The fear's as bad as falling.' Beasts no longer impress unless they have more than four legs or less than three: let a thought of Nature's fearful list of parasites suffice; or of the invisible sub-vital 'life' of viruses. Think of what the Black Death was, and what poliomyelitis is—or might be—a creeping terror that walks by day. And then of human rage, obsession, mass-hysteria; of heartless craft and treachery; of politic lying by those

[1] *Timber*, No. xx.
[2] See *All's Well*, II. iii. 1–6, quoted at p. 259.

who know their own mendacity and its cheating-value; and of that quintessence of the urge to hurt and destroy which invades all minds behind the 'pride, pomp, and circumstance, of glorious war'. All those are part and parcel of *Nature*: and there is no escape but by death or lunacy—unless into the various sorts of fools' paradises (which amount to being dead without having the manners to admit it). This terror in Nature is only an element in the whole, but one which caught some of the great sixteenth-century artists by the throat and bore them away: as the author of *Job* was borne, when the Lord answered Job out of the whirlwind, and when (among many terrible and admirable things) the Voice said: 'Upon Earth there is not his like, who is made without fear.'

In Shakespeare that terror is epitomized in *King Lear*. The play is not an allegory, but we can allegorize it without distortion. The magical King, who is Order and Right Reason, tears out the keystone of Authority; and the arch of State, of piety (in the widest sense) and Kind-liness (affection *and* nature, the 'law of Kynde') collapses. But Nature is double; and from this collapse an *under-nature* surges over the world, making good, as it were, Edmund's claim: 'Thou, Nature, art my goddess', and also his kind of priority, for he is a 'natural son'. He, Goneril, Regan, Cornwall and Oswald represent types of an 'old law of Nature' which has reasserted itself: and the resulting chaos is not only in the State and family; it is equally in the storm and in 'the tempest in my mind'—is, indeed, madness. The heath-scenes show Lear as 'unaccommodated Man' in a natural universe where all the gods have failed. It is this total disintegration, this retrogression to 'the natural' (of the 'old law') which Timon calls down as a curse on Athens.

Madness includes the terrifying unbalances of hysteria which may lead to it: the unexplored country which Brutus only glimpses, when he likens mental conflict to man's 'little kingdom' suffering 'the nature of an insurrection'. In *Julius Caesar* it is derangement in the State of Rome which releases the 'under-nature'. The human stuff which explodes in Cade's rebellion and in *Coriolanus* is also 'Nature': Nature which has 'lost its head'—not merely in our sense, but in the Tudor one. All Shakespeare's mob-scenes relate more closely to his intuitions of *nature* than to 'political' thinking; hence Caliban ('high-day, freedom! . . .') is a species of mob.

In *Measure for Measure* we see the 'under-nature' breaking out all over the play. But here lust's dominion in Angelo is *comically* paralleled by its domination in the underworld of Vienna. The duplicity of sex—as deadly sin and dirty joke—enables Shakespeare to use that kind of deflationary or derisive comparison. The equation of lust and death by the plot emphasizes the fear-element. But there is also a kind of fear in the apposite thoughts of the two French Lords in *All's Well*:

> Now, God delay our rebellion! As we are ourselves, what things are we!
> Merely our own traitors. (IV. iii. 18–20)

Angelo, Claudio, even Lucio and Pompey are their own traitors; and, in different kinds, sex is the cause. And sex is Nature.

Sex, with its concomitants of self-betrayal (loss of reason by 'infected will'), and venereal disease as part of 'the order of Nature', may have brought great shocks to the speculative mind of 1600. We need not make too much of venereal disease: though we should note the tone of *horror* that surrounds it in Shakespeare, rare outside him. Rather, sex generally is for him a symbol of disorder. Not only Vienna's 'corruption . . . boils' (how it terrifies Isabella!); but 'rebellious hell' mutinies in Gertrude's bones; Othello's imagery ('goats and monkeys' and the rest) is sex-obsessed; in *King Lear* the 'small gilded fly' and the 'fitchew' are wrenched from wild nature's economy to lash on the hysterical one-eyed contemplation of Centaur-woman: 'There's hell, there's darkness, there is the sulphurous pit'; and so to Timon's 'Maid, to thy master's bed. . . . Down with the nose.' The theme is not limited to the Problem Plays: although, as products of intellectual uneasiness, most obvious in them.

Over Shakespeare's scattered omni-present intuitions of Nature we can have no doubts: his heart goes with them. We can see one Romantic catching a glimpse of this fullness and depth of Nature—and quite independently of anything *we* may associate with Darwin or nineteenth-century science—in Keats's *Epistle to J. H. Reynolds*. He writes of a 'mysterious tale' of which he has read 'the first page'

> Upon a Lampit rock of green sea-weed
> Among the breakers . . . . . .
> . . . . I was at home
> And should have been most happy,—but I saw
> Too far into the sea, where every maw
> The greater on the less feeds evermore.—
> But I saw too distinct into the core
> Of an eternal fierce destruction,
> And so from happiness I far was gone.
> Still am I sick of it, and tho', to-day,
> I've gather'd young spring-leaves, and flowers gay
> Of periwinkle and wild strawberry,
> Still do I that most fierce destruction see,—
> The Shark at savage prey,—the Hawk at pounce,—
> The gentle Robin, like a Pard or Ounce,
> Ravening a worm,—Away, ye horrid moods!
> Moods of one's mind! You know I hate them well.[1]

And he would 'sooner be a clapping bell/ To some Kamtschatcan Missionary Church', than be left with them. Keats, the Romantic, dismisses the book with page one. And page one looks like a recollection of a couple of lines from two Fishermen in *Pericles*:

> Master, I marvel how the fishes live in the sea.
> Why, as men do a-land—the great ones eat up the little ones.
> (II. i. 27–8)

But I am not content to leave Wordsworth with Shakespeare pointing an ironic finger at him and mispointing his own lines: 'There are more things in heaven and earth [William] than are dreamt of in *your* philosophy!'

[1] *Epistle to John Hamilton Reynolds* (25 March 1818), l. 88 f.

In *The Prelude* Wordsworth runs up towards the terror-element in Nature, almost or quite touches it (it certainly touches *him* in the early books) and then withdraws. But it is there, if looked for, as something more than and very different from what he calls, in *Michael*,

> A pleasurable feeling of blind love,
> The pleasure that there is in life itself.

By 'terror' I do not mean what scares us out of our wits: rather, what jerks us into them. It need be no more than the lightest touch of Nature's inalienable strangeness: that 'otherness' to which the mind itself must be subject (whether it is germane or opposed, still subject), unless man, inwardly contemplated, is no part of Nature; and that means with no dependence on his physical body.

The touch of that otherness is what is great in the lines in *The Prelude* about the Boy 'of Winander' who 'blew mimic hootings to the silent owls' to fool them into answering:

> Then sometimes, in that silence, while he hung
> Listening, a gentle shock of mild surprize
> Has carried far into his heart the voice
> Of mountain torrents. (v. 406–9)

Through ear and eye he receives—and *we* receive—the impact of a barely-apprehended world upon awakened sense. The same voice of the earth speaks (but how differently) in the tremendous vision on Snowdon, where the moonlit mist parts in a blue chasm through which

> Mounted the roar of waters, torrents, streams
> Innumerable, roaring with one voice. (XIII. 58–9)

I cannot particularize further, only point to the well-known episodes in the early books: the stolen boat—leaving him haunted with an 'undetermin'd sense/ Of unknown modes of being'; the boy-poacher pursued by 'sounds/ Of undistinguishable motion'; the few lines on bird's-nesting on a windy crag, his ears blown through with 'what strange utterance' of the loud dry wind; and the ineffable scene of 'visionary dreariness' in Bk. xi.[1] Moreover, Wordsworth generalizes for me:

> Fair seed-time had my soul, and I grew up
> Foster'd alike by beauty and by fear (I. 305–6: just before the poaching episode);

and, again, where the 'Wisdom and Spirit of the universe' has 'intertwined' the passions for him, 'purifying' the elements of feeling,

> And sanctifying, by such discipline,
> Both pain and fear. (I. 439–40)

Wordsworth recognized the terror-element in his intuition of Nature; but he backed away. Part, at least, of the explanation can be found in Bk. xiii. There, returning thanks to Dorothy, he says that despite her 'sweet influence',

> Even to the very going out of youth, . . .
> I too exclusively esteem'd that love,
> And sought that beauty, which, as Milton sings,
> Hath terror in it. Thou didst soften down
> This over-sternness; but for thee, sweet Friend,
> My soul, too reckless of mild grace, had been
> Far longer what by Nature it was framed,
> Longer retain'd its countenance severe,
> A rock with torrents roaring, with the clouds
> Familiar, and a favourite of the Stars. (XIII. 222–32)

But, he adds, 'thou didst plant its crevices with flowers'—and after a century, one can reasonably complain that you cannot see the rock for daffodils. In the 1850 version, Wordsworth added to the address to Coleridge which followed this some new lines:

> Thus fear relaxed
> Her overweening grasp; thus thoughts and things
> In the self-haunting spirit learned to take

[1] Wordsworth, in my opinion, turns this into a demonstration of a stupidly self-evident psychological platitude: to the effect that places look and feel quite different according to our moods. But the misuse does not affect the poetry.

> More rational proportions; mystery . . .
> Admitted more habitually a mild
> Interposition.
>
> (*Prelude, 1850*: XIV. 282–9);

and I feel justified in saying that both style and substance have 'gone soft'. In effect, even in the 1805 version, his palinode gives the pattern for the later revisions: away from paganism and towards Anglican orthodoxy, in the shape of the mid-nineteenth-century belief in a providential Creator who has devised Nature as an educational convenience.

Critics differ very much about this; but I cannot dissociate from this turning away from 'terror' Wordsworth's omission from *The Prelude* of the episode of Annette and his illegitimate daughter. He told the tale—very ill indeed—in *Vaudracour and Julia* (which de Selincourt has put into Bk. ix., where it belonged). I leave it with but two points. The shamed embarrassment of his own words about 'some unguarded moment that dissolved/ Virtuous restraint' does not accord well with his creed of passionate human feelings. With 'Nature never did betray . . .' it accords not at all. Nature *does*; Nature *did*. But Wordsworth only responded with a lot of pathetic poems on deserted and miserable women and children; and we are left to guess if some sense of Nature's not being all so divine and good was contributory to the fading of 'the visionary gleam'.

Yet the gleam had been there: we can still revisit his 'spots of time', and find still valid his approaches to a mysterious, half-awed, delighted 'under-revelation'. But it is not a revelation of that '*under-nature*' which is as great a part of our universe as it was of that of the sixteenth century. Put Wordsworth's Nature beside Shakespeare's, and he is a poet of *mood*. There is no 'Heart of Darkness' in him. Thus I admire him at his best; but I cannot persuade him far into the mountains—not even into his own mountains, small enough in all conscience.

To put it all as briefly as possible, if cryptically, and come back to Shakespeare. T. S. Eliot wrote of Leonardo: 'He lived in no fairyland, but his mind went out and became a part of things.'[1] It is perhaps only active men—sailors, miners, men who know deserts or jungles, soldiers and (when things go wrong enough) climbers—whose minds see to the bottom of Lear's 'Pour on; I will endure.' Except poets who hold the Globe in their hands.

[1] 'Imperfect Critics': *The Sacred Wood*, p. 24.

Index